Principles of Hotel Management

PRINCIPLES OF HOTEL MANAGEMENT

Sujit Kumar Dwivedi
Simran Kaur Julka

NAMAN PUBLISHER & DISTRIBUTORS
NEW DELHI

Published by
Sangeeta Jain for Naman Publisher & Distributors
7360-B, Prem Nagar,
Gali No.1, Shakti Nagar,
Delhi-110007
PH: 23823642, MOB.: 09013478302
E-mail: rajivjain72@ymail.com

First Published – 2011

ISBN–978-81–920935–2-9

Published in an association with **HLDC**, Agra.

SOLE DISTRIBUTOR
JINDAL BOOK SERVICES
LG-4A, Ganpati Bhawan,
4675-B/21, Ansari Road,
Darya Ganj, Delhi - 110002

Jacket Designed by :
S.M. Graphics

Printed by:
Sachin Printers, Delhi, India

Preface

Hotel Management is a multi-disciplinary field of study with the purpose of preparing people with the expertise, commitment, and skills for management, marketing, and operations positions in the expanding industry that provides food, accommodations, and tourism services to people away from home. As a field of study, Hotel Management is inter-disciplinary. It draws upon a wide range of basic disciplines to provide the fundamental knowledge and skills that are required to fulfil the diverse demands placed upon individuals in management positions within the hotel industry.

Recognizing that the individual educated for today is soon out of date, the academic emphasis of the programme is on principles, analytical tools, processes, and systems. These change relatively slowly. However, it is recognized that at least a minimal exposure to the skills and knowledge which make up the present state of the art is necessary to understand the principles. Likewise, it is recognized that the students in the programme are composites of many talents, and that in hospitality and tourism, pure academic ability cannot predict professional success.

Students majoring in hotel management may elect a concentra-tion in Food and Beverage Management (Commercial and Non-Commercial), Club Management, Casino Management, Lodging Management, and

Tourism, Convention and Event Management. Detailed information about the programme and courses is given in this book.

The book contains nine chapters on various aspects on principles of hotel management, i.e. Hotel Development Process; Organisational Design; Responsibilities of Hotel General Manager; Management of the Front Office; Housekeeping Management; Managing Food and Beverage Operations; Hotel Sales Organisation and Operations; Financial Control; Strategic Management of Human Resourcesnine.

We hope this text book meets its intended purpose as a practical resource, and serve as a vehicle for promoting the professionalism of this important segment of the Hospitality Industry.

SUJIT KUMAR DWIVEDI
SIMRAN KAUR JULKA

HERITAGE

LEARNING & DEVELOPMENT CENTER

Heritage Learning and Development Centre (HLDC) is an extended arm of Heritage Institute of Hotel & Tourism (HIHT). Heritage Institute of Hotel & Tourism is an Institute of excellence of the upcoming chain of Management Institutes, founded by D. K. Singh, President. At HIHT, our endeavour is to take education to the higher domains of never ending success. Heritage Institute of Hotel & Tourism provides the best possible infrastructure for pursuing best quality Hotel Management Education. HIHT has three campuses Agra, Shimla and Goa and proposed campuses at Kolkata, Pune, and Singapore.

In the modern era, Hospitality Industry is a reality, fighting for extremely challenging phase and getting into a stability mode. There are SMILES everywhere and this is relatively controlled and guarded, a sign of maturing and learning of Hospitality, which is cyclic in nature. The Hospitality Industry reflects a bright future. Earlier days, hospitality was synonymous with only hotel industry, but today this industry holds its important place with tourism. Hospitality academic in India is still in its nascent stage when compared to the west.

HLDC has been developed through the inputs from the industry and experts from the academics. This panel of experts have gone through the book and made suggestions which were incorporated. Every attempt has been made to thoroughly cover the day to day problems faced in the profession. In this field, as in most any other, it is prudent to remember the old adage, actions speak louder than words. The information given in this book makes the students fit for the industry. It provides about technical skills, personality and soft skills and ability to think and make decision.

This book is designed and presented in an easy to read and easy to understand format. It will be beneficial to both aspiring professionals and those already in the industry.

We hope this text book meets its intended purpose as a practical resource, and serve as a vehicle for promoting the professionalism of this important segment of the Hospitality Industry.

Contents

1

Hotel Development Process

During the second half of the 20th century, the hotel industry underwent a subtle but certain change in concept. In fact, this concept first originated in the manufacturing industry-that of line production, which was first initiated at the Ford Motor Company, where it proved to be very successful. This heralded a change in focus from individualised attention to mass production, which led to enhanced productivity and greater economy of scale. Most industries immediately adopted this concept.

The hotel industry too found it to be more profitable to put up rooms that were easy to construct, easy to maintain, and easy to duplicate rather than create high-cost, one-of-a-kind rooms that can be very expensive to maintain and refurbish. This led to the rise of several hotel brands that offered similar rooms and services throughout their chain. This was an attempt to standardise their offering so that guests knew what to expect when they walked into any of that brand's hotels.

This also enabled hotels to set up centralised purchase systems and departments that would buy for the entire chain, thus receiving more competitive prices, greater bargaining power with vendors, and less administrative activity at the individual hotel level. This led to significant savings, a portion of which was then passed on to guests.

As time passed, a segment of travelers became weary of hotel rooms that all looked the same and had no character, and started seeking other options.

In an attempt to capture this market niche that was willing to pay higher for a differentiated product, a number of hotels entered the market with a different product offering. These hotels offered unique styles and a high degree of personalised attention. And most importantly, each property had a character of its own. These hotels were soon called "boutique hotels" and the name stuck to them.

Boutique hotels are able to achieve such high rates due to a number of different factors. First, they target a more influential segment of travelers who are ready to pay more for a better product and who are willing to try out different hotels offering different experiences. As this segment pays higher rates, they obviously expect more personalised service. Boutique hotels might provide old-fashioned personal service, but this is not possible without the state-of-the-art property management systems that are used to track and record guest preferences, right from the type of room they prefer to the way they like their eggs cooked for breakfast. The availability of this information empowers hotel employees to provide the high degree of personal attention that is expected of them.

Guests who walk into such hotels are greeted by name if they have stayed there before and might even receive enquiries as to the welfare of their spouses and children. To guests who may have resigned themselves to disinterested front desk personnel constantly asking them for their reservation confirmation numbers at check-in, such a welcome comes as a pleasant surprise. Boutique hotels constantly aim at surprising and delighting their guests in this manner throughout their stay at that property.

As the number of boutique hotels accelerates, competition will also rise, and these hotels will have to target their market segments more aggressively. While there might be a move towards more competitive pricing, hotels are expected to focus on differentiating their product offering rather than reducing prices for a segment that is not price-conscious.

New supply invariably threatens the stability of an established hotel. The older the hotel, the more likely the threat of lost market share and profitability will be realised. Regardless of flag, location or reputation, hotels are vulnerable for the simple reason that trying a new hotel is a safe form of adventure for a frequent traveller.

Making of Good Relationship with Customers

Knowing the identities of your best customers is the first step towards keeping them. Successfully retaining customers when new competition enters the market is also a function of the quality of your relationships with them. Many relationships with customers evolve from vendee/ vendor into a meaningful commitment in these ways:

— Recognition: Nothing makes a more powerful impression on a customer than being greeted by name or thanked by an employee that he has never met before. The ability to communicate the identities of your best clients through the ranks creates a point of difference.

— Authenticity: To paraphrase Albert Schweitzer, certain infrequent events reveal the true essence of people, like a lightning flash in a pitch-black sky. A spontaneous situation that calls for empathy, candid honesty, or taking responsibility can enhance a client relationship if handled well or abruptly end a relationship if mishandled. When the unexpected happens and management has the chance to demonstrate good faith to a customer, the payback usually exceeds the investment.

— Personal Stakes: When customers contribute ideas and suggestions to improve the operation, they inevitably take a personal interest in the outcome of their ideas. If a valuable customer has a history of active involvement with you, switching to a new hotel will feel like an act of abandonment. An active process that facilitates client input is a defensive measure that protects your best assets, your customers. Conversely, the more you understand your customer's viewpoint, the more he sacrifices by switching to the competition.

— Ability to decide: When a customer needs an answer to a difficult request, he should have access to a person with the authority to give him one at once. Immediate response creates client loyalty; bureaucracy destroys it.

Making of Good Staff

The cost of employee turnover is great to both profit and quality. Retaining staff is not an isolated case of compensation, although that is precisely what a new competitor will use to lure them away from you. If management recognises achievement, shows an active interest in career growth gives responsibility that reflects expertise and provides a professional work environment, money alone will not be persuasive enough to lure away your staff members.

— Recognition: The quickest way to get rid of the best staff member is to make him the employee of the year. Nobody wants to admit it, but conventional employee recognition tactics do not work. Reward and recognition programmes like "employee of the month" used in most hotels are stale. Many employees react cynically to them because they sense an absence of sincerity and authenticity. Genuine recognition is a form of empathy.

If management really understands the difficulties of the work and expresses genuine appreciation consistently, good employees will respond. Employee recognition is also a daily practice as opposed to a monthly luncheon or an annual awards banquet. Whether a general manager works the floor when a restaurant is slammed, hands out fifty dollar bills after a record breaking month or gives a banquet houseman a day off with pay after a difficult convention, the message resonates that management cares. Demonstrations of gratitude, empathy and respect beat a wooden plaque every time.

— Career: If an employee is performing at a level that is clearly different and better than the standard and management wants to retain that employee, it is management's responsibility to initiate discussions regarding the future with that person. Retaining great customers requires both understanding and fulfillment of their needs. So does retaining great employees. Demonstrating a sustained, proactive interest in the future success of a great employee is an unmatchable advantage over a potential new employer. Showing a sincere interest is often all that is necessary.

— Responsibility: Successful people crave responsibility. Giving it to them, however, contradicts the need to control. The risks of mistakes and unexpected results are magnified if authority to make decisions is spread out. By limiting power to a select few, results are predictable. The benefits of limiting control are dwarfed however, by the reality that deprivation of responsibility, authority and latitude disconnects talented employees from their work. Lack of substantial responsibility makes the decision to leave a job to go to a competitor much less complicated. There is nothing at stake to give up by leaving.

— Professional Environment: Regardless of a hotel's sector, segment, brand affiliation, geographic location or size, professional standards matter. The environment can quietly but emphatically suggest that you have to be a pro to belong. When everyone looks immaculate, acts professionally and works toward the same goals, jumping ship to join a competitor becomes anathema. When true outstanding performance is recognised and rewarded all of the time, the employee mindset evolves from "doing the job" to striving for excellence. When people without dedication, commitment or the best skills leave, the powerful implicit message is that you have to be excellent to stay.

Spend more Money

When demand is strong, sales people spend most of their time fielding inquiries, evaluating leads, and trading function space. The idea of prospecting for new business is absurd from their viewpoint. Why go through the drudgery of making cold calls when they cannot get through the message stacks on their desks from customers that already want to book? Is performance measured by prospecting or sales results? The unpopular answer is that it is necessary to do both; sales people must promptly return inquiries as well as consistently prospect for new accounts. The reasons include:

— When demand diminishes because of increased supply or a downturn in the economy, the hotel will certainly lose business. Customer defections, tightened travel budgets, the perceived need to try something new, the negative impact will be reduced if a sustained effort to attract new customers is in place.

— Business that comes from inquiries fills the most popular dates and arrival/departure patterns. Prospecting is necessary to create opportunities to fill the least popular patterns and down times. Prospecting for qualified clients whose requirements match up to a hotel's needs only makes sense. Las Vegas is the only place on earth where the hotels routinely run 100%, and those days are numbered.

— Returning messages is fundamentally passive. The buying ability of the customer is unknown and can easily lead to unproductive time management.

If sales performance evaluations are based strictly on results, little motivation exists to prospect in an active market. To make prospecting matter, evaluation criteria for sales people must include a structured, quantitative set of sales activity goals that are reported and used to judge performance. Monthly goals for telephone calls, solicitation letters, proposals, site visits, entertaining customers and outside sales calls that are tracked and reported lend a meaningful structure to the work done in the sales department. When results decline, quantitative information about the work habits of the sales staff can be used to help them break out of slumps.

New Innovations and Publicity

New hotels illuminate the obsolete characteristics of their competitors. Limited service hotels that can offer low rates and brand new facilities will take away customers from a twenty-year old full service hotel in spite of its existing clientele and established reputation. In order to protect market share in the face of new competition, hotels must recreate and re-enforce their image constantly by means of innovation and publicity.

Telephone greetings, restaurant menus, billing presentations, uniforms, bathroom amenities, promotional events, leisure and business packages, message taking procedures, front door service standards, coffee service; constant, evident improvement in every detail of the guest experience is the weapon that must be used to do battle with a new competitor. Obviously, big-ticket capital improvements are crucial to compete effectively, too. However, if innovation can become a daily way of life among the hotel staff, service levels, work environment and guest satisfaction all stand to continually improve.

Equally important is the effort made to publicly communicate the improvements. The effective combination of press releases, direct mail, advertising, promotions and direct sales must be dedicated not only to creating new customers but also to keeping current customers. One message required to do the latter is an impressive track record of constant innovation.

Effective Competitive Position

Public, easily accessible information that covers key competitors' pricing, future sold out dates, group clients, marketing alliances, customer incentive programmes, product and service improvements, advertising media placement, marketing collateral materials and news releases is invaluable. A hotel can effectively manage its competitive position by reviewing this body of information regularly and making the appropriate adjustments.

The hotel industry is engrossed in the idea that brand equity and global market share are the instruments of success. From the perspective of the battleground where the daily fighting for the end-user takes place, reality takes on a different appearance.

— Taking care of the individual guest.

— Employing people in a way that provides meaning and fulfillment.

— Finding new customers every day.

— Making innovation the highest valued achievement in the organisation.

— Using competitive intelligence shrewdly, effectively and constantly.

Over the next year or two, a handful of global giants will emerge. There will always be opportunities for smaller niche players to carve out attractive and profitable industry roles for themselves. But the big players will likely have a stronger hand in shaping the industry's future. Industry convergence may also play a hand in shaping the future. With the potential for non-lodging companies to further buy their way into the lodging business. It could also be within the realm of possibility that multifaceted consumer-based financial services companies and consumer products companies could also venture into the lodging business.

Integration Process in Lodging Business

There are three major stages to the integration process:

— value preservation,

— value realisation,

— value creation.

Value preservation is the preservation of value erosion: value realisation is the achievement of cost savings: value creation is the design of a new entity which differentiates itself from the competition.

While doing the deal to combine two hotel companies is a daunting challenge, it is overshadowed by the more difficult task of integrating the two companies. Those organisations which successfully integrate the businesses and execute appropriate business strategies to create enhanced shareholder value will be the winners in this arena.

Development, Marketing and Sustainability

As hospitality firms reach maturity in their own markets they expand overseas into new markets. In doing so, such firms need to make choices as to which countries they select for market entry. There is a wide range of criteria for making such entry decisions.

International Hotel Chain

An international hotel chain can be defined as a firm which has direct investments and other major forms of contractual agreement (such as franchises or management contracts) in more than one country. The number of such companies is growing considerably. Few however have reached global status—that is to say they have hotel properties on at least five of the six economically viable continents.

Expansion strategies of such global chains falls into three main groups. Asian hotel companies had relatively few properties when compared with European and American chains, but a high degree of internationalisation, as measured by the proportion of chains located outside their home country. North American chains (Choice, Hyatt, Sheraton, Marriott and Radisson) were the least international, with a relatively low proportion of hotels outside the USA, although some groups are actively pursuing internationalisation strategies. For instance, Marriott's corporate franchise deal with Whitbread Hotels in the U.K. Finally European chains, have been more international than American chains but less so than Asian ones.

Since 1995, this situation has not changed very much despite the significant amount of merger and acquisition activity within the industry. In 1995 there were only 9 hotel companies with representation in more than 30 countries and this was the same in 1998. Of the world's ten largest hotel chains, in 1998 four chains have more than 90% of their rooms in the USA. So it is clear that internationalisation and size are not related. It is clear therefore that some hotel chains have decided to be represented outside their home country as a matter of deliberate policy and others have concentrated on their home market.

Strategic Choice

Once the decision to 'go international' has been made, a chain then has a choice with regards to which countries or destinations to prioritise and what 'entry mode' to adopt. Market entry can be achieved with minimal operational activity and no investment in a country through franchising, or with operational activity but no or limited investment through a management contract, or with operational control and direct investment through the development and ownership of a hotel property in the target country. The decision which of these entry modes to adopt is influenced by two main criteria, those external to the firm and firm specific.

External criteria are those that derive from the attractiveness of a country or location with respect to hotel market entry; whereas firm specific criteria are those determined by the firm with regards market entry policy. Some firms are completely ruled by such policies, i.e. they adopt a single mode of entry. For instance Hyatt operate solely on a management contract basis. It seems likely that these two decisions about entry and mode of entry are highly iterative, and may vary from chain to chain. However, we shall now consider each of these in turn in relation to Southeast Asia and Indo-China.

Potentials of Hotel Development

Hotel chains have to make a basic decision as to whether

to have representation in a country or not. There are a number of ways for countries to be indexed in terms of their potential for market entry. There is evidence to suggest that hotel companies do not rely solely on these general criteria but take account of other specific factors. For instance, hotels do not solely rely on internally generated demand.

Clearly, the rankings that emerge are greatly influenced by the relative weighting of the various factors. The weighting presented here is based on the authors' opinion. Quite clearly a new ranking emerges. China emerges as the most attractive country for hotel entry. Korea is an attractive country for general investment, it is less attractive to hotel chains; whereas Thailand is more attractive to hotel entry than general investors. Indonesia has the least potential in both cases.

Choice of Entry Mode

There are various forms of entry that reduce the level of risk such as license agreements and joint ventures. Indeed there are some countries, such as China, which place legal restrictions on foreign investment and ownership. The hotel industry has a long history of developing alternative forms of management or 'affiliations', which comprise two broad categories namely management contracts and franchises. It is generally agreed that direct ownership and management of a hotel property carries the highest risk, a management contract less risk, and franchising even less. Hence hotel chains may decide to enter markets that are deemed to be risky by using an entry mode that reduces this risk.

The only large-scale, empirical study of hotel market entry mode choice is that by Contractor and Kundu. They adopted a transaction cost analysis approach, which identified 12 potential influences on the entry mode choice made by hotel chains. These can be broken down into country-specific variables, firm structural factors, and firm strategy and control factors (as perceived by executives).

The factors that were found to most influence market entry mode were country risk, level of development, international experience (measured by number of years since first overseas development), extent of foreign business (% of hotels outside home country), strategic control over quality and reservation system and brand. Cultural distance, penetration by foreign businesses, size of the chain, need for size, economies of scale and investment in training were not significant.

Asian hotel chains do not have a major presence across the region and tend to be concentrated in their home market, such as Oberoi. Two European chains do operate one-third of the hotels in the region, but Bass does so largely through its Holiday Inn brand, which was originally an American chain. The history of chain ownership and recent merger and acquisition activity suggests a more detailed analysis is required before any assumptions can be made about exactly how the country of origin affects market entry in the industry.

There are certainly some countries, such as Bangladesh, with considerably fewer international chain hotels. A larger, if not complete, sample might provide a more accurate assessment. Another reason may be that although these countries are different, the range of difference is not so great that hotel chains discriminate between them to prioritise one country over another.

India's hotel industry has entered the global stage, supported by its growing economy and the development of the 'Incredible India' tourism brand. Previous security concerns due to the Kashmir situation have reduced due to improved relations with Pakistan. Meanwhile the cost of travel has fallen following the government's liberalisation of the airline industry. Given that these two main barriers to travel have been tackled, not surprisingly, hotel performance has benefited.

With India capturing the attention of the world, Deloitte has responded by dedicating the 18th edition of the HotelBenchmark™ Survey to report each month on the country's hotel performance. To put the size of India's gigantic domestic market into perspective, it equates to over one third of total international arrivals received by all markets globally. While current mid-market players like Choice Hospitality India, Best Western, Fortune Park and Sarovar Park Plaza have catered for domestic tourism for some time—this market has recently exploded and demand is growing.

As the domestic market continues to expand, the escalating economy provides the rising middle classes with increased disposable income. The arrival of low cost airlines and the associated price wars have given domestic tourists more options than ever before. The 'Incredible India' destination campaign has also helped the growth of many domestic markets including religious tourism. As a next step, the government has recently launched the 'Atithi Devo Bhavah' (ADB) campaign aimed at increasing awareness of tourism in India.

To respond to the needs of this growing giant, companies like Choice and Best Western plan to significantly increase their portfolio over the next two years, by 100% and 50% respectively. Other hotel companies have also taken steps to ensure they benefit from the country's huge domestic demand. Indian Hotels launched its IndiOne brand with huge success last June in Bangalore.

Accor has entered into a joint venture with InterGlobe Enterprises to introduce 25 Ibis branded hotels, the first will arrive in 2006. InterContinental Hotels Group is also introducing their economy brand, Holiday Inn Express, with ten properties planned, starting later this year. Marriott has also announced plans to introduce the Courtyard brand in India.

Despite the international market being significantly smaller than India's domestic market, it also shows promising growth. The country's appeal to international visitors has previously been affected by the political situation in Kashmir as well as the global events of the past few years. However this has now improved due to relative geo-political stability and international economic growth. Tourism in India is also benefiting from the stronger economies of India's two major source markets, the United Kingdom and the United States. The peace talks with Pakistan have also improved the situation, with the ongoing cricket test series between the two countries further instilling confidence of future harmony.

Currently corporate travel dominates the international arena. The Indian subsidiary of Kuoni estimates that 80% of foreigners staying in their hotels are there on business. While corporate business will naturally continue to expand as the economy grows, there is enormous untapped potential in the country's leisure market. "Incredible India" has focused not only on promoting traditional holiday attractions and cultural experiences, but on defining unique markets from medical to religious tourism. In fact, India has already seen growing Japanese arrivals due to the promotion of Buddhist travel.

But India still faces many challenges in attracting the international traveller. This will continue whilst the government addresses the quality of India's infrastructure. Although the World Travel and Tourism Council rated India second in price competitiveness (after Brazil) there are many factors which need to be dealt with to encourage foreign visitors. Poor roads, overstretched railways and old airports discourage international travellers. Add to that hotel taxes higher than most Asian countries and a bureaucratic visa process - and you start to get a clear picture of the challenges facing India.

According to the new India edition of the HotelBenchmark™ Survey by Deloitte, the growth in hotel performance is impressive. As indicated in the graph below, all markets tracked by the survey reported double-digit growth in the twelve months to February 2005 compared to the same period the previous year. This is not surprising given the global economic growth in 2004, India's bustling domestic economy and reduced travel barriers.

Amongst the unique features of the hotel industry in India is the sheer volume of the domestic market. Hotels receive twice as many domestic guests as international guests. With most branded supply in India sitting in the top tier of the market, the hotel industry is currently very top heavy. While many companies are addressing the needs of the growing domestic market for more economical hotel products, most projects are still in development. Future growth of the hotel industry will not be helped by archaic land laws that make construction of new hotels time-consuming and expensive.

What is interesting to note, is that the demand for hotel rooms far exceeds the country's supply. While an opportunity exists to develop the hotel industry to meet this demand, India experiences large seasonal shifts in demand and corporate travellers currently represent the bulk of guests. Due to the lack of a widely distributed business mix, annual occupancies and average room rates in India did not rank very high in the 2004 HotelBenchmark™ Global Ranking Index. The industry must explore ways to seize untapped potential demand whilst addressing the down-time to maintain profitable operations. Developing a more diverse business mix is key.

Airline Industry

The opening up of the aviation industry in India brings exciting opportunities for hotels; as they rely on airlines to transport 80% of international arrivals. Increased airline activity has stimulated demand and has helped to improve India's troubled infrastructure. Increased competition will lead to the development of new and improved services. In addition to new aviation brands, many existing companies have ordered new planes. This is long overdue considering state-owned Indian Airlines has not purchased a new plane in 16 years.

The open skies policy has benefited both international and domestic travel. On the international front, the capacity and availability of destinations serving India continues to grow. In late 2004, India and the UK agreed to double (in phases) the number of direct flights per week. Earlier this year, Malaysia Airlines announced their plans to add 18 new routes in India within the next five years. Jet Airways and Air Sahara, two privately owned airlines have launched services to other South Asian destinations, and will shortly launch services to Singapore.

The increasing competition in the domestic airline industry will continue to drive the growth of India's domestic market. In May, two new private domestic airlines (SpiceJet and Kingfisher Air) are expected to enter the market. They will compete head on with current operators Jet Airways, Air Sahara and Air Deccan. It is expected that the tumbling cost of travel will continue, given the growing number of seats available.

The government has expanded the scope of airline liberalisation with its approval in January for private airlines to fly all international routes excluding the Gulf. To qualify the government requires a company to have a fleet of at least 20 planes and five years domestic experience. Jet Airways and Sahara will be able to benefit immediately. In three years time India's state-run carriers will also have to share their Gulf routes. These routes currently earn them most of their operational revenue and profit. The recent IPO (Initial Public Offering) by Jet Airways was over-subscribed several times - indicating the confidence this industry has gained over recent years.

Opportunity knocks

The aviation industry in India will drive future tourism growth, with the continued increase of flights and options for travel. But the question remains, can the country's accommodation meet the increasing expectations of the global traveller? Hotel supply must catch up with demand whilst creating a healthier business mix. Mid-market properties especially need to respond to the growing middle class. But even as the hotel industry joins the airlines in responding to India's thriving economy and driving future tourism growth—infrastructure challenges could still prevent India from grasping its full tourism potential.

Encouragingly major government initiatives such as 'Incredible India' and tax policy revision are well underway. With the growth of the economy expected to continue, and considering the size and dynamics of the domestic market, Indian hotel performance will be exciting to watch over the coming years. Future performance should reflect a country of vast opportunities, especially as mid-market products develop to satisfy the country's thriving domestic market.

Inter-Continental Hotels and Resorts

This international chain has more than 30 hotels and resorts in major Asian business centres and leisure destinations. Recent expansion has centered around joint venture agreements in Malaysia and China, which added nine hotels to the portfolio in 1996. The Forum brand remains an under-developed brand in Asia, although destined to grow. Four projects with a total of 1,456 rooms are currently under construction.

The company currently has 21 hotels with more than 5,300 rooms in Asia. Lai Sun Hotels' recent 51 percent acquisition of Century International Hotels will provide the management company with further financial backing to expand throughout the region. Century International Hotels has been fully committed to developing mid-market hotels in this region as its only brand. The group plans to expand its midmarket portfolio to 60 hotels with 18,800 rooms by the year 2000. Immediate plans call for expansion in Indonesia, Malaysia and Thailand.

A major player in Asia, Shangri-La Hotels & Resorts is rapidly expanding its portfolio of deluxe city hotels and resorts. Shangri-La presently operates 35 properties with a total of 17,000 rooms. Shangri-La Asia Ltd. recently acquired Slim, the privately held hotel management and marketing operation arm of the Kuok Group, which manages all Shangri-La and Traders hotels. Shangri-La has current plans to add 11 hotels with a total of 5,718 rooms in Asia, mainly in primary and secondary cities of China. Westin Hotels & Resorts currently manages 16 hotels with more than 7,000 rooms in Asia. Five hotel projects with some 2,354 rooms will come on stream in the next two years.

Clearly, some markets are experiencing severe financial problems, the most serious being in Thailand and Malaysia. This will likely interrupt domestic developments for the time being until financial institutions have identified a new way forward. This comes at a time when both markets suffer from growth in tourism and a substantial oversupply in the firstclass and luxury segment of the hotel market. This time of uncertainty and volatility is bringing with it opportunities for investors as distress sales and acquisitions are likely to follow in select Asian markets during the next 9 to 18 months as some owners and operators may default on their payments.

This will create opportunities to buy hotel properties at minimal replacement cost primarily in Thailand, but possibly in Malaysia as well. This will occur as hotel owners are forced to adjust their assets to today's market value, and financial institutions seek buyers to purchase assets newly acquired by default. Lending for new construction will be very hard to come by, while new regulations will need to be put in place to reduce the lending risk for banks and other financial institutions going forward.

At the same time, intra-Asian business travel is on a rapid rise as the business interests of major Asian and international corporations drive further expansion in the region. A rapidly growing middle class in countries such as Indonesia and China also will assure the need for more affordable accommodation in the region, especially for individual leisure travellers. Owners and operators in Asia will increasingly face the following challenges:

Productivity and Training

Shortage of skilled labour in almost all Asian markets remains a serious problem for the foreseeable future as new hotels come on line. This will inevitably drive labour costs higher as a percentage of revenue. Hotels will need to review and increase the productivity of all staff, from rank and file to executive, to stave off this rise in costs. Profit margins will inevitably slide if hotels do not reinvent their primary processes and eliminate services not sought by today's travellers. The high staff room ratios of the past may well decline during the next five years to levels much closer to what is common in Europe and the United States.

Training is another major challenge, more so than ever, and must become an integral part of the human resource strategy. With turnover often exceeding 30 percent annually, training still focuses on getting newcomers assimilated to the company as quickly as possible. Limited funds are typically made available for training and developing existing staff to improve knowledge and productivity. Unless the industry embraces training and measures monetary pay- offs, service quality, productivity and turnover are unlikely to improve in the region.

Marketing and Distribution

Increased marketing activities in main feeder markets and alliances with key suppliers of demand (such as wholesalers and airlines) will become critical in the future due to intense competition. In addition, electronic distribution systems, still in the infancy stage in Asia, will gain in significance. Often up to 70-80 percent of hotel bookings are currently made by phone or fax directly with the property. This must change. An interface with Global Distribution Systems (CDS) is one of many competitive advantages of international hotel management companies, yet their impact is reduced in Asia as travel agencies and wholesalers do not use the technology to the same extent as their counterparts in Europe or the United States.

This is significant as the percentage of intra-Asian travel is rapidly increasing—with the ultimate effect of reducing dependency on overseas feeder markets during the next five to 10 years. Investments in Central Reservations Systems (CRS) will allow hotel chains to control inventories and pricing through sophisticated yield management systems, as well as offer a one-stop shop for travel agencies to make bookings for the entire hotel portfolio. An interface with a recognised GDS is the next step only if a) the non-Asian business mix justifies the investment in added distribution and cost; and b) the Asian travel agencies use the available GDS technology to book hotel rooms in larger quantities.

Branding and Mergers

Branding will become one of the most important issues facing Asian-based owners and operators, many of whom have accumulated portfolios of assets without a proper framework for growth. Asset management and hotel management are two distinct businesses requiring different resources. Some Asian-based companies are trying to do both at the same time, often with disappointing results in developing a strong brand with a critical mass of properties.

The global trend of mergers and acquisitions will continue regionally with further rebranding and reorganisation of hotel property portfolios of Asian-based companies into two single asset and hotel management entities. Don't be surprised, however, if a seemingly "small Asian fish" swallows a "big Western fish" in the not too distant future as pockets are deep in this part of the world.

Diversification

With an oversupply of first-class and luxury hotels in most Asian cities today, the development of new mid-market hotels has the greatest potential, especially in population - rich countries such as China, Indonesia and India. Supply of internationally operated hotels does not currently meet the demand in these countries. International operators are eager to introduce their mid-market brands to the Asian market. For the past decade only Accor and Holiday Inns have made major strides in the region in the mid-market sector. Much competition is now expected from ITT Sheraton's "Compass," Marriott's "Courtyard," Shangri -

La's "Traders" and Inter-Continental's "Forum" brand, which will push hard to get a market presence.

Secondary cities are also on the screens of international operators to guarantee management fee growth as primary Asian cities seem to enter the bottom of the cycle. These secondary cities are likely to gain in importance as a sound strategy to grow market share and a balanced network with all of the obvious economies of marketing and operational scale. Although the payoffs are usually longer-term in secondary markets, rapid growth in the economy and population (especially the middle class) should support future profitability.

India and China are in desperate need of hotels in secondary cities, yet more often than not first-class and luxury hotels in Asia enter the market first followed by the mid-market properties years later. Given the rise of an Asian middle class and the desire of Western tourists to look for culturally rich and less crowded vacation spots, Asian resorts are providing major international operators with additional growth opportunities. Four Seasons is expanding its resort portfolio in Bali and India. Sheraton and others have made similar strides to increase their resort portfolios.

Although pristine destinations are harder to find, the future of the resort industry, especially in Malaysia, Indonesia and the Philippines, should be bright. Serviced apartments is another sector of significant potential growth. Despite high yields available, most international hotel operators have stayed clear. Given the scope for growth, however, their absence may not last for long.

Impact of Internet and Technology

Technological innovation through Internet and electronic commerce solutions is one way in which the lodging business is changing rapidly. Electronic commerce on the

Internet is already proceeding at a rapid pace. Rapidly expanding uses will include paperless electronic transaction processing, electronic storefronts, on-line guest services and information publishing in-room entertainment and virtual training for employees.

Security Management

Hotel protection management is one of the most important factors in the lodging industry, one must learn to integrate guest protection techniques and practices into the normal management approaches. It consists of an integrated management model and series of approaches which, when properly applied, allow for the establishment and maintenance of an acceptable level of protection. And at the same time the image of hospitality is maintained.

A model hotel manager's tools are the same tools every manager has to some degree. They are called the "M" tools and they are the tools he uses to accomplish tasks. The four "Ms" represent Money, Methods, Machinery and Manpower. To one extent or another, these are the tools which every manager has as he strives to accomplish his objectives. He learns to influence and motivate and make most productive his "Manpower" tools and leads.

In virtually every organisational model, responsibility and accountability go hand in hand. This concept is no less true in the lodging industry. For example, the food and beverage manager is responsible for ensuring that quality meals are served to guests. If guests are satisfied, the food and beverage manager receives the credit. If the guests express dissatisfaction with their dining experience, the same manager is subject to criticism. Unfortunately, the same management scheme is not applied to security, which is often either ignored or ill-managed, leaving gaping holes in guest protection.

To address the problem, a new approach to hotel security—which the author calls hotel protection management—is being explored. It is the basis for an academic model under consideration at scores of colleges and universities that offer hotel management degrees. And the author suggests that it should also be adopted as a new management tool by hotels. This unique management approach entails decentralising the security function—making it the responsibility of all departments.

The rationale for adopting this potentially controversial management concept is that hotel security—or more accurately, guest protection—cannot hope to succeed to the level mandated by the courts unless specific security duties belong to the designated nonsecurity personnel most able to ensure their completion. In addition, each department manager must be accountable for the successful accomplishment of those assignments.

Hotel protection management takes an approach contrary to the "bigger and expanded security department" thinking that has permeated lodging security for decades. It improves security's reach and effectiveness by a different course. Some security professionals may initially react to this new approach with the dismissive view that "On my property, everyone is already responsible for guest protection." In practice, however, without the requirement of protection task accountability, the "everyone is responsible" scenario results in a situation in which no one is responsible.

So how can accountability be ensured? The first step is to focus senior management's attention on the hotel's legal responsibility. As security professionals know, the courts have determined that the lodging industry must provide a specific level of protection to guests—that being the duty of "reasonable care." This tenet forms the basis of hotel protection management; everything builds from there.

Stated another way, hotel protection management takes the unusual position that every function within the hotel—from the food and beverage department to housekeeping to sales and engineering—ought to be viewed as, in some sense, subordinate to guest protection. That extraordinary position is based on two facts: the aforementioned legal duty to protect the guest, and the proposition that the guest is the asset most critical to a hotel's business success. It is then logical to determine that protecting this paramount asset, the guest, must be the prime concern of a property.

For the traditional hotel security manager, this may, at first blush, seem to be a gift from heaven—security elevated to its rightful position. But properly implemented under the hotel protection management model, this restructuring has far-reaching implications—and some security managers may not embrace them. Essentially, hotel protection management takes the position that guest protection is simply too complex and too vital to be the exclusive responsibility and domain of a security department.

The responsibility must be borne—both functionally and from an accountability standpoint—equally by all departments. To this basic assumption, the traditional hotel security manager might balk. However, the theory of hotel protection management is that the hotel security manager who adapts to this approach will be elevated along with his or her function.

Protection Management Committee

At the heart of this new approach to security is the protection management committee. Traditionally, safety committees have been responsible for reviewing safety concerns and recommending remedial action when appropriate, but their agenda and authority have often been limited. The new model suggests replacing this type of committee with a proactive protection management committee that has expanded responsibility, specifically with regard to crime against the guest.

This committee, which should at a minimum include the head of each department, should be led by the hotel's general manager. The general manager will use this committee as an accountability tool to force every manager to give security the priority it must have if guest protection is to succeed. Typically, a large hotel has eight departments, each with a manager or director who reports directly to the general manager. Departments include food and beverage, personnel, engineering, front office, sales, controller, housekeeping, and security.

The food and beverage manager is responsible for the conduct of that department and held accountable when and if problems arise—and so on for each department. But when a guest is assaulted or property is stolen from a guest room, who is held directly accountable? In practice, no clear lines of responsibility exist under traditional security structures. Using the hotel protection management approach and the protection management committee, a general manager can ensure accountability.

Traditional security strategies still apply, but are given a slightly different twist. For example, it is traditional to begin with a security survey. That is also the first step under hotel protection management. Before responsibilities can be assigned through the committee, the hotel must do a security survey to identify and examine the assets in need of protection. Next, a threat assessment determines the threats to which assets are or may be exposed. But hotel protection management holds that these first two steps should be carried out by the general manager—perhaps with the security manager—but they should not be conducted by the security manager alone. The reasoning is as follows: while most general managers argue that they know their property thoroughly, most do not.

Hotel protection management takes the position that this void is unacceptable, that the general manager must be made to know the property intimately. By conducting the initial security survey, the general manager sees firsthand the specific profile of the assets to be protected, the identity and nature of the threats that may, or indeed do, threaten those assets, and the countermeasures currently in place. Because "seeing is believing," general managers who walk the property may be more committed to allocating funds and other resources to address security's weak points.

In part, hotel protection management is also based on the premise that general managers of the future will have had, as part of their college curriculum, courses that give them a foundation in security issues. Where that is not the case, the security manager's assistance during the survey, threat assessment, and countermeasure phases will be critical.

Action Plan

The survey itself is diagnostic, not remedial. After the survey and threat assessment have been completed, the general manager, with the assistance of the committee, is ready to develop a menu of countermeasures to minimise the threats. The diagnostic survey and analysis are presented to the committee for its evaluation and action. The group then determines not only whether existing countermeasures are appropriate and effective but also whether any countermeasures should be eliminated, added, or modified.

For example, the survey may reveal that security lighting is adequate but that replacing fixtures is costly. The committee may then direct the person in charge of lighting to find a way to extend the life-span of fixtures or to investigate whether alternative fixtures might be more cost-effective. The action plan that will guide the committee is founded on the hotel protection management tenet that there are eight—and only eight—countermeasures management can use to counteract the threat of crime. (These also are the eight countermeasures against which the general manager measures his property during the security survey.) They are:

— preemployment screening
— staffwide training
— access control
— lighting
— key control
— security officers
— guest room protection
— emergency response

Security professionals are familiar with each of these, although they may not necessarily have categorised them exactly this way. The hotel protection management model proposes that general managers be taught—as part of their college curriculum—how each of these countermeasures relates to hotel security. They would, for example, learn the importance of training the entire property staff—not just security personnel—in the methods and techniques of guest protection. Such training in the following scenarios would be appropriate:

— Training the housekeeping staff to allow only specifically identified authorised persons into rooms.
— Training the front desk staff in proper guest confidentiality techniques such as not verbalising the number of the room being rented to the guest.

- Training maintenance and engineering personnel in proper guest room key production and storage control. For example, emphasising that blank, extra, and unused keys be stored in a secure, locked cabinet, and that the number of employees with access to the cabinet be controlled.

With the survey and threat assessment data in hand, the protection management committee must:

- Examine each threat vis a vis each asset, including foreseeability issues and considering existing countermeasures.
- Determine collectively the validity and completeness of the general manager's findings.
- Determine which of the countermeasures are appropriate, which are adequate, and which are lacking.
- Decide under the direction of the general manager, and often with the assistance of the security manager, which countermeasures are to be the responsibility of each manager.

In response to this last point, traditionalists in the security field may cry "heresy." They will object to "protection by committee." The assignment of a countermeasure—complete with responsibilities for its installation, maintenance, and continued effectiveness—must not be haphazard. When possible, each security assignment should complement other duties.

Consider the countermeasure of guest room protection. Historically, this responsibility has fallen under the purview of the security manager. But the hotel protection management model poses the question, "Who is better qualified than the executive housekeeper to manage this countermeasure?"

No one knows the rooms better than the housekeepers who tend them. No one is inside each and every room more than the housekeeper. No one has a bigger stake in the housekeeping of rooms than the executive housekeeper.

Similarly, one might assign the countermeasure of preemployment screening to the security manager. Initially, the personnel manager might seem to be the more logical choice. However, the security professional's investigative skills, database resources, and general eye for detecting "red flags" make him or her better able to weed out problem candidates.

Accountability

The final step under the hotel protection management model is for each manager to actually carry out the protection duties in each assigned area—to be responsible and accountable for the installation, maintenance, and continued working order of the relevant devices and measures agreed to by the committee. Each department head should be diligent in overseeing and monitoring whether procedures suggested by the protection management committee are being followed.

The committee should meet monthly to reassess the appropriateness of countermeasures, discuss changes in assets or threats, and address performance of duties to ensure accountability. The responsibility for each security item should be a line item on each department's or manager's performance report, making security a quantifiable and documented responsibility for every manager—not just the security manager.

Perhaps it would help if this approach is thought of not as protection by committee but rather as protection by cooperation, by joint effort, by validation and mutual assistance. Hotel protection management might also be thought of as a way of bringing to hotel security the empowerment and team-building models that are being used effectively elsewhere in the business world to enhance productivity and worker participation.

While the traditional security professional might initially view this approach as cause for concern—because of the implicit loss of control—the result is more likely to be that, with the elevation of protection to the highest concerns on a property, the security manager's experience and knowledge will be in greater demand and his or her advice will be more readily sought and appreciated. Most importantly, security managers will be surrounded by allies.

The general manager will convey the important premise that every department on a property has a part to play in guest protection. The hotel management protection strategy will help ensure that those roles are understood and that proper training is provided, along with clear assignments of responsibility and accountability, making everyone a partner in the protection program.

Guest Protection

The underpinnings of our entire approach to the provision of guest protection is constituted mainly by four phases. Built on the basic canon that guest protection is an absolute requirement, they are the following:

Phase I: In any high-tech manufacturing and production facility, assets which require protection will most certainly include the products, proprietary production processes, highly confidential technological research-and-development procedures, and of course, the buildings, equipment, furnishings, and that all-important, highly trained, virtually irreplaceable assets, the employees. When visualising this protection approach, it is important to realise that these assets, collectively and individually, are unique to this facility. They differ in importance, in priority, in scope, and in description from the assets of any other facility.

Phase II: In any high-tech facility and considering the assets, one would consider that threats to those assets would include product theft, industrial espionage, fire exposure to the buildings, and accidents or crimes against persons. It is absolutely vital that one remember that when identifying these threats, they are as unique to this location as the assets are.

Phase III: Once the assets and threats to them have been identified, the manager must embark on the process of identifying those particular, individually selected countermeasures, which are specifically designed to minimise the specifically identified threats to which those specifically identified assets are exposed.

Phase IV: The manager must then integrate his specifically selected countermeasures into his overall property-management scheme, and establish accepted management-science umbrellas over them. He will then assign responsibility demand accountability, and establish training and continuity. At this point, the lodging manager can be said to have begun the establishment of protection management.

Yet there are several major real-world problems which present themselves when such an all-encompassing approach to management is attempted. The important points to be noted are given below.

— Managers often have a built-in bias against security. They find it uncomfortable to accept and difficult to deal with. Of course, they often fear the issue of expense.

— Managers often have difficulty in accepting security on the same management terms and at the same management level as other functional management endeavours such as sales, production, transportation, housekeeping, etc.

— Managers often fail to realise that such protection must be property-wide and property-specific.

All of these dispositions manifest themselves when the lodging manager is faced with the challenge of guest protection. He is burdened with outdated thinking and the short-sighted and limiting usage of what is known as security. He has been too long exposed to traditional thinking which holds to the mind set which leads him to consider protection only after a crime has occurred. And because of outmoded thinking, what is the solution most often considered when reacting to a protection problem? If it ever worked, that state approach was weak at best, and it is woefully inadequate and counterproductive today. It is inadequate because it is reactive.

It is counterproductive because random countermeasure selection either invariably will bring about too much protection. Selection of particular countermeasures must come only after a systematic and thorough analysis of the first two considerations or phases, which are: (i) the assets which need protection, and (ii) the threats against which those assets must be protected. Each property is unique, it follows that the protection scheme designed to protect such an entity against threats which also are unique to the property, must be unique. This individuality must be taken into consideration long before plans are formulated as to what types of protection to apply.

Different cities, different neighbourhoods within the same cities, even different locations within the same neighbourhood have different threats. Different styles of building construction invite different threats. Different construction, different furnishings and different employees all impact to produce different threats. For example, the high-tech plant would require a different protection profile if it were located in a high-crime, urban slum area, as opposed to the exact duplicate facility located in a low-crime, low population, well-protected rural setting.

Guests are as unique both individually and collectively as are hotelier's properties, and as such, require unique protection. For example, if a property caters to a young, high-energy clientele, then it is obvious that the protection profile we seek must differ from that which we would establish if the clientele consisted primarily of senior citizens. We might well pay attention to proper liquor-serving training in the former, and pay more attention to slip-and-fall protection in the latter.

HOTEL BOOM IN ASIAN COUNTRIES: STUDIES IN BANGKOK, KUALA LUMPUR, MANILA AND HONG KONG

In Asian countries, tourism has posted double-digit increases in recent years even with the reduced annual growth rates since 1995. Vietnam reported an increase of 18.9 percent between 1995 and 1996, while the Philippines posted a 16.4 percent rise. Tourist arrivals in Hong Kong and Japan have been near 14.7 percent. Not all countries, however, showed record gains. Thailand's arrivals lagged with only a 3.5 percent increase, while Malaysian visitor arrivals actually declined by more than 4 percent in 1996. Just as significant, tourism receipts for the region rose at a faster rate than arrivals in 1996, demonstrating the positive economic impact of tourism in Asia.

Tourism receipts climbed a healthy 12.8 percent for Asia / Pacific from 1995 to 1996.[2] It is indeed very encouraging to see China, for instance, registering a 20 percent growth in tourism receipts, totaling almost US$10 billion. Singapore (14.6 percent), the Philippines (13.9 percent) and Hong Kong (12.8 percent) all experienced a significant increase in tourism receipts. Yet Malaysia and Thailand again suffered, showing a mere 0.4 percent and 1.2 percent improvement respectively.

Regional markets in Asia / Pacific offer dramatically different profiles when it comes to new hotel development. East Asia and the Pacific registered the fastest increase in hotel accommodation measured by bed-places, adding 2.9 million beds between 1980 and 1995. This represents a compound annual growth rate of 10.9 percent. This trend will continue especially with China becoming the major source for supply growth in north Asia. South Asia - India, Myanmar and Nepal, among others has seen only minimal growth in hotel supply given both inadequate economic and political policies in recent years. This is likely to change as we enter the 21st century, with these three countries showing exceptional opportunities for hotel development.

Bangkok

In the past five years, the Bangkok hotel room supply nearly doubled from 10,608 in 1992 to 19,323 in l9%. Given only modest demand growth over the same period, this has led to an oversupply of rooms with occupancy rates at about 65 percent. The occupancy rate in 1995 and 1996 showed only slight improvements, and this occurred only because room rates were eased. Bangkok had become one of the most affordable destinations in Asia even before the currency devaluation of the Thai baht. The daily room rate of luxury hotel rooms has averaged US$75, and demand is not likely to increase as prices are already rock-bottom. It is anticipated that room rates will decrease slightly in 1997 with occupancy unchanged. Furthermore, additional supply during the next two years will reduce the bottom line even more in an already depressed market.

Kuala Lumpur

Malaysia, along with its capital city, Kuala Lumpur, have suffered from minimal increases in tourist arrivals during recent years compared to other Asian destinations, with slower growth straining the hotel and tourism industry. To prepare for the 1998 Cornrnonwealth Games, the government has initiated a tax incentive scheme, which has led to a "development frenzy" in Kuala Lumpur. New supply in the firstclass and luxury segment is projected at more than 3,400 rooms by 1999. This additional supply, primarily in the up-market segment, is likely to further depress occupancy and room rate growth during the next three to five years. Hotel occupancy rates fell from the mid-80s to high 70s between 1995 and 1996, as did the average room rate. Tourist arrivals also dropped in 1996 from the preceding year.

Manila

A total of 60 hotels and 12,112 rooms were in operation in Manila in 1996 - an increase of 7 percent from 11,321 rooms in 1994. Strong economic growth supported improved performance in Manila's hotel market, with occupancies reaching 69.1 percent in 1996 compared with the 62.2 percent occupancy rate in the previous year. The number of rooms available also fell with hotels under renovation, including the Dusit Hotel Nikko, EDSA Plaza Hotel, the Heritage Hotel, the Manila Hotel and the Westin Philippine Plaza.

Between 1997 and 1998, 12 hotels and four extension projects totaling some 2,347 rooms - will come on stream, increasing the supply in Metro Manila to 14,089 rooms, about a 20 percent gain. These hotels, generally not managed by an international operator, are mainly mid-market.

New first class and luxury hotels planned for Manila include a Ritz-Carlton and a JW Marriott in Makati, as well as a hotel development by Mega World in Manila Bay reclamation area. None of these hotels, however, will open before the year 2000. Further supply of at least three Luxury hotels is expected in the new development of Fort Bonafacio with opening dates beyond 2001. Given literally no additional supply during the next two years, both Makati (next to the financial center and thus frequented by the business travelers) and the bay area (where most leisure travelers stay) should see further growth in occupancy and average rates, especially if tourism arrival growth continues at a 16 percent pace as was the case in 1996.

Hong Kong

As of December, 1996, the Hong Kong hotel market comprised 33,530 rooms and 88 properties. With growth in hotel demand outweighing supply, Hong Kong has enjoyed tremendous success as occupancy rates have climbed to 85 percent on average during the last five years and average room rates have risen to some of the highest in Asia. Supporting this economic success story are the commercial redevelopments of the Lee Garden, Victoria and Hilton hotels, which have been an economic benefit for other currently existing hotels. A mid-market hotel is able to demand at least US$125, first-class hotels US$190 and the luxury segment US$300 a night. Hotel profitability has thus increased substantially during the past five years as labour costs fell as a percentage of revenue.

As the price gap between the leisure and business segments has narrowed, Hong Kong is now facing a major challenge to further expand the leisure sector. Recent arrival figures, however, have been discouraging and the 100-day, posthandover public relations campaign by the Hong Kong Tourism Association had no immediate impact on business. With bargains on shopping becoming more and more difficult to find and no additional tourist attractions on the drawing boards, Hong Kong may see a long-term decline in leisure travelers unless new strategies are put in place by both the public and private sectors. High prices in Hong Kong are one reason for the drop in tourist arrivals.

The devaluation of major Southeast Asian currencies during recent months will also force Hong Kong to review its future pricing policy. Most Asian travelers have seen their local currency drop more than 30 percent against the U.S. dollar and the Hong Kong dollar. In addition, Hong Kong developers have 9,000 rooms on the drawing boards before the year 2,000, a 27 percent increase - pushing supply from 33,536 to 42,685 rooms. Given recent political and economic developments, however, it is unlikely that all projects will remain on time, while some may never materialise. The majority of the new developments are planned along the new MTR railway to the Chek Lap Kok airport opening in mid - 1998. Given that this new supply is primarily in the mid-market sector, leisure travelers now staying at firstclass hotels may find themselves trading down in their accommodation once these new properties open. The growth in business travelers to Hong Kong should remain strong as the city will continue to benefit from being the financial and business center of Greater China.

Future Trends in the Hotel Industry

The organisation and business operations of hotel companies will be reshaped to satisfy the changing needs of constituents. This is due in part to rapid technological advances in information and communications, as well as a transformation of the capital base of the hotel industry. Customers and stakeholders will demand seamless access to hotel company business information and processes.

Heightened business interdependencies between hotel companies, their suppliers, and marketing and service representatives, will undoubtedly blur corporate lines. Major changes will take place in the way the hotel industry accesses and deploys financing and venture capital.

Nearly every business and most individuals in the United States have already entered the electronic age of information and communications. Laptop computers, cellular telephones, beepers and interactive communication devices have all become commonplace tools are heavily. Within the next few years, consumers will have unlimited direct access to most channels of market and business information and distribution.

Consumers will want to handle daily activities and business transactions without leaving their homes or offices using their own personal computers. Buying and selling goods and services, paying bills, researching topics of interest, handling banking transactions, and planning daily personal and business activities are all part of this change.

What implications does this have for the hotel industry? Well, for starters, many individuals will want to book personally-tailored vacation packages and business itineraries using direct links through their own personal computers. This will require full access to on-line facility data bases and vacation catalogues, as well as price lists. Also, they will need direct access to hotel and airline rooms and seat inventory control systems. This alone could revolutionise the marketing and sales paradigm for the hotel industry.

Technological advances in information and communication will cause hotels to make dramatic chances in the way they serve and physically accommodate guests. Count on it, interactive computing and multimedia devices will be as commonplace in hotel rooms of the future as present-day remote control televisions and touch-tone telephones. Guests will want the option of avoiding interaction with hotel service and clerical personnel by using these devices. Just think, no more waiting in line to check in or out of your hotel room.

No delay while waiting for the hotel operator or some other service clerk to answer the telephone to schedule your wake-up call, take your room service order or book your restaurant reservation. No need to call for additional towels, or to order a shoe shine or dirty laundry pick-up. You can do all of this by touching a few icons on your television screen.

Technological advancements may alter the physical design and space allocation of hotels in the future. Quite possibly, a computing and multimedia room will be required on every floor of every full-service hotel.

Possibly, the amount and size of meeting rooms and auditoriums will change as guests wishing to participate in large conferences from the comfort and convenience of their guest rooms, may wish to use interactive video conferencing devices and remote response terminals, to participate. Another possibility is that the front desk area could be cut hack to a small greeting kiosk and the remainder of the space put to more productive use such as retail space.

Many new sources of revenues could result from these changes. Direct guest room linkups to a wide variety of online entertainment and informational networks will be a standard requirement in the future. This could mean large access fees for hotels. Rental or usage charges for peripheral devices could also mean big business.

A number of hotel companies presently are focusing their attention on redesigning or participating in new global distribution systems. These will better link hotel companies, airlines, travel companies, and rental car companies to each other--but not directly to the consumer.

Just think of the marketing opportunities that exist today for hotel companies to reach customers directly using international computer networks, on-line bulletin boards, and direct "E-mail" advertising. A few innovative hotel companies have already seized this opportunity.

Role of Stakeholders

Owners, investors, lenders and suppliers all want and are demanding more timely information on which to base their business decisions and monitor their business interests. Many hotel companies are finding that stakeholders particularly owners and lenders- want to check-in directly to the flow of business and financial information. Think about demands for information that might come up in the future. Hotel lenders may want on-line access to hotel treasury and cash management systems to daily sweep bank accounts and monitor compliance with covenants of loan agreements.

Investors may want up-to-the-minute financial statement information to gauge investment performance and make daily investment decisions. Suppliers may want on-line access to perpetual inventory records to automatically trigger purchase orders and shipments. Already, travel agents, meeting planners and tour wholesalers want on-line access to room inventories and pricing information. To accommodate these needs, major changes in the business and accounting information systems of hotels and hotel companies will have to be implemented.

Organisational and Operational Changes

Sweeping organisational and operational changes will

occur in the hotel industry. The need for large headquarters facilities with multiple departments and large technical support staffs will greatly diminish because of technological advancements in information and communications. In marketing and sales, huge competitive advantages can result from setting up state-of-the-art" customer databases with interactive communication linkups.

Through the use of wide area networks and other linkages, individuals will be able to share information and experiences between locations rapidly and set up multi-location workgroups to facilitate problem-solving. This will significantly reduce the need to cluster technical support staffs under one roof. The ability exists to link suppliers seamlessly with hotel companies using "E-mail" and knowledge management software.

For the first time, outsourcing for a wide variety of technical and business support functions, such as payroll and personnel management, purchasing and new business development, is a viable option for most hotel companies. For hotels, the entire organisational and operational structure may change as a result of technological innovation. Front-office functions could be minimised or eliminated. Universal service representatives could tend to virtually every guest need from a single work station.

Guests will likely be able to initiate many service functions directly using interactive guest room devices. This could change the service staffing requirements and mechanical resources to more productive activities such as better execution of guest requests. This also holds true for many back-office functions. Through better uses of technology, many hotels can approach elimination of many of the clerical functions presently performed in the back offices of hotels.

Capital Access and Deployment

The capital base of the U.S. hotel industry is quickly shifting from Main Street to Wall Street. More and more hotels are being acquired by large investment funds. They typically match small amounts of equity with large amounts of secondary funds obtained from the sale of debt and equity securities on Wall Street. This includes funding from REMICs, REITs, initial public offerings and high-yield note offerings. These sources of funding will continue to be the most viable and efficient means of raising capital for the hotel industry in the future.

In addition, traditional funding sources such as banks, credit companies, and insurance companies are already returning to the market to make loans. However, they too are planning to raise funds for lending through the sale of mortgage-backed securities on Wall Street.

The shift in capital is expected to have a dramatic effect on the future underwriting of hotel loans and investments. No longer will the game be to convince the lender's credit committee or the investor's capital committee to do the deal. Now the game will be to convince the independent agencies rating the securities that the deal is good, since they are the ones that Wall Street investors rely on to rate the underlying securities.

Underwriting parameters will continue to be tough in the future since virtually all loans will ultimately be sold in pools to investors as securities. Lenders will want to be sure that every loan meets the minimum underwriting criteria set by the investment bankers who sell the loans to investors. After the loan is made, a far greater amount of periodic business and financial information will be required from the borrower. This is to allow for secondary sales of the mortgage-backed securities on Wall Street.

Foreign capital will continue to play a very important role in the U.S. hotel industry. If the equity for a deal is not coming from Wall Street, chances are pretty good it is coming from Europe, the Middle East or Asia. This is particularly true for deals involving large luxury hotels in major U.S. cities. For budget and limited service hotels and motels throughout the United States. Asian-American investors account for a large portion of the capital. In the future, we may see capital increasingly coming from ibis group for middle market and luxury properties.

Growth of Supply

Regional markets in Asia / Pacific offer dramatically different profiles when it comes to new hotel development. East Asia and the Pacific registered the fastest increase in hotel accommodation measured by bed-places, adding 2.9 million beds between 1980 and 1995. This represents a compound annual growth rate of 10.9 percent. This trend will continue especially with China becoming the major source for supply growth in north Asia. South Asia—India, Myanmar and Nepal, among others has seen only minimal growth in hotel supply given both inadequate economic and political policies in recent years. This is likely to change as we enter the 21st century, with these three countries showing exceptional opportunities for hotel development.

A profile of the hotel boom in Asia also reveals that the region's primary cities—including Bangkok, Kuala Lumpur, Manila and Hong Kong are at different stages in the development cycle. In many cases, these differences are dramatic, reflecting a wide range of supply - and - demand characteristics.

In the past five years, the Bangkok hotel room supply nearly doubled from 10,608 in 1992 to 19,323 in 19%. Given only modest demand growth over the same period, this has led to an oversupply of rooms with occupancy rates at about 65 percent. The occupancy rate in 1995 and 1996 showed only slight improvements, and this occurred only because room rates were eased.

Bangkok had become one of the most affordable destinations in Asia even before the currency devaluation of the Thai baht. The daily room rate of luxury hotel rooms has averaged US$75, and demand is not likely to increase as prices are already rock-bottom. It is anticipated that room rates will decrease slightly in 1997 with occupancy unchanged. Furthermore, additional supply during the next two years will reduce the bottom line even more in an already depressed market.

Malaysia, along with its capital city, Kuala Lumpur, have suffered from minimal increases in tourist arrivals during recent years compared to other Asian destinations, with slower growth straining the hotel and tourism industry. To prepare for the 1998 Cornrnonwealth Games, the government has initiated a tax incentive scheme, which has led to a "development frenzy" in Kuala Lumpur. New supply in the firstclass and luxury segment is projected at more than 3,400 rooms by 1999. This additional supply, primarily in the up-market segment, is likely to further depress occupancy and room rate growth during the next three to five years.

Hotel occupancy rates fell from the mid-80s to high 70s between 1995 and 1996, as did the average room rate. Tourist arrivals also dropped in 1996 from the preceding year. This year is expected to show a further erosion of profitability in Kuala Lumpur, particularly given the recent devaluation of the Malaysian ringgit, with average occupancy dropping to the low 70s. Given the additional supply at the top-end of the market and resulting labour demand, a further increase in salaries and wages is expected. Kuala Lumpur's hotel sector appears set to follow in Bangkok's tracks.

A total of 60 hotels and 12,112 rooms were in operation in Manila in 1996—an increase of 7 percent from 11,321 rooms in 1994. Strong economic growth supported improved performance in Manila's hotel market, with occupancies reaching 69.1 percent in 1996 compared with the 62.2 percent occupancy rate in the previous year. Between 1997 and 1998, 12 hotels and four extension projects totalling some 2,347 rooms—will come on stream, increasing the supply in Metro Manila to 14,089 rooms, about a 20 percent gain.

These hotels, generally not managed by an international operator, are mainly mid-market. New first class and luxury hotels planned for Manila include a Ritz-Carlton and a JW Marriott in Makati, as well as a hotel development by Mega World in Manila Bay reclamation area. None of these hotels, however, will open before the year 2000. Further supply of at least three Luxury hotels is expected in the new development of Fort Bonafacio with opening dates beyond 2001. Given literally no additional supply during the next two years, both Makati (next to the financial centre and thus frequented by the business travellers) and the bay area (where most leisure travellers stay) should see further growth in occupancy and average rates, especially if tourism arrival growth continues at a 16 percent pace as was the case in 1996.

As of December, 1996, the Hong Kong hotel market comprised 33,530 rooms and 88 properties. With growth in hotel demand outweighing supply, Hong Kong has enjoyed tremendous success as occupancy rates have climbed to 85 percent on average during the last five years and average room rates have risen to some of the highest in Asia.

Supporting this economic success story are the commercial re-developments of the Lee Garden, Victoria and Hilton hotels, which have been an economic benefit for other currently existing hotels. A mid-market hotel is able to demand at least US$125, first-class hotels US$190 and the luxury segment US$300 a night. Hotel profitability has thus increased substantially during the past five years as labour costs fell as a percentage of revenue.

As the price gap between the leisure and business segments has narrowed, Hong Kong is now facing a major challenge to further expand the leisure sector. Recent arrival figures, however, have been discouraging and the 100-day, posthandover public relations campaign by the Hong Kong Tourism Association had no immediate impact on business. With bargains on shopping becoming more and more difficult to find and no additional tourist attractions on the drawing boards, Hong Kong may see a long-term decline in leisure travellers unless new strategies are put in place by both the public and private sectors.

High prices in Hong Kong are one reason for the drop in tourist arrivals. The devaluation of major Southeast Asian currencies during recent months will also force Hong Kong (whose currency is pegged to the U.S. dollar) to review its future pricing policy. Most Asian travellers have seen their local currency drop more than 30 percent against the U.S. dollar and the Hong Kong dollar.

In addition, Hong Kong developers have 9,000 rooms on the drawing boards before the year 2,000, a 27 percent increase—pushing supply from 33,536 to 42,685 rooms. Given recent political and economic developments, however, it is unlikely that all projects will remain on time, while some may never materialise. The growth in business travellers to Hong Kong should remain strong as the city will continue to benefit from being the financial and business centre of Greater China (Hong Kong, China and Taiwan). The IMF and World Bank meetings this year have underlined the fact that Hong Kong remains the principal economic gateway to China.

In almost every Asian country, there is a strong presence of independent or family-owned hotels with long traditions and are thus well established in the market. Yet international chains are dominating the major developments in Asia through their proven track record, management skills and access to international financing.

Accor Asia/Pacific—which manages hotels under the brand of Sofitel, Novotel, Mercure, Ibis and Formula I - currently operates 75 hotels in Asia. Under an aggressive expansion plan, Accor will add 34 hotels with 6,053 rooms to its 75 property portfolio during the next two years alone. Expansion focuses primarily on Indonesia, the world's third largest country, Thailand and Vietnam.

2

Organisational Design

Newly built hotels are being admired throughout the world by travelers and architects, and this strikingly illustrated survey features the best new designs. An interesting evolution in hotel design over past several decades. At the beginning of the 20th century, the wealthy traveled in grand style at a leisurely pace, with vast amounts of luggage and, quite frequently, large numbers of staff.

The design of the hotels that catered to them reflected that style, in size, proportion and atmosphere. The tumult of the 20s, 30s, and 40s disrupted travel patterns, but when people began traveling more consistently in the ensuing years, the look and feel of hotels changed.

Opulence and exclusivity are associated with innovative and somewhat theatrical design, rather than traditional signifiers like Persian carpets and wood paneling. Built-in case pieces, flat-screen televisions and simplified bedding materials are used to maximise guestrooms space. Furthermore, bathrooms have become more spacious and an important part of guestroom design. What worked a decade ago for the guestroom does not work today. The concept of 'zones' within the room has not changed, there is still a sleeping, relaxing, working, dressing and bathroom 'zone' but the way in which these zones are now laid out and have started to overlap has changed and is continuing to evolve with the increased focus on guest 'life-style'.

The guestroom must be able to function on a number of levels in addition to providing a comfortable place to sleep. For the business traveler, the room should be able to function as office and meeting space. At then end of the day, literally, it should also feel more like an entertainment area than strictly a bedroom. Technological capabilities that enable the guest to accomplish various tasks from the privacy of the room are highly desirable—Interactive in-house television systems that let the guest review the bill, order movies, check e-mail and check out are increasingly popular.

But it certainly is not just the guestroom that is critical to effective design. Public areas are increasingly being incorporated into the rhythms of the guest experience. "Many newer hotels use their lobbies or spaces immediately adjacent as gathering places, most frequently putting a bar or lounge next to or in the lobby. The activity is now seen as fashionable, where a hushed, silent lobby remains at a minority". "The creation of large scale residential settings where the guest almost feels like they are at a party at a friend's house is becoming a concept for hotel lobbies and public area spaces.

The set area boundaries of the past are melting away to give us the ability to cross-utilize spaces depending on the demand for each area at different times." There are also critical elements of the exterior design which are different now from ten years ago and can have an impact on customer perception. With increased competition, hotels must be creative in attracting guests' attention, before they even enter the lobby. wwsith so many new hotels around the world in mixed-use complexes, the entrance to the hotel are often the only exterior part of the hotel the guest sees.

Many popular, luxury properties are housed in buildings whose overall appearance is very plain. Chic resort hotels, particularly in warm climates, have definitely pushed owners towards more innovative architecture and the use of more luxurious materials. In addition to spas which have become increasingly popular in recent years, other amenities, such as media rooms, libraries, screening rooms and full-fledged theaters, are now being considered as developers are looking to add new dimensions to the guest's perception of overall value, and which lend a unique aspect to the hotel atmosphere.

These areas offer obvious benefit to the individual traveler, but can also be used very creatively for groups and incentives as ways to generate additional revenue. The guest is better traveled, more educated, sophisticated and surrounded by design elements through all forms of media therefore the expectations are far more difficult to meet. Another trend in hospitality design is the "designer' touch. Armani just announced the opening of its new hotel in Dubai, following the Palazzo Versace and Bulgari openings.

In any case or era, the success of a hotel's design can be gauged by how well it has anticipated and met the tastes and needs of its guests. More importantly, the continuing success of an innovative change lies in how functional that change is. New just for the sake of being new doesn't last long. "Comfort and practicality are all important, and this is often forgotten in striving to achieve avant garde and stylish design. The architecture creates the base, whether the building is an old or modern one, and defines the overall feel of the hotel. Some hotels are architecturally beautiful but lack a human dimension.

Design has to create a sense of intimacy and proportions to which the guest can relate, leaving him in comfort and at ease. A touch of excitement and glamour will also help. Good design should be visually exciting and original. It should be functional but above all it should offer great comfort.As is true of any successful business person, hoteliers must know and anticipate what their guests want. Whatever changes are instituted, they must continue to fulfill their brand promise to the customer. This is not to say that very forward-thinking innovations won't work, but they must be delivered in a context which is consistent with the customer's expectations. Any design component must be regarded from the point of view of how it will enhance the overall guest experience, and how will it augment guest satisfaction.

Changing Face of Hotel Industry

No hotel company operating today can be unaware of the swift pace of global change and its impact on every facet of the hospitality industry. With just five years left in this century, we can expect change to be the only constant. New business practices are evolving virtually as fast as our technologies, while resistance to change has become one of the primary causes of business failure.

The future success of hotel organisations will be driven in large part by the ability to foresee—and capitalise – on change. Beyond this truism, however, there is an urgent need to identify what will be required in the competitive environment of the future with its intense focus on serving customer needs. The hospitality industry—as is the case with business generally—is subject to deep currents of change set in motion as economic and social systems shaped in the industrial era evolve to a knowledge-based era driven by technology advances.

In this period of global transition, it behooves hotel organisations to examine the key factors that will not only define success, but the ability to survive in coming years. Its mission was to identify the characteristics needed to lead successful businesses in the next century. These executives offer a number of compelling messages regarding the key success factors of the future.

Customers will have the strongest influence on the corporation in the year 2000. Indeed, these executives believe that the customer will be "king" in the new century. Exceptional leadership was by far the attribute most frequently cited by CEOs and senior executives; the consensus appears to be that successful companies in the year 2000 will be led by corporate visionaries.

A strategic planning focus is not only essential, but must embody a concept of planning for the future that anticipates change, rather than being based exclusively on historical models. In structuring organisations for the future, companies must build management capabilities to deal with one of the most critical challenges—diversity in the marketplace. Employing information technology to drive business success in this information-driven era is not only the path of least resistance, but vital to virtually every aspect of operations.

Customer Focus: Recognising that the hotel industry has a somewhat split personality reflecting the inherent conflicts between its real estate and operational aspects, it is important to understand the industry's real estate origins and how they are shaping the challenges ahead.

The origins of the industry's real estate persona are embodied in the classic theory of location - "if we build it, they will come." As a result of this "building" complex, the industry has tended to have a real estate and asset orientation, rather than a customer focus. From the hotel company perspective—especially that of the brand-oriented "chain"—the varied interests of a diffused property ownership group can be quite different than the singular interest of the chain that operates and markets the properties.

Even when the ownership of geographically dispersed hotel properties is controlled by a single hotel organisation, the financial structuring tends to be property-specific. Corporate financial strategies are frequently subjugated to the needs of the last property deal brought into the company's fold. Each property in a so-called "chain," is frequently the subject of a unique and distinctive ownership and financial structure. This phenomenon—quite common in the real estate sector, but unusual for business enterprises generally—makes for elusive economies of scale in the structuring and financing of property-driven expansion.

Collectively, these factors have produced low comparative returns in real estate, although criticism leveled at commercial real estate returns is somewhat less germane to the hotel industry, where management and franchise fees can produce high returns for those companies where property ownership is held by third parties. While hotel chains have adopted traditional corporate frameworks, there are a number of predominantly real estate-driven, family-owned businesses in the hotel sector that continue to operate as relatively unstructured organisations. In meeting the future, these businesses will need plans, people and processes in order to establish viable corporate forms that can compete in tomorrow's marketplace and capitalise upon its opportunities.

In today's changed environment, the hotel organisation must deal with a number of new realities. Investors in our industry are no longer satisfied with long-term capital appreciation and psychic income that heretofore were often the justification for otherwise seemingly uneconomic investments in hotel property or, indeed, hotel chains. The first reality is that there is a very specific and identifiable relationship between bottom line performance and value. Improvements in business operations raises values. It is not surprising, therefore, that the new owners attracted to this industry in recent years have new sets of demands.

This transformation from an old-guard group of investors and owners to income and return-driven newcomers has meant that the once "quiet enjoyment" of operators in their management of hotels for third parties is being disturbed, interrupted and overturned. These challenges all take place in an environment where capital has become extremely selective in markets that have little stability. A global shortage of capital will not remain a short-term problem, and future hotel organisations must have a stronger alignment to capital providers—a critical "customer" group. Hotel companies will need to compete by offering better returns and performance than in the past.

Hotel chains have found their development timetables quashed in recent years, making it difficult to achieve goals of critical mass often required to improve performance. These factors are driving consolidation in the brand "sweepstakes." Capital markets, therefore, continue to favour well-established companies, a reality that must drive entrepreneurial organisations to meet the future now by planning for an evolving corporate context in which to operate.

Hotel developers, owners and management companies will all need to develop new strategies, skills and processes that look forward to the competitive demands of the future. These ultimately must address issues related to vision and planning, as well as organisational skill sets and processes to attract and retain customers. To stake a claim in the future, current business practices should be examined in light of what can be expected to be the key success factors in the year 2000.

Embrace a global change orientation: As the information age produces greater worldwide integration of business activities, a global knowledge base will become invaluable. Success in local and regional hotel markets will be shaped decisively by a global business environment that defines capital movement, customer expectations and applications of new technologies.

Focus on the Customer: If the customer is king in the 21st century, hotel organisations will be best served by focusing less on their hotel assets as measures of success, and more on their customers.

This involves a fundamental shift in viewing the real estate asset as the wealth creator—to the customer as the key to building shareholder wealth. A customer focus must imbue business decisions at all levels of developing and operating a hotel organisation. Pursuing such a course will inevitably impact shareholder wealth. To accomplish this, however, customers need to participate in the product development process.

Fully realising a customer focus in the industry poses a significant challenge. The hotel industry must confront problems due to conflicts between operational needs and real estate goals. Quite simply, an operator must remain customer-focused, but the short-term strategies to meet these needs may be inconsistent with the long-term objectives of property owners. Balancing those goals will be essential.

A customer focus implies a significant shift in what drives hotel development—placing primary emphasis on the customer with the locations to follow. Nevertheless, a hotel organisation with its large investment in fixed assets—the real estate—can never be as nimble as a consumer products company in adjusting products and services to match rapid shifts in the marketplace.

The Japanese taught us that the concept of zero defects" in products and services can yield tremendous benefits. But today an even more rigorous standard dominates—quality that surprises. In practical terms, the hotel industry finds it extremely difficult to meet the standard of zero defects in service. Hotel services are based primarily on people, not computers or other equipment. Quality that surprises takes the concept of zero defects a step further. Yesterday's surprising product or service is today's status quo.

Twenty years ago, a business executive did not expect a consistent and predictable level of service wherever he or she traveled in the world. Today that is a standard—not the exception—as is the expectation for sophisticated technology in hotel rooms to support business needs. With customer discrimination so acute, it is not surprising that brand loyalty is a diminishing "commodity" in the hotel industry.

Find the ingredients for visionary leadership. Today's hotel organisations need to recognise the need for visionary leadership. The ability to forecast the future—to anticipate change rather than react to it—will be one of the single greatest determinants of market dominance in the years ahead. The old "command and control" model of leadership is giving way to a focus on leadership in ideas, information, inspiration, vision and teamwork. "For the most part, failing organisations tend to be over-managed and under-led. The leader sets the tone for the moral character, the vision, the corporate culture and the fiber of the institution."

While visionary leadership is essential, it must be linked to business operations and foster a risk bias, rather than a procedural bias. This will allow the organisation to stretch and, in turn, change. And it must be shared by empowered professionals and staff throughout the organisation, including those who meet the customer.

Overcoming the resistance to change can be a daunting task, particularly in large hotel organisations in which diversions from the status quo may threaten established management lines. It suggests that a culture based on conformance may need to be replaced by an emphasis on flexibility, learning and cooperation.

Management competencies will need to be aligned in order to achieve the desired result. For many organisations, this may mean a shift from traditional hierarchies typical of companies in an industrial era to a flatter organisation with a more transparent interface between leadership, organisational functions and employees. Create a defensible position through corporate strategy. For many of the industry's leaders, vision is driven by the strategic planning process, a function which has become critical for success.

Strategic planning, however, has at times been a step-child in the hotel industry, and it is often the first to be cut when organisations are downsized. It is clearly in transition. There also has been a tendency to decentralise and simplify this function—both actions of potential benefit. Strategic planning must be led by the top people in the organisation—the CEO and COO. On the other hand, it should be close enough to the customer to ensure that planners can "listen" to and be influenced by customer needs.

Empower Management: Beyond the ability to envision the future, core management capabilities will make the difference—they are essential. A clear vision without the management skills to support it cannot be a recipe for success. First and foremost, hotel management must have strategic development skills and the ability to integrate complex factors affecting success. Market volatility has become the norm, in part caused by the rapidly changing tastes of customers. Customers are increasingly approaching the hotel industry with widely different social, economic and political backgrounds, to say nothing of employees. Being able to deal with these diversities in a positive and constructive fashion that capitalises on the differences, rather than working to find ways to mitigate them, is the clear path for successful management in the future.

The organisation will also need to be imbued with a sense of entrepreneurship that reacts proactively to the market's diversity. Traditional organisations that follow well-documented rules must give way to leaders who can balance a sense of discipline with that of flexibility. Talent and resources must be marshaled and leveraged. In an industry with high fixed costs and labour intensity, the concept of leverage in the hotel business is an all-important one. Improving labour productivity through technology must be a goal for today's forward-looking hotel organisation.

Management must also be able to narrow the gap between the employer and the employee, forcing a flatter organisation in the process. This will put management closer to the customer and speed the two-way communication process up and down the organisation.

Be in the information fast lane: The traditional role of information technology (IT) as a back office support for accounting and bookkeeping has clearly moved front and center stage. IT today influences all aspects of business from corporate strategies to organisational structure—and from the very business processes it is designed to support to performance measurement. In a world where the customer is "king," IT must also deliver in two critical areas: sales and marketing and customer service.

Technology was once viewed as a way to reduce costs by replacing people. That attitude has been firmly supplanted by one that seeks IT support for the creative work that all organisations must pursue. IT must allow organisations to react more speedily to market needs and, of course, produce the fulfillment of customer demands both quickly and accurately. To do this IT must operate on a decentralised basis. IT delivers, but it has to be the right information to the right people, and it needs to be done on a timely basis.

Steps to Starting A Hotel Business

The hotel business has picked up pace with more and more people taking to traveling. Steps for start a hotel:-

— Do proper market analysis and feasibility study

— Make sure that the hotel is located strategically and is easily accessible to the tourists

— Make sure that the hotel is located strategically and is easily accessible to the tourists

— Hire a specialist interior designer to design your hotel to suite a specific theme

— If you are planning to open a luxury hotel then be sure to choose a location within the main city near major attractions.

— In case of a cheap hotel the best place is on the outskirts of the city where more tourists looking for a cheap accommodation are likely to come

— Make sure to provide online hotel reservation services with proper cancellation rules

— Be sure to open an online website for your hotel and register it with travel services like expedia.com, Travelocity.com, orbitz.com and beststay.com

— Make sure to offer special discounts and best deals on a regular basis

— Offer combination deals by partnering with l ocal car rental companies and airlines

How to start a hotel business is not very important; though the part that plays the most important role is the planning.

How to Build a Hotel

If you are planning to build a hotel then there are certain steps that you need to follow. Steps are

- First and most importantly you should do a market analysis and feasibility study. The best way to do this is by hiring an independent consultancy. The hotel planning should be carried out based on the study
- Making use of the study report layout a plan for your hotel, that includes the hotel location hotel architecture, rates and amenities to offer
- After determination of these key factors hire an engineer to build your hotel. Interior designers can be consulted to fix the hotel design
- Frame proper laws and regulations for your hotel along with getting proper registrations and rights
- Promote your hotel online by opening a websites and submitting the links to the databases of online reservation services like expedia.com, travelocity.com, hotelsanddiscounts.com, orbitz.com etc
- Make sure to provide online reservation facilities for you hotel in your website
- Offer best deals and special offers on a regular basis

Hotel Development Cost

One of the least understood terms in the hotel/real estate business is "feasibility." Some analysts evaluate feasibility by calculating an internal rate of return (IRR) and seeing if the resultant return is sufficient to account for the potential risks. An easier procedure is to compare the economic value of a proposed hotel upon its opening to its total development cost. If it costs more to build than it is worth, then the project is not feasible. When a hotel opens and its value is greater than the cost to build it is considered feasible.

A developer wants to sell the completed hotel for a price that actually exceeds the development cost so a profit can be realised. This profit factor is called a "developer's profit," which typically ranges from 10% to 25%. Considering that most people want to make a profit for their effort, it is normal to include a developer's profit on top of the total development cost when evaluating feasibility.

The process of developing a hotel requires packaging five components—land, improvements, furniture and equipment, pre-opening and operating capital—in a manner that meets the needs and desires of travelers visiting the marketplace. This delicate balancing act requires precise coordination of design, function and cost. The hotel development process starts with the land acquisition. Generally, the land component cost represents between 10% to 15% of the total project cost. When land cost exceeds 20%, project feasibility could be in doubt.

The improvements represent the actual building with all its mechanical, electrical and plumbing systems. The cost of the improvements is directly related to construction quality, spatial utilisation, design consideration and the local development cycle. During the building boom of the late 1980s and, to a lesser extent, today increased construction activity produces a more rapid rise in building development costs.

The large amount of furniture and equipment within a hotel is unique to this form of commercial real estate. Depending on whether the property has foodservice or not, the furniture and equipment component generally represents between 10% and 20% of the total project cost. As hotels start installing more expensive technology, expect these percentages to increase, which could affect the balance between cost and value. Another two components unique to the hotel industry are pre-opening expenses and operating capital.

Pre-opening costs include items such as initial marketing, recruiting and training. For large convention hotels, these, activities can occur years before the property opens and often represent a significant expenditure. Operating capital is the money needed to purchase inventories and supplies. Once a hotel becomes operational, its actual working capital diminishes.

Public Sector Financing

When government has commonly stepped in, support has focused on the development of key hotel properties deemed essential to stimulate business travel and tourism, and create new jobs. Formal public/private alliances in these cases have often opened the door to lower-cost financing of hotel development, as well as a host of other incentives to stimulate private investment.

Public entities have at their disposal a wide array of programmes and financial vehicles that can assist in making a hotel project feasible and thus contribute to an area's overall economic well-being. The potential to access lower-cost financing, tap redevelopment incentives, structure favourable land lease terms, secure site improvements and other alternatives should not be overlooked by hotel developers when development projects have a clear link to public interests.

The interdependent economics of convention centers and the hotels that serve them create opportunities for public/private partnerships of benefit to government entities and private investors. The evolution of public/

private partnerships to support development of convention headquarters hotels, as a result, offer an excellent foundation for examining how public sector financing and other incentives can support private hotel investment.

Most cities require a convention headquarters hotel to market their convention center successfully. Yet many mid- to upper-tier cities often lack sufficient hotel inventory that can be specifically committed to this purpose. Conversely, room nights generated from a convention center are often insufficient to exclusively support a convention headquarters hotel serving the meetings and trade shows so important to local economies. Further complicating the problem, convention headquarters hotels often incur higher than typical development costs due to the amount and quality of public areas required.

A need for public/private partnerships to support the economic feasibility of a convention headquarters hotel. This hotel, in turn, will support the public investment made in a convention center, as well as generating other local economic benefits. They also evidence the range of options available to the public sector to support private hotel development. While these types of incentives most often may be used to support convention hotels, they may also be important tools for other types of hotel projects in which there is a strong relationship between public interests and private investment.

Convention facilities in these cities may be located in areas peripheral to hotel concentrations. In addition, existing hotel operators are often reluctant to commit the room inventory required to serve convention delegates—typically offered in package deals at lower room rates—while simultaneously reducing rooms available to serve guests that make up their core business. The basic economics in hotel development and operations pose additional challenges. Convention-oriented hotels are typically 10 to 20 percent more expensive to develop than a comparable size, group-oriented hotel.

At the same time, room rates for a convention hotel's core market segment may run 20 to 30 percent below comparable business hotels due to discount package deals negotiated for delegates as part of convention attendance. To remain successful, a convention center must attract annual national bookings in the range of 25 to 30 events that have a minimum of 2,500 participants each. These bookings, however, on average support occupancies of only 30 to 35 percent in terms of total room nights. As a result of these factors, convention center hotel properties must either achieve higher average occupancies, develop other sources of business or realise higher room rates attributable to non-convention guests to succeed.

Convention hotels can often attract alternative sources of revenue, including sponsoring convention and meeting trade separate from a convention center. Sources of business may include smaller group business, commercial activity, and wholesale and tour operator business. Nevertheless, the hotel is in most cases fundamentally dependent on the convention center for its core business. To entice new development, local government entities must often work jointly with hotel developers to overcome the obstacles that tend to make these hotels more costly to develop and less profitable to operate.

What tools can government bring to bear to attract private hotel investment by improving their economics. The city acquired land, provided a 45-year lease with attractive terms and furnished off-site improvements, as well as site utilities. The hotel additionally was awarded the food & beverage concession for the convention center, and real estate property taxes were abated during construction.

Tax increment financing was used to support public improvements, while real estate taxes were abated. In addition, the hotel was supplied with convention center-owned parking at prevailing market rates. More recent public/private partnership successes include the Westin Hotel venture in Providence, Rhode Island, which involved a $290 million bond issue, that covered the convention center, hotel and parking. A Sheraton Hotel at the Jefferson Center in Birmingham, Alabama, involved a $148 million low-interest bond offering, guaranteed by JCA and supported by city and county occupational taxes.

Convention and Visitors Bureau has contended that a convention hotel within walking distance is required to make the city more competitive for attracting large conventions. Yet the downtown Los Angeles hotel market has been weak since the onset of the recession early in this decade, a condition which has been further exacerbated by the Los Angeles riots in 1992 and the Northridge earthquake last year. Downtown's primary convention hotels, all located within seven blocks of the convention center, collectively posted occupancies in the mid-50 percent range last year (up more than six occupancy points from one of the worst years in recorded history) with projected occupancies edging toward 60 percent this year. Thus far, it has been concluded that a major new convention hotel is not economically feasible, even with generous public incentives.

These initiatives demonstrate the range of strategies available to the private sector to attract private hotel investment—as well as the pitfalls that can create obstacles. At their best, these partnerships make it possible to reduce hotel development costs, set the stage for more profitable hotel operations, and allow a government jurisdiction to safeguard public investment and achieve local economic development goals.

Generally, public contributions that can drive development of a hotel may include land at favourable lease terms, off-street parking facilities, construction/use rights of public space and marketing support. Hotel developers may also be granted the convention center's food and beverage service concession. This ancillary revenue can be an important step to offset the lower room rates often associated with delegate business. Among the contributions made by the hotel developer are equity funding, the track record of team members, a superior product development plan, and strong management and marketing.

In addition, the public and private entities must have controls in place to ensure that relationship objectives are maintained. A convention headquarters hotel, for example, must commit room nights to the convention center, even at the cost of displacing higher rated business. Conversely, the convention center must book events, which generate room nights, perhaps foregoing higher revenue-generating consumer shows that tend to be oriented to a local audience. A range of successful private/public techniques are available to further these partnerships:

Site Control: Land values in urban or resort environments are generally very high with these costs typically representing a significant component of hotel development. Government participation is often essential, either by writing down the market value of a property or purchasing a property to lease to a hotel owner on a long-term basis at an economic cost.

Miami Beach's experience is instructive. The city in 1992 expanded its existing convention center located near City Hall, a location remote from Miami Beach's highly developed existing hotels. No new major hotels have been developed in 27 years. Studies commissioned by the city addressed several pivotal issues. It was determined that none of the existing hotels—clustered primarily at some distance along the coastline—would or could continuously sell room nights to major national conventions that desire to book the city's convention center. Additionally, major hotel developers would be unlikely to develop a new hotel away from the beach area without significant incentives.

To advise the city on incentive parameters required to entice developers and financial institutions in the development and financing of the 800-room hotel. Among the most important of the incentives was site control. Arthur Andersen advisors concluded that the city's purchase of the site adjacent or proximate to the convention center was essential. It was further determined that the hotel site should have ocean-front exposure. After analysis of three potential locations, the city purchased an ocean-front site at a cost of $24 million. The site is five blocks from the city's convention center.

Low-cost Financing: In the past five years, new full-service hotels have been extremely difficult to finance. Convention hotels, furthermore, are generally regarded as being of even higher risk—a result of the uncertainty related to occupancies and above-average development costs. As a result, public financing can be the key element in making a convention center hotel feasible.

Again, a number of options are available to the public sector. While tax- exempt public bond issues are subject to 'private purpose' limitations, there are techniques which can blend in public funding to privately owned and operated hotel ventures. These include financing and leasing back the 'public' areas of a hotel (or a parking, etc.) facility. Public revenues from hotel taxes or real property taxes may be designated for the facility through non-tax exempt issues. In addition, cities, counties and other government entities may offer certain operating guarantees, such as payment of debt service, for a specified period of time.

In some cases cities have made equity investments in convention hotels. The municipality may become the junior equity partner in the hotel with 'first-in' risk capital, and 'last-out' return. In a broad policy sense, the city's rate of return is potentially greatly enhanced by an improved local economy, higher visitation and associated tax revenues. Bond financing, and public ownership of the asset, for example, is a cornerstone of the financing structure for a new convention center hotel at McCormick Place, the final phase of its exposition center.

Other Public Incentives: Local governments also have incentive options that will have significant impact on the economies of building a convention headquarters hotel. These include incorporating public spaces and amenities, such as joint parking or meeting facilities to reduce the overall cost of the convention hotel. Municipalities may also provide property tax abatements, as well as redevelopment zone benefits such as expedited permitting and access to other public funding sources.

From a development and operational standpoint, there are a number of challenges facing hotel companies as they consider convention headquarters hotels. In addition, many deals have failed because a city has insufficient resources to close a transaction, or lacks an understanding of the resources it can bring to bear in support of these developments. What is fundamentally at stake is shifting a portion of the risk from the developer to public entities, since the public jurisdiction stands to benefit economically if the hotel is a success.

More than a standard Request for Proposal (RFP) to attract a quality developer is often needed. The public sector must understand what types of incentives it has available to drive a project—and the best way to frame the RFP process. And it will clearly require specialised expertise to ensure that financial incentive structures make

Improvements in business operations raises values. It is not surprising, therefore, that the new owners attracted to this industry in recent years have new sets of demands. This transformation from an old-guard group of investors and owners to income and return-driven newcomers has meant that the once "quiet enjoyment" of operators in their management of hotels for third parties is being disturbed, interrupted and overturned.

These challenges all take place in an environment where capital has become extremely selective in markets that have little stability. A global shortage of capital will not remain a short-term problem, and future hotel organisations must have a stronger alignment to capital providers—a critical "customer" group. Hotel companies will need to compete by offering better returns and performance than in the past.

Hotel chains have found their development timetables quashed in recent years, making it difficult to achieve goals of critical mass often required to improve performance. These factors are driving consolidation in the brand "sweepstakes." Capital markets, therefore, continue to favor well-established companies, a reality that must drive entrepreneurial organisations to meet the future now by planning for an evolving corporate context in which to operate.

Successful Organisation Strategies

Hotel developers, owners and management companies will all need to develop new strategies, skills and processes that look forward to the competitive demands of the future. These ultimately must address issues related to vision and planning, as well as organisational skill sets and processes to attract and retain customers. To stake a claim in the future, current business practices should be examined in light of what can be expected to be the key success factors in the year 2000.

Embrace a global change orientation. As the information age produces greater worldwide integration of business activities, a global knowledge base will become invaluable. Success in local and regional hotel markets will be shaped decisively by a global business environment that defines capital movement, customer expectations and applications of new technologies.

Create a defensible position through corporate strategy. For many of the industry's leaders, vision is driven by the strategic planning process, a function which has become critical for success. Strategic planning, however, has at times been a step-child in the hotel industry, and it is often the first to be cut when organisations are downsized. It is clearly in transition. There also has been a tendency to decentralise and simplify this function—both actions of potential benefit.

Empower Management. Beyond the ability to envision the future, core management capabilities will make the difference—they are essential. A clear vision without the management skills to support it cannot be a recipe for success. First and foremost, hotel management must have strategic development skills and the ability to integrate complex factors affecting success. Market volatility has become the norm, in part caused by the rapidly changing tastes of customers.

Customers are increasingly approaching the hotel industry with widely different social, economic and political backgrounds, to say nothing of employees. Being able to deal with these diversities in a positive and constructive fashion that capitalises on the differences, rather than working to find ways to mitigate them, is the clear path for successful management in the future. The organisation will also need to be imbued with a sense of entrepreneurship that reacts proactively to the market's diversity.

Traditional organisations that follow well-documented rules must give way to leaders who can balance a sense of discipline with that of flexibility. Talent and resources must be marshaled and leveraged. In an industry with high fixed costs and labor intensity, the concept of leverage in the hotel business is an all-important one. Improving labor productivity through technology must be a goal for today's forward-looking hotel organisation. Management must also be able to narrow the gap between the employer and the employee, forcing a flatter organisation in the process. This will put management closer to the customer and speed the two-way communication process up and down the organisation.

Be in the information fast lane. The traditional role of information technology (IT) as a back office support for accounting and bookkeeping has clearly moved front and center stage. IT today influences all aspects of business from corporate strategies to organisational structure—and from the very business processes it is designed to support to performance measurement.

Technology was once viewed as a way to reduce costs by replacing people. That attitude has been firmly supplanted by one that seeks IT support for the creative work that all organisations must pursue. IT must allow organisations to react more speedily to market needs and, of course, produce the fulfillment of customer demands both quickly and accurately. To do this IT must operate on a decentralised basis. IT delivers, but it has to be the right information to the right people, and it needs to be done on a timely basis.

Business to Consumer (B2C)

Diverse factors are driving the successful 20th century

businesses in hospitality and travel to reinvent themselves for the 21st century using eBusiness. But the drivers of change differ in Business to Consumer (B2C) and Business-to-Business (B2B) spaces. In the B2C arena, the desire to strengthen customer relationships, develop new revenue streams, enhance profit margins and create more value are all motivating rapid change. The foundation of success increasingly is the ability to create new business models that leverge Internet technologies to deliver unique value to customers.

The business has moved rapidly and successfully in building high levels of brand awareness out of the starting gate. Loyalty programmes targeting Web-site purchases have now evolved. This new brand awareness and loyalty is a direct threat to the decades of investment in the bricks-and-mortar brands of the industry. As online clearinghouses (businesses selling distressed room inventory) appeal to a growing number of customers, they are directly challenging the hotel brands.

Customers' needs do not stay the same. The hotel industry meets the core need of providing a safe and secure home-away-from-home for the business and leisure traveller. But an increasing number of guests—business and leisure, domestic and international—require high-speed Internet access and related capabilities. Guests expect remote-office (and entertainment) environments no less functional than they have at home or in the office.

The new intermediaries have used technology to create other revenue generating tools. There has always been distressed inventory, but networked technologies are allowing the industry to sell it effectively rather than let it perish. There has always been the aspirational non-user of hotel product and services. Now technology is allowing the industry to sell attractively packaged offerings to a market that heretofore has been difficult to identify and reach. Used intelligently, these businesses are adding a further arrow to the marketer's quiver—enabling the industry to add occupancy by targeting specific (and new) market segments.

The extreme last-minute decision-maker and the highly price-sensitive traveller are both in this category. Growing numbers of consumers now compare room facilities and rates, and they are learning to bid for rooms and spare seats on aircraft. A third-party can do the aggregation and the constant updating. It can also act as a brand buffer allowing companies to discount unsold seats or unsold rooms indirectly. Even with concerns about the competition, why let the value leak to the middleman?

The Internet's cost efficiency appeals to companies that currently manage travel offline, and it should lead to an increase in the number of companies that manage travel overall. We have seen the successful hotel businesses of the old economy partnering to compete with the start-up businesses of the new economy. As these ventures get off the ground, they have the potential to cut deeply into the revenue streams of the new Internet businesses, which have relied on commissions and on the sluggish response to market threats of the airlines and hotel companies.

It will not be that easy to get companies with an ethos of confidentiality to cooperate with competitors—in the process promoting transparency to common customers. But by pooling their resources, the major hospitality and travel chains can develop portals quickly and at lower risk to compete in this dynamically changing market.

Corporate Traveller

The corporate traveller is a key segment targeted by almost all the major brands. Corporate policy, rather than individual choice, increasingly dictates business travel. According to Forrester Research, Inc., companies eager to save travel and processing costs will mandate the use of

Web-based corporate booking engines. The few remaining unmanaged business travellers will buy their business travel online as leisure bookers do.

Corporate policies will increasingly require travellers to use company-approved online booking engines. These engines deliver two elements to improved margins—directed use of a company's negotiated room rates with their preferred suppliers, as well as reduced service charges for making employee travel reservations. Due to the self-service nature of online business travel booking, companies and travel suppliers must increase efforts to encourage continued use.

The Internet's cost efficiency appeals to companies that currently manage travel offline, and it should lead to an increase in the number of companies that manage travel overall. Companies with larger travel budgets can be expected to be the first to shift their travel buying online with 70 percent of Fortune 1,000 companies making this migration by 2002, says Forrester. Larger accounts that are currently unmanaged will increasingly buy online and thus will soon adopt managed travel.

Even smaller firms will move their business travel online as well, first encouraging individuals to use any Web interface, then gradually adopting targeted services. Each managed traveller's company computer will include a desktop icon, which, after entering a user name and password, will link directly to a personalised profile within the travel site. Once business travellers sign on to corporate travel sites, entire trips can be booked with one click on the desktop icon, eliminating the need to re-enter login information. On the road, managed travellers will have the ability to research upcoming trips, check on late flights or change an existing hotel reservation.

Due to a combination of new bookers and the increasing amounts consumers are spending, the online travel market continues to boom. Travel sites, however, face the same challenges that online retailers struggle with—most consumers are not loyal. Web travellers rely upon the convenience, abundant information and low prices found online, and they are willing to research multiple sites for the best deals.

B2B applications are even bigger accelerators of change than those in the B2C space when it comes to how hospitality and travel companies will do business in the years ahead. Even though many customers aggressively seek choices to meet their needs, some sites attract more loyalty than others. The one-stop-shop nature of online travel agencies effectively attracts bookers that rely on one site for all their booking needs.

Hotel chains, on the other hand, may have a harder time attracting loyal bookers because they are offering only one element of the travel package. Hotel chain web sites can lure disloyal bookers away from agency and consolidator web sites with special room rates and upgrade perks available exclusively online. Although portals have the greatest reach of all travel sites, they get the lowest percentage of bookers from all three segments.

To combat online booker disloyalty, hotels, agencies and portals must take lessons from online retailers on how to encourage loyalty. Suppliers must establish dynamic partnerships with suppliers in other travel categories that allow consumers to book flights, hotels, and car rentals at the same site. Hotel chains must sell adjacent categories of products and services. Portals should let the agencies and hotels fight over bookers and instead focus on what portals do best—offer information to consumers.

Business to Business (B2B) Application

B2B applications are even bigger accelerators of change than those in the B2C space when it comes to how hospitality and travel companies will do business in the years ahead. The B2B space is populated by many types of companies, including links among supply chain partners and market exchanges selling products and services online to businesses. eProcurement is one example of a growing B2B space in the hotel industry. Adoption of B2B strategies that connect businesses in varied ways is being driven by a number of factors:

Simplifying IT Infrastructures

Yesterday's information technology (IT) model was based on each hotel and/or hotel group maintaining an in-house IT team, which owned and managed the business's hardware and software. Tomorrow, most businesses will have migrated to an Application Service Provision (ASP) model.

Under the ASP model, providers offer a variety of applications and services to companies, which these clients can access with nothing more than an Internet link to the ASP site. This marks a dramatic change from the traditionally defined "service bureau," which once involved the transmission of operational data to an outside agency for management by a remote application. More recently, the explosion of Internet-based software applications and services by ASP providers has caused old economy and new economy businesses alike to revisit off-premises application processing. The processing of unit-level data at a distant site via an ASP provider may well represent one of the most important ways to obtain mission-critical IT solutions in the hotel industry on a cost-effective basis.

Micros-Fidelio, for example, introduced the OPERA ASP application at HITEC. Serious concerns remain about data ownership and the risk of whether the public Internet offers the speed, data security and reliability to support a highly interactive PMS application. But this is a dynamically changing area, and companies can expect to see ASP technology being introduced to radically simplify IT infrastructures. The ASP model will most likely be successful in the case of vendors offering a complete range of outsourced products—not just a PMS or CRS, but the complete systems operation for properties.

Wireless Application Protocol (WAP)

Mature businesses are not simply assuming that a focus on eBusiness is enough. The wireless market will introduce new competitive elements. Wireless Application Protocol (WAP) is a global specification that gives wireless devices—including mobile phones, personal digital assistants (PDAs) and computer terminals—access to the Internet. The distinguishing feature of wireless service is the ability to identify a user's location. The network seeks out the mobile phone to complete the call and knows where the holder of the phone actually is. This offers advertisers a dream channel to target customers in a personalised, time and location-specific way.

In the administrative areas, WAP technology can be applied to interface the mobile sales force with the centrally held customer relationship management (CRM) database—linking the revenue generating and cost generating systems in the bedroom (e.g. telephone, mini-bar, air-conditioning) to the centrally hosted property management system.

Realistically, none of this will be available until 2002, but progressive businesses will be determining what strategies to follow, seeking expert advice, and will begin demanding these applications of their vendors as technology progresses and the wireless market, particularly in Europe, develops.

3

Responsibilities of Hotel General Manager

Hotel managers are responsible for operations, including reservations, food services, housekeeping and conventions. In a small hotel, one manager usually makes all the important daily decisions, whereas in a large establishment, a general manager hires a number of managers to be in charge of individual departments.

— Ask yourself if you have excellent interpersonal, communication and organisational skills. They are necessary for a successful hotel management career.

— Obtain a college degree in hotel management or restaurant management. Remember that a food services department contributes greatly to the profits of a hotel; a successful restaurant manager can his or her career advance quickly.

— Take advantage of work-study programmes offered by many colleges so that you will gain solid experience working in hotels.

— Expect to go through a hotel's training programme once you are hired after college. During the first couple of years you will be handling only relatively mundane duties, instead of providing your input on issues such as staffing, hotel decor or conventions.

— Understand that you might be offered a position as a front office manager, a food and beverage manager, a convention services manager, or any of a number of administrative positions after your training period. If you are successful at different managerial positions, your career will benefit in the long run.

— Be aware that a promotion might require you to relocate for a few years if you work for a hotel chain that has properties throughout the country.

Characteristics of a Good Manager

The mark of a good manager isn't how well things run when you're there. It's how well things run when you're not there. Managers must hire the right people; people who care and show a willingness to care for others—that's what hospitality means. Then, they must train their employees in the rudiments of the job and later, coach them to do their job well in a positive environment that inspires and motivates teamwork.

Training and coaching are not the same things. Training teaches skills. Coaching teaches the application of those skills; and training must always precede coaching. Finally, the manager needs to get out of the way and let people do their job. Delegate tasks, authority and decision making, but don't abdicate them. Hold people accountable for their actions. Cultivate and nurture key players and you will develop winners along the way. The manager who works seven days a week to make sure things get done right has missed this important attribute of leadership.

On the other hand, managers who are never around while the department is in a state of chaos have equally missed the point. People do what they do because of what they get after they do it. People behave within an organisation a certain way because that is what is being culturally reinforced. Culture is nothing more than the collective attitudes of those who hold power. Managers who are not leaders and leadership that does not preside has abdicated power, but power will still be held by someone within the organisation, and usually by tenured employees with lower standards than their customers.

Leadership's role is to use its authority as a means to influence behaviour. Reward is the only thing that initiates lasting changes in behaviour and in order for reward to succeed, it must be positive, immediate and certain. Giving reward is a Leadership behaviour that acknowledges someone for having done something correctly. Unfortunately, many managers see their role as correcting behaviour only when it is wrong. We've all worked for the manager that was always on our case when we made a mistake, was slow to give praise for having done something right and rarely said, "Good job."

Good Leadership is always noticing when someone does something right and makes mention of it. Reward need be nothing more than a smile and a few kind words, but given routinely and as soon as a positive act is observed, it will set the culture moving in the right direction. Do it. Do it right. Do it right now. Leaders act. Leaders get it right the first time. Leaders take action the moment it is required and inspire others to do the same. If you've ever had a complaint, then explained the complaint to a frontline clerk only to be told that you'll have to see the manager, you might understand the importance of this Axiom. There probably is no more important place in a hotel where this Axiom is needed than in the Sales office.

A hotel where Leadership has a certain operational intensity and sense of urgency about getting things done has embraced this philosophy, which is a hallmark of good Leadership. The attitude of any staff reflects the attitude of their leader. If a front desk crew is friendly and vivacious, their leader is, too. If a restaurant delivers outstanding service, you can bet that the leader exhibits the same attitude toward serving the customer. Leaders, by their very attitude, set the standard by which others will behave.

"Leadership by example" is a kindred Axiom. People tend to follow those who expect exactly what they give; someone who no less asks another to do anything that he or she would not do themselves. Left unmanaged, moments of truth regress to mediocrity. If you don't define precisely what is supposed to happen when a customer encounters an organisation at any given point, then the experience will at best be mediocre. Mediocrity is a natural state. It tends to exist without influence, but Leadership inspires something beyond mediocrity.

Leadership sets an expectation, creates an environment where that expectation is routinely met and ensures that it will endure over time. This means managers have to be willing to deal with the nitty-gritty and the fundamentals of their department. Every service encounter that an employee will make and every expectation that Leadership has must be communicated and reinforced. You can grow, or you can be comfortable, but you cannot do both at the same time. Leadership isn't a state that is suddenly attained, at least not for most of us. And while it is true that great leaders are born, they still have to learn an awful lot about channelling their innate ability to become great leaders.

Leadership is a path of continual enlightenment that occurs over a lifetime. That path is often difficult. Hotel managers don't have an easy job, but any level of discomfort may well be precisely because that path has been taken. All leaders reach certain plateaus in the course of their development: that's called experience. But learning never stops and it's never very easy. Managers who rest in their comfort zone will eventually fail because the world all around them isn't static. The market isn't; the competition isn't; customers aren't and neither are employees. Leaders must continually challenge themselves to compensate for the changing environment and learn new ways to gain market share, beat the competition, find new customers and retain good employees. People don't always do what you expect. They'll do what you inspect.

Checking behind your crew doesn't mean you don't trust them; it just means you accept your Leadership role. General Managers in particular should never stop checking rooms and you can almost always tell the hotels where they have. At the heart of business is the need to be fiscally healthy and it is Leadership's responsibility to guide the organisation toward that state. Junior managers in particular sometimes lose site of the fact that their decisions, on an hour-by-hour basis, are having financial impact on the hotel, both good and bad. Yes, put people before money and recognise that the organisation deals with human issues every day; Leadership must always be caring and compassionate. But absent financial success, the business will fail, and then, all human conditions fall prey to unfortunate and often unsavoury outcomes: lay-offs, litigation, foreclosure or take-over.

General Managers are being asked more and more often to assume responsibility for management of the sales staff. It is a job for which they have received little training and for which they have a number of challenges. Five years ago, when demand was high and the sales function was relegated to answering the phone and taking the order, it was relatively easy for General Managers to keep an eye on things in the sales department.

Unemployment was at historic lows and in order to keep positions filled, we were reluctant to expect too much or discipline an under performing employee. There was a tendency to keep the chair warm rather than let a position go unfilled. Times have changed both in terms of demand of demand and the employment pool but often the attitudes of management have not. Sales people represent a distinct management challenge. The good ones are bright, aggressive, able to sell their managers as well as their clients but they are also very human. They like most other employees will take the path of least resistance, need to have expectations made clear and have objective standards of performance by which they are evaluated.

The fact of the matter is that no one does what no one checks! Sales people (like everyone else) do not perceive the importance of job duties that are not monitored by their supervisors. In addition, there has to be the WIIFM factor, 'what's in it for me'. If an employee, sales or not, is going to take home the same paycheck whether or not they achieve their goals, why would they do more that the minimum requirements. GMs have a particular challenge in that they work long hours and very closely with their sales staffs, especially the DOS. It is difficult to maintain an objective and professional distance that allows for the kind of management that gets results.

There are a few simple steps you can take to make your monitoring of the sales effort more effective. They may also make the sales effort more effective. Refrain from Cronyism—Simply put, this means do not get too close to your DOS or any member of the sales department. It is difficult with a DOS who has worked for you for a long time. It is also difficult with the long hours required working in close quarters in this industry. There has to be a line of familiarity that you don't cross. It negates your ability to lead and manage effectively.

Have regular sales meetings with a fixed agenda. It should occur at least once a month, preferably once a week at a time when it does not interfere with Prime Selling Hours. This provides a structured environment in which you can ask the 'tough' questions without sounding picky and irrational. To a sales person, if you just casually ask a question about an account or ask for numbers, they are likely to feel that you are just in a bad mood and it will pass.

Take a course in sales. If you come from another discipline in the industry, learn about basic sales. Read a book, take a course—take a course in sales not related to the industry. There are many fine resources for hotel sales available especially now when that function has become so challenging. Sales people who have worked on commission 'get it'.

Set realistic goals and involve them in the process. Goal setting should be an objective process. When you let them know what they need to produce and why, then involve them in figuring out how they are going to get there, they understand and ideally buy into the plan. Be supportive but expect results! Your head is on the line here too!. If your sales staff is making a ton of calls but producing few results, it could be a skills problem. Offer them some training. When a reasonable amount of time and training effort has passed, don't be afraid to make the tough decision. The fact of the matter is they are uncomfortable at their non-performance and may be happier and more satisfied in another position.

Role of Lodging Managers

A comfortable room, good food, and a helpful staff can make being away from home an enjoyable experience for both vacationing families and business travellers. While most lodging managers work in traditional hotels and motels, some work in other lodging establishments, such as camps, inns, boardinghouses, dude ranches, and recreational resorts. In full-service hotels, lodging managers help their guests have a pleasant stay by providing many of the comforts of home, including cable television, fitness equipment, and voice mail, as well as specialised services such as health spas.

For business travellers, lodging managers often schedule available meeting rooms and electronic equipment, including slide projectors and fax machines. Lodging managers are responsible for keeping their establishments efficient and profitable. In a small establishment with a limited staff, the manager may oversee all aspects of operations. However, large hotels may employ hundreds of workers, and the general manager usually is aided by a number of assistant managers assigned to the various departments of the operation. In hotels of every size, managerial duties vary significantly by job title.

For example, general managers have overall responsibility for the operation of the hotel. Within guidelines established by the owners of the hotel or executives of the hotel chain, the general manager sets room rates, allocates funds to departments, approves expenditures, and establishes expected standards for guest service, decor, housekeeping, food quality, and banquet operations. Managers who work for chains also may organise and staff a newly built hotel, refurbish an older hotel, or reorganise a hotel or motel that is not operating successfully. In order to fill entry-level service and clerical jobs in hotels, some managers attend career fairs.

Resident managers live in hotels and are on call 24 hours a day to resolve problems or emergencies. In general, though, they typically work an 8- to 10 hour day and oversee the day-to-day operations of the hotel. In many hotels, the general manager also is the resident manager. Executive housekeepers ensure that guest rooms, meeting and banquet rooms, and public areas are clean, orderly, and well maintained. They also train, schedule, and supervise the work of housekeepers, inspect rooms, and order cleaning supplies.

Front office managers coordinate reservations and room assignments, as well as train and direct the hotel's front desk staff. They ensure that guests are treated courteously, complaints and problems are resolved, and requests for special services are carried out. Front office managers may adjust charges posted on a customer's bill. Convention services managers coordinate the activities of various departments in larger hotels to accommodate meetings, conventions, and special events. They meet with representatives of groups or organisations to plan the number of rooms to reserve, the desired configuration of the meeting space, and the banquet services.

During the meeting or event, they resolve unexpected problems and monitor activities to ensure that hotel operations conform to the expectations of the group. Assistant managers help run the day-to-day operations of the hotel. In large hotels, they may be responsible for activities such as personnel, accounting, office administration, marketing and sales, purchasing, security, maintenance, and pool, spa, or recreational facilities. In smaller hotels, these duties may be combined into one position. Assistant managers may adjust charges on a hotel guest's bill when a manager is unavailable.

Computers are used extensively by lodging managers and their assistants to keep track of guests' bills, reservations, room assignments, meetings, and special events. In addition, computers are used to order food, beverages, and supplies, as well as to prepare reports for hotel owners and top-level managers. Managers work with computer specialists to ensure that the hotel's computer system functions properly. Should the hotel's computer system fail, managers must continue to meet the needs of hotel guests and staff.

Because hotels are open around the clock, night and weekend work is common. Many lodging managers work more than 40 hours per week. Managers who live in the hotel usually have regular work schedules, but they may be called to work at any time. Some employees of resort hotels are managers during the busy season and have other duties during the rest of the year. Lodging managers sometimes experience the pressures of coordinating a wide range of functions. Conventions and large groups of tourists may present unusual problems. Moreover, dealing with irate guests can be stressful. The job can be particularly hectic for front office managers during check-in and check-out time. Computer failures can further complicate an already busy time.

Lodging managers held about 69,000 jobs in 2002. Self-employed managers-primarily owners of small hotels and motels-held about 50 percent of these jobs. Companies that manage hotels and motels under contract employed some managers. Hotels increasingly emphasise specialised training. Postsecondary training in hotel or restaurant management is preferred for most hotel management positions, although a college liberal arts degree may be sufficient when coupled with related hotel experience. Internships or part-time or summer work are an asset to students seeking a career in hotel management.

The experience gained and the contacts made with employers can greatly benefit students after graduation. Most bachelor's degree programmes include work-study opportunities. Community colleges, junior colleges, and some universities offer associate's, bachelor's, and graduate degree programmes in hotel or restaurant management. Combined with technical institutes, vocational and trade schools, and other academic institutions, over 800 educational facilities have programmes leading to formal recognition in hotel or restaurant management. Hotel management programmes include instruction in hotel administration, accounting, economics, marketing, housekeeping, food service management and catering, and hotel maintenance engineering.

Computer training also is an integral part of hotel management training, due to the widespread use of computers in reservations, billing, and housekeeping management. Additionally, over 450 high schools in 45 States offer the Lodging Management Programme created by the Educational Institute of the American Hotel and Lodging Association. This is a two-year programme offered to high school juniors and seniors, which teaches management principles and leads to a professional certification called the "Certified Rooms Division Specialist". Many colleges and universities grant participants credit towards a post-secondary degree in hotel management.

Lodging managers must be able to get along with many different people, even in stressful situations. They must be able to solve problems and concentrate on details. Initiative, self-discipline, effective communication skills, and the ability to organise and direct the work of others also are essential for managers at all levels. In the past, many managers were promoted from the ranks of front desk clerks, housekeepers, waiters, chefs, and hotel sales workers. Although some employees still advance to hotel management positions without education beyond high school, postsecondary education is preferred.

Restaurant management training or experience also is a good background for entering hotel management, because the success of a hotel's food service and beverage operations often is important to the profitability of the entire establishment. Graduates of hotel or restaurant management programmes usually start as trainee assistant managers. Some large hotels sponsor specialised on-the-job management training programmes that allow trainees to rotate among various departments and gain a thorough knowledge of the hotel's operation. Other hotels may help finance formal training in hotel management for outstanding employees. Newly built hotels, particularly those without established on-the-job training programmes, often prefer to hire applicants who have hotel management experience.

Large hotel and motel chains may offer better opportunities for advancement than small, independently owned establishments, but relocation every several years often is necessary for advancement. The large chains have more extensive career ladder programmes and offer managers the opportunity to transfer to another hotel or motel in the chain or to the central office. Career advancement can be accelerated by the completion of certification programmes offered by various associations. These programmes usually require a combination of course work, examinations, and experience. For example, outstanding lodging managers may advance to higher level manager positions.

Employment of lodging managers is expected to grow more slowly than the average for all occupations through 2012. Additional job openings are expected to occur as experienced managers transfer to other occupations or leave the labour force, in part because of the long hours and stressful working conditions. Job opportunities are expected to be best for persons with college degrees in hotel or restaurant management. Increasing business travel and domestic and foreign tourism will drive employment growth of lodging managers.

Managerial jobs are not expected to grow as rapidly as the hotel industry overall, however. As the industry consolidates, many chains and franchises will acquire independently owned establishments and increase the numbers of economy-class rooms to accommodate bargain-conscious guests. Economy hotels offer clean, comfortable rooms and front desk services without costly extras such as restaurants and room service. Because there are not as many departments in these hotels, fewer managers will be needed.

Similarly, the increasing number of extended-stay hotels will temper demand for managers because, in these establishments, management is not required to be available 24 hours a day. In addition, front desk clerks increasingly are assuming some responsibilities previously reserved for managers, further limiting the employment growth of managers and their assistants. Additional demand for managers is expected in suite hotels, because some guests-especially business customers-are willing to pay higher prices for rooms with kitchens and suites that provide the space needed to conduct meetings.

In addition, large full-service hotels-offering restaurants, fitness centers, large meeting rooms, and play areas for children, among other amenities-will continue to provide many trainee and managerial opportunities.

Manager's Role in Hotel Security

Security encompasses areas such as security of the property itself, company assets, employees' and customers' personal belongings and valuables, life security, personal security, and job security, among others. Let us take one "security example" related to employees' personal belongings and valuables in a hotel environment: In all workplaces management stipulates that it is not responsible for valuables and employees personal belongings. Yet management must take all possible measures to prevent theft among employees and of employee belongings through its hiring practices and through the implementation of effective management, human resources and operational policies, such as:

— Background checks of selected applicants

— Policies related to employees' entry to, and exit from, the workplace

— Spot checks of locker rooms and lockers

— Effective supervision and control during the work cycle
— Policies related to the discovery of criminal records and wrongdoing among, and by, employees
— Control of people entering and exiting the workplace

With regard to guest valuables, management informs guests that the hotel is not responsible for valuables left in the room, advising them to secure these in safety deposit boxes provided by the hotel. Besides taking care of security issues related to the people they employee, management must undertake some necessary measures, among which:

— Providing "secure" (safety) deposit boxes and areas to keep valuables
— Policies and practices to ensure the security of these boxes and areas
— Management and operational policies regarding the security of guest rooms
— Management and operational policies regarding the security of public areas
— Security policies and practices for the back-of-the-house areas
— Employment and training of security personnel
— Policies and practices to minimise the "presence" and "patronage" of "shady characters" and criminals, verification of registration and check-in personal data and documentation submitted, and curtailing free movement of unknowns on the premises, as well as direct, free flowing communication with local, national and international security authorities)
— Training of staff in guest and valuable security Effective supervision and control procedures.

When we take the same hotel as example, it is

management's duty to ensure "safety" in several areas, such as:

— The structure itself
— Installations and fixtures (check electrical, plumbing, air-conditioning and other installations)
— Public and work areas (e.g. slippery floors, hazardous obstacles in traffic areas), safety of furniture, equipment, appliances, and utensils.

This is followed by:

— Health safety (nontoxic cleaning material and detergents used)
— Good quality air (what we breathe, dependent upon the type of equipment, installations and fixtures used, and regular repairs and maintenance)
— Food safety (a whole world in itself including sanitation, food quality, food spoilage, correct handling procedures, allowable and recommended temperatures, etc.), and checking and control procedures.

An important "preventive measure" is eliminating the possibility of communicating contagious diseases. Even if local regulations do not require it, it is recommended to send food and beverage handlers for regular medical checkup. Another preventive measure is the formulation and implementation of policies and procedures related to employee accidents which may present a threat to food sanitation.

Culinary staff who cut themselves accidentally at work, as often happens while slicing food products, have to immediately stop handling food, and report to their Executive Chef and to the person in charge of First Aid in their company for preliminary treatment and handling. Healing and precautionary measures are taken before they

included bombings, hijackings, strikes/protests and sabotage. The database does not capture every event, and consequently the statistics should not be viewed as comprehensive. However, they do provide a picture emphasising the need for attention to risk by hospitality industry managers.

During October 1997, terrorists attempted to place a truck bomb at a five-star hotel in Colombo, Sri Lanka, but were stopped by hotel security from gaining entrance into the parking lot. The terrorist thereafter parked the vehicle near two other five-star hotels, detonating the device causing major damage to the hotels and surrounding buildings and killing eleven people and wounding 105. The hotels were located near government buildings.

The second most frequent offenses reported after bombings. Not included on the earlier table because of the difficulty of capturing total data, assaults take the form of shootings, murder and physical assaults on a person. Various police jurisdictions report high numbers.

According to Sao Paulo, Brazil police records, for example. 4,778 people were murdered in Sao Paulo in 1997, averaging 13 homicides per day. The Brazilian Ministry of Justice reported that 31 of every 100,000 Brazilians are murdered compared to 20 per 100,000 in Mexico and 10 per 100,000 in the United States. The records of the Colombian National Police reflected 31,808 murders or 87 per day in 1997, as well as 204 muggings or assaults committed in Colombia every 24 hours. Mexico City reports more than 250,000 crimes annually or approximately 700 per day.

This threat has emerged as a problem worldwide, reaching critical levels in Colombia and Mexico. Kidnappings are conducted by terrorists, criminals and others acting for political reasons. Most of the kidnappings are motivated by economic reasons, but in some cases are undertaken to effect political change in a country. Most are resolved peacefully, but some have tragic results.

The International Monetary Fund, World Bank and Inter-American Development Bank are all addressing the issue as it relates to projects with which they are involved. For an industry involved in operating buildings, the fact that corruption is extensive in the construction area should be of particular concern to hospitality managers. Where building inspectors are paid to overlook poorly constructed buildings or lack of compliance with building codes, there is a potential for disaster.

Such activity has resulted in a number of incidents, including building collapses resulting in injury and death. Clearly there are risks for hospitality companies "going global," particularly in markets where there is a history of political and economic instability. Hotel organisations frequently rely on security systems that are transplanted from property to property. But hospitality managers should consider a number of pertinent questions.

— When was the last complete security survey completed for all facilities?
— Is the system sufficient to the threats in the local area?
— Have new risks developed since the last surrey?
— Is there an effective emergency management plan in place?
— Will staff be proficient in its execution?

Building Design

New construction should include a crime-prevention design audit. Design for crime prevention in hotel development can he highly beneficial. To be considered are such factors as the relationship of buildings to parking areas and structures, lighting, perimeter views and protection, and security systems. Pre-Employment Screening/Training All hotel employees should have a thorough background check conducted. There have been a number of instances in which hotels have hired individuals with criminal records in illegal drug sales or theft. Incidents of drug dealing, time-clock tampering and guest theft are relatively common problems that can be greatly mitigated with thorough employment and criminal checks. This process is especially important when selecting security personnel.

Training programmes should be developed to enhance security among all hotel staff. In addition to the security force. Employee training should not only include a focus on hotel functions, but security awareness as well. As is the case at most hotels, the security staff is limited and is sometimes strained due to commitments and shrinking staff. By providing the entire hotel staff with training in the identification of security issues, a description of operational methods, where to report information, and periodic updates on security advisories. Management can in effect add additional "eyes" and ears to the organisation.

Security Planning and Operations

It is important to broaden the focus of risk and systematise processes. Each hotel, for example, should have a detailed bomb threat plan that covers procedures to include:

— the reporting person;

— execution of the search plan;

— what to do if a suspect package is found; and

— evacuation plans.

The process is critical because time is always of the essence. Many bomb threats are made for the purpose of disrupting a company's operations. Needless evacuation of a facility can play into the hands of the person making the threat. On the other hand, information must be properly handled because of the scope of the potential damage.

Special Events Planning

These events often involve government dignitaries, officials and organisations, senior management, associations that may be embroiled in controversial policies or business transactions that can elevate the security threat. In some cases, police or other government agencies provide security, but this does not obviate hotel responsibility. The example of the bomb threat at the banking conference in Colombia, for example, was augmented by exposure of detailed conference plans on the Internet. The hotel needs to track where information has been distributed, including the Internet, to determine the level of risk that may result.

Companies establishing new operations in other countries must begin by understanding the risks inherent in these locations. Taking "local knowledge" too much for granted can be costly. If an incident does occur, the consequences can be extraordinarily high. Compounding the threats to people and buildings are the prospects of financial loss. And yet the protection of insurance coverage should not reduce the sensitivity of hospitality managers to these risks, which can have completely unforeseen consequences. Negative publicity or litigation arising from such incidents can have an adverse effect on a company's reputation, stock price, employee morale and future business relationships.

By focusing on proactive safeguards, rather than reactive measures, hospitality companies can reduce risk efficiently and cost - effectively. The important point is not to wait until a major incident shatters the status quo. The time to assess risks and build security and crisis management systems is before-not after-an emergency.

Security has always been a key issue for hoteliers. The events of the past seven months have only heightened awareness for proper security and the need for upgrades in equipment, where required. Technology plays a major part in meeting today's security requirements, but there are other important factors in implementing effective security measures. The people link to technology is critical in the successful use of any security system. The attitude of the hotel staff must be oriented toward security and the proper use of the equipment that is installed. A case in point is the use of closed circuit television (CCTV). Even the newest, most sophisticated equipment must be monitored, and when there is an incident, a prompt review of the recorded media is required. CCTV certainly is not a new platform. The earliest models consisted of a camera fitted with a special lens and connected to a monitor (a television without broadcast reception capability).

Systems were later created that added multiple cameras that used switches to rotate the images that were shown on the monitor. The next enhancement came in the form of a video recorder, which captured images on videotape. The original models were reel-to-reel, just like the original audio tape recorders. Later models utilised the same type of video cartridge used by VCRs; in fact, the unit was a modified VCR. Today's systems include all the above features along with digital colour cameras and images recorded to the hard disk of a personal computer. These images can be retrieved by various criteria and can be archived onto digital audiotape (DAT), CD (RW), DVD or any other digital media.

Since retrieval from hard disk is random and not sequential, the time required to review images is greatly reduced. It is important to understand the difference between time-lapse recording and full-motion recording. Time-lapse is actually full motion, but the recording speed is fewer frames per second. The advantage of this technique is a significantly greater length of time can be recorded on either tape or hard drive; however, if the frames per second are set too low a subject could actually pass through an area and not be recorded. There are many CCTV systems in the marketplace including those from JVC, Panasonic and Sony.

Most systems offer high-resolution digital cameras with a motion detector terminal output included. A zoom lever is used to adjust the range of fixed cameras. Other types of cameras feature automatic zoom lens operation. Day and night operations are programmed to detect light levels. Some cameras are infrared sensitive for use in virtual darkness. Digitisation of the signal enhances image quality. The recording devices use a digital hard drive to store images. Some recorders can store up to 160GB online, with even more capacity available with optional add-on features.

An Ethernet network interface device is available for LAN, WAN or Internet connections. This allows monitoring with a conventional Internet browser from any network connection. It is becoming more common for CCTV services to be offered in a package with other applications. Internet-enabled video security is a product offered by StayOnline. The company is a provider of high-speed Internet access for hotels and provides CCTV as part of its services. The service can use existing cameras and multiplexer by adding a digitiser and installing a video server (PC). The server has an Internet connection that provides recording.

The cameras can be monitored from any PC equipped with an Internet connection and a Web browser. This is accomplished by logging on to a secure Web site. This approach offers several benefits including no archiving required on property, providing an alert should cameras be moved or disconnected, and the ability to survey multiple properties from a central location.

Integrated with the TimeLox DC-One system, it has the capability for a security officer to hear a doorbell on a computer, view a live picture of the person at the door, and open the door lock from the computer. The system can use either the hotel's local area network or an Internet connection. The cameras are manufactured by Axis Communications, a worldwide supplier of security and other products. Network cameras have their own IP address and connect directly to a network without using a multiplexer or digitiser. More advanced cameras can detect motion, alarm input/output signals and even send e-mails.

No matter what approach is taken for utilising CCTV, proper installation is essential. The correct wiring must be used, cable-TV COAX for older, analog cameras and CAT-5e for more modern, digital cameras. Wiring requirements may vary, however, so the installer must verify the type of wire required with the camera's manufacturer. Training is also a key element to the successful installation of any security equipment. The staff must have an in-depth knowledge of all features and functions. While CCTV is an integral part of hotel security, guestroom locks and safes are equally important. Below is a sampling of some available products. SAFLOK's Select MT lock offers many attractive features. The lock has the ability to use magnetic stripe, smartcard or memory card technology.

The lock itself is a robust one-inch, steel reinforced bead bolt with a three-fourths of an inch latch bolt, creating a double deadbolt effect. An optional automatic deadbolt is also available. Security Innovations, Incorporated (SII) specialises in online and real-time access control systems for the lodging industry. SII provides security products that integrate standard electrical and building specifications. Current products include Access-Plus® online access control featuring Sensor-Lock deadbolt technology, credit card keys and the ability to choose any combination of reader technologies. Options include energy management, paging alerts and secondary annunciation of smoke detection. Future releases will include CCTV integration, property mapping and automatic alarm paging.

VingCard offers two significant products, The DaVinci Locking System and the Elsafe Infinity Series of electronic safes. The contemporary design of these products has bridged the gap between form and function. As an example, the DaVinci series locks come in six different finishes and also offer six different handle designs. This hardware is modular, therefore, offering many different configurations in both appearance and functionality. The Infinity collection of safes feature a Windows CE-based PDA that can interrogate the safe and provide a 100 event audit trail. The safes can be equipped with a multi-voltage outlet so that laptops can be recharged while secured in the safe.

One technology that has been proposed for hotels is the use of biometrics to profile guests and identify those that may be involved in some form of criminal activity. These technologies have no place in the hospitality industry. They are intrusive and subject to error, not to mention expensive. Security is critical in today's environment, be sure your hotel is not behind.

Managers Making Mistakes

Every hotel and motel manager makes mistakes; that's just part of being human. All mistakes are costly; but some have a greater financial impact than others do. The following list cites potentially costly security gaps most hoteliers are not aware of or haven't focused on-and should.

Never cut back on security personnel: In these times of cost containment and budget controls, security is the one area of your budget that should never be cut. The financial impact of reducing or eliminating your security staff would be tremendous should a guest or employee be injured or damage to property occur. In addition, eliminating or reducing security personnel sends the wrong message to staff members, namely that their safety is not of the highest importance to your business and that you are not watching them as closely.

Have an evacuation route posted in your meeting room space: Meeting rooms serve as gathering places for large groups of people who will most likely panic in the event of an emergency such as a hurricane, earthquake, bomb threat and so on. In the event of a crisis, will your group function attendees know where to go and what to do? Have evacuation routes posted in meeting rooms for group attendees to see, and ask your sales and catering personnel to have detailed discussions with the meeting planners about evacuation procedures.

Increase lighting throughout your property: Look for physical areas on or around the property that do not have adequate lighting or are not secure, and address these issues immediately. Check your parking lots for areas where lighting needs improvement. Ask your local law enforcement agency to do a security audit on your property. Don't wait until someone falls or is injured to protect your guests, employees and your business.

Continuously train employees: When it rains or snows and a guest slips and falls on your property, do your employees know the proper steps to take to protect the injured guest, not to make casual comments admitting liability and how to handle the situation? Who is responsible for their training? Make it your objective to ensure that your employees receive adequate training on procedures for handling guest injuries. Initial training and continuous ongoing training are critical. One hour of training is not enough. Keep detailed records of the procedures and training which can be used in your efforts to convince a litigious opposing party, and a judge, of your due diligence in safety training.

Comply with Occupational Safety and Health Administration standards: Make sure all OSHA requirements and standards are met. If you are not sure that you have all the latest information, take an updated course on compliance efforts. The Internet has many resources for OSHA compliance courses available for hotels and motels. Visually inspect to see that all necessary notices and posters are current and displayed appropriately, and not stuck behind other notices on the bulletin board.

Keep back-up data off property: Keep a copy of all property operations data stored off-site in a safe and secure location. Do not rely on someone's personal computer to house your employment, financial and guest data. It is imperative to have access to guest records at all times—especially in the event of an emergency.

Install phones in fitness centers: All exercise or fitness rooms need to have a phone available to all guests that will dial immediately to the front desk. A security camera should also be installed so that injuries and problems that occur within the fitness facility can be immediately detected and addressed. If security cameras are used, written procedures for their use must be in place. Also: Are the cameras staffed with trained professionals viewing the scene? How often is the videotape reused? Are the cameras in good working order or are they simply mounted as a decoy to provide a false sense of security to guests and employees?

Perform background checks on employees before hiring: All managers, front desk personnel and security officers must have their background history checked to eliminate or minimise any unknown and undesirable discoveries once employed. An Internet search can assist in accomplishing this task very quickly. Check driving records on employees hired to transfer guests to and from the airport or surrounding areas. Select the best employees now and avoid future trouble.

Check detection devices regularly: Are sprinkler systems and smoke detectors working and in place, on all floors, in guestrooms and in all public spaces? Is an emergency lighting system in place along with an emergency generator? When was the last time you had these items checked? What is your back up plan if these devices should fail? All such items need to be tested and certified on a monthly basis and the inspections need to be properly documented in writing.

Check on emergency equipment periodically: Does your property have automatic external defibrillators and oxygen tanks on site and are they in working order? Have employees been trained to use these devices? Make sure you conduct monthly inspections on these types of equipment, and have at least one CPR-trained employee on staff at all times. These are but a few of the safety precautions being overlooked by many hotel and motels around the country. Preventative measures are always preferred over litigation strategies. Your guests and employees expect and want an injury-free experience and work environment. Implementing these steps, and reviewing them on a continuous basis, will go a long way in protecting your business.

Role of Executive Housekeepers

An Executive Housekeeper describes someone who is hired by a household to oversee the overall cleanliness of a formal or multi-staffed household. An Executive

Housekeeper has specialised knowledge in cleaning and caring for fine furnishing, valuables and artwork. They must have excellent English skills, a professional demeanor and appearance.

An Executive Housekeeper is responsible for the overall appearance of the household. A housekeeper's duties may include any of the following:

— Cleaning the interior of the home and the immediate areas outside (patios, porches, decks, walks)

— Kitchen maintenance—dishes, cupboards, pantry, counters and floors.

— Laundry (Clothing & household linens)

— Bed making, routine bedding & linen changes

— Meal Preparation & Service

— Assisting with the cooking and serving for special events

— Grocery shopping and other household errands

— Keeping the household supplies fully stocked

— Receive & serve guests

— Pet care

— Plant care (household)

— Silver Polishing

— Secure/supervise tradesmen/contractors

— House-sitting while the employer is out of town

— Occasional childcare

— Household bookkeeping and/or accounting tasks

A housekeeper may supervise other household staff, but this is not the norm. A housekeeper may be assisted in the performance of his/her duties by a maid.

Salary for an Executive Housekeeper is based on the amount of experience the candidate brings to the position and the duties and hours included in the job description. The benefits for full-time Executive Housekeeper may include paid sick days, paid holidays and two weeks paid vacation. Other benefits may encompass medical insurance and reimbursement for automobile expenses.

A housekeeper is a domestic service professional who has general responsibility for the maintenance and cleaning of a private household. A housekeeper's primary job responsibility is to maintain the employer's home in a clean and presentable manner at all times. A housekeeper may live in or live out, and may be employed on either a full time or a part time basis. A housekeeper is 'hands on' in the performance of his/her job responsibilities.

How to Avoid Mistakes

— *Maintain safe conditions*: Keeping your premises safe can save lives. It can also help in defending against allegations of negligence should a disaster occur. Consider the lesson of the hotel that let dust and linen accumulate in linen chutes: when the accumulation caused an otherwise containable fire to spread and cause substantial damage, they were held liable.

— *Test the alarm and emergency communications systems regularly*: During an emergency, you must be able to alert your guests, deploy personnel, and summon emergency services quickly. For example, checking to see how bad a fire is before calling the fire department may make fighting the fire more difficult and subject the hotel to liability.

— *Keep emergency plan current*: The evacuation guides on the back of hotel room doors do not constitute an "emergency plan." Your plan should ensure that guests receive adequate warning of an emergency and provide for their effective evacuation. Your plan should provide for ongoing education to employees and for conducting periodic drills to ensure compliance with the plan. Hotels may be held liable for losses caused by a disaster if they don't have a plan, if the plan is inadequate, or if they fail to follow the plan.

When disaster strikes:

— *Warn guests of the emergency*: You have a duty to warn guests of an emergency: do not delay! Hotels can be held liable for a failure to warn guests of an emergency or for an unduly delayed warning. You may not have to physically accompany guests out of the hotel, but you can be held liable if blocked exists or inadequate lighting in halls and stairwells impedes evacuation.

— *Call for medical assistance:* Hotels have a legal obligation to call for medical assistance when a guest is seriously ill or suffers serious injury. Unnecessary delays in summoning emergency help can subject the hotel to liability. Also keep in mind the hotel that provided a physician's assistant to treat guests was held liable when the assistant prescribed the wrong medicine resulting in the death of the guest: be wary of providing your own medical care.

If your hotel is safe, don't raise the rates. If your hotel survives a disaster and other hotels in the vicinity do not survive, the market value of your safe hotel rooms will skyrocket. However, think twice before raising your rates. Hotels may be held liable for price gouging under state law and be ordered to refund the costs of rooms to customers. Hotels may also be held liable for deceptive business practices.

Demonstrate goodwill: If your hotel is no longer able to house and provide services to guests after a disaster, it is unlikely you have a legal obligation to find your guests other housing. Of course, in the interest of customer relations and goodwill, providing as much service as possible is the wisest course for those in the hospitality industry.

Role of General Manager in Environmental Issues

General Manager's office is the central point for all policy decisions, implementation and monitoring in the hotel. The GM has to get the Environment Management System (EMS) prepared, put the systems and funds into place for its implementation. The GM should appoint an environment coordinator who would normally be the Chief Engineer/Head of Engg. This person could also be a full time person in the hotel who will be responsible to prepare, coordinate and monitor implementation of the EMS, and prepare detailed action plans for each department, with the approval of the GM.

General Manager will also be well advised to from an Environment Management Committee on which key HODs and Financial Controller will be represented. This Committee and in some cases GM will take key policy decisions including approvals for implementation of proposals and funding of specific purchases. The Environment Coordinator, with assistance and concurrence of Financial Controller, will also prepare data on return on investments for various funding proposals so that financial benefits of such proposals can be clearly proved. This will be helpful in getting their approval.

It has been demonstrated by many hotel companies around the world and by research organisations that most purchase decisions for equipment and re-modelling connected with environment conservation and resource usage have a short buyback period which varies from 3 months to 3 years. Environment coordinator and concerned HODs should work out their proposals, specially involving investment of funds, with figures on return on investment, benefits and pay-back period.

Role in Administrative Offices

Administrative offices though not large consumers of energy, still have a role to play. They house the general manager and heads of departments who should practice what they preach and set example for others. These areas consume electricity by lighting and other appliances such as computers, printers, and copiers. They generate solid waste such as wastepaper and stationery, copiers and printer's cartridges.

Heating and cooling systems can affect the offices' indoor air quality. These offices should run their operations in an environment-friendly manner: reduce energy consumption, recycle and reduce solid waste, reuse recycled materials, revise its purchasing procedures, and freshen air quality in the premises. People in this area tend to prefer artificial lighting to natural light.

Procedures must be set up and implemented for using daylight as far as possible. An energy-saving programme in offices is easier to ignore than in other departments. As people in offices think that they are small uses of energy and water. But every kw/hour of electricity and every drop of water counts and adds up to the overall consumption in the hotel.

Energy Management

Kitchens

Kitchens consume considerable amounts of energy and water. Energy management in Kitchens is crucial because of the variety of demands placed on the facility, and the numerous opportunities that exist for wastage of energy.

Apart from lights, fans, HVAC, kitchens use a large number of energy-intensive equipment. Care has to be taken in purchase of such equipment and in saving energy in all kitchen operations. Apart from energy, kitchens use a large amount of water.

The main types of water-using equipment found in kitchens are dishwasher, faucets, ice-making machines, and garbage disposers. Additional kitchen water uses relate to food preparation like thawing frozen food, rinsing vegetables, cooking, steam tables and washing activities. Chefs and kitchen staff can guide and assist purchase managers in eco-purchasing by buying less packaged food products and reusable supplies that can successfully reduce and control the volume and toxicity of wastes generated.

Banquet Halls and Restaurants

Banquet halls and Restaurants use substantial amounts of energy. Air Conditioners, heaters and lighting are used in guest areas. Restaurants are generally lit brightly and decorative lighting also increases the overall load. Energy can be saved by good practices like controlling thermostat, cleaning condensers, coils and filters, controlling leaks in refrigerant lines etc. Energy can also be saved in lighting by using Compact Fluorescent Lamps (CFLs), electronic chokes instead of copper chokes, dimmers and motion sensors.

Lighting loads can also be reduced by switching off lights in unused areas, monitoring electric consumption monthly through sub-meters etc. All stand alone banquet halls and restaurants are connected to kitchens and the same measures and precautions are to be taken in their kitchens, as in the kitchens of hotels. Restaurants also use lot of water in kitchen and toilets which needs to be controlled through installing aerators, infrared activated faucets in toilets and sinks and through good practices in dish washing. Solid waste in restaurants needs to be separated in dry and wet garbage and grease traps need to be installed.

Housekeeping department

The housekeeping department provides clean accommodation to guests, and affects the impact the hotel has on environment. A laundry system can consume large quantities of energy and water, a regular guest-room can generate various kinds of solid waste, and the air ventilation system can affect the guest room's indoor air quality. The housekeeping should run its operations in such a way as to reduce consumption of energy and water, recycle and reduce solid waste, reuse recycled materials, revise purchasing procedures and freshen guest-rooms' indoor air quality.

Housekeeping can influence the success of a hotel's energy management programme because guest-rooms and guest corridors consume more than 20 per cent of the total energy bill of the hotel. With an effective energy management programme, which includes employee education and training, housekeeping staff can reduce energy consumption as part of their daily routines. Housekeeping is also a major user of water in hotels, the main uses being by guests and in room cleaning. Conservation of water in housekeeping can offer considerable bottom-line savings. Good quality water saving fixtures work just as well for the staff and guests as conventional fixtures, while reducing your water usage and your water bill. Rooms generate large quantities of solid waste.

Housekeeping sections should have proper segregation, recycling and waste disposal procedures to protect environment and reduce operating expenses. Poor indoor air quality leads to a loss of housekeeper's productivity, has negative health effects on guests and employees, and increases building's energy and maintenance costs.

Laundry operations have an enormous impact on environment too. Various cleaning and finishing processes use vast amount of energy and water while use of chemicals causes air pollution, toxic waste and sewage problems. Various studies reveal that it is drying and finishing that take the major share of the process energy rather than washing. Water and energy can be saved in laundry operations by proper care in purchases, operations, and procedures.

The engineering and maintenance department controls and manages the hotel's heating, ventilation and air-conditioning systems, lighting, hot water & steam systems, kitchen and cooking equipment, and refrigeration systems. All these equipment and systems are energy consumers. Engineering and maintenance staff should make an all-out effort to incorporate every feasible measures to reduce energy consumption without compromising the quality of services and comforts provided, since a resources-efficient hotel is one in which quality services and quality environment go together.

Engineering has to study and understand new innovative equipment coming into the market, energy saving devices, concepts like buyback periods for new equipment and investments, energy and water saving procedures during operations of all departments. These actions save resources, reduce pollution, protect environment and employee health, reduce operating costs, improve hotel's image among customers, increase employee loyalty, and increase profit margins. Engineering also provide guidelines and monitoring systems for energy conservation and environment protection to other departments. The head of engineering can be appointed as environment coordinator for the hotel.

Recreational areas

Most hotels provide recreational facilities, such as swimming pools, water sports, game rooms and fitness centres. A fitness centre consumes large quantity of energy, a swimming pool needs tonnes of water, and the air ventilation system can affect the recreational areas' indoor air quality. A swimming pool's water filtration and circulation system uses electricity continuously.

Indoor air quality is an important consideration for a health club, since guests breathe more air into the lungs, and produce more carbondioxide. Poor indoor air quality leads to a loss of optimum exercising efficiency, negative health effects for both customers and employees, and increases building's energy and maintenance costs.

Stores and purchases

The responsibilities and initiatives of stores and purchasing are fundamental to environmental management in a hotel. Every other department relies on stores and purchasing to achieve green targets. Products can be identified as green by being environmentally sound or environmentally packaged or both. Value for money, quality and convenience were traditionally considered important when making product purchases.

However, eco-purchasing considerations should figure in all purchase decisions. This will not only conserve environment but will also lead to bottom line savings. Eco-purchasing should not only involve assessment of the products in terms of their raw materials, production process and eventual disposal but also their impact on other resources like water, energy and efficiency in operations.

4

Management of the Front Office

Until the 1960's, nearly all hotels were operating under the manual system. At late 70's, with the introduction of computers, hotels shifted to semi-automated systems. Nowadays, most of the five-star hotels operate under the fully automated system. Below is a brief description of the three different systems under which hotels might operate.

— *Non-automated [manual] systems*: This very system is the one characterised by the sole usage of hands. In fact, all formats, procedures, and different kinds of calculations are done manually.

— *Semi-automated [Electro-mechanical] systems*: This system gets use of some Electro-mechanical equipment. In fact, under the semi-automated system, each department might have its own computer system under which it handles all its operations.

— *Fully automated [computer based] systems*: That's the best system ever used in the hotel industry. In fact, it is characterised by the excessive use of departmental software package programs integrated and connected to a main frame or terminal situated at the front office department.

Guest Cycle under Three Different Systems: Following stages of the guest cycle under the three different systems do not conflict with each other. In fact, the only differences are due to the nature of the system use. Therefore, what will be discussed above is not the repetition of the sequence; rather only differences will be highlighted.

Non-automated Systems

Pre-arrival activities: At the pre-arrival stage, reservation requests should be introduced in a loose-leaf notebook or index card. Moreover, only reservations up to 6 months horizons shall be honoured. Lastly, it is not practical, under this very system, to issue reservation confirmation numbers, initiate pre-registration activities (at the exception of VIP and groups) and prepare occupancy forecasts. The reason is, time and money loss along with insufficient labour force to manually conduct all the above mentioned activities.

Arrival activities: At the arrival stage, guests shall either sign a page in the registration book or fill manually a registration record. Under this very system, the most widely used front office equipment is the room rack, in which registration records are inserted to serve as room rack slips. Moreover, registration books and records shall be time stamped as an internal control proving when the guest exactly came, who registered him/her. Lastly, guest folios shall be opened for each registered guest.

Occupancy activities: Under the occupancy activities, registration records shall be prepared with multi-copies. In fact, one copy shall be distributed to room rack, another stamped to the guest folio, another given to switchboard operators, and a final copy handed to the uniformed service personnel. Lastly, guests with charge privileges charges and payments shall be posted to respective guest folios.

Departure activities: At departure stage, cashiers should settle each guest account's outstanding balance and get room keys back from guests. Moreover, cashiers shall notify the housekeeping department that the room is no more occupied (i.e. room status change) to let this very department clean the room and prepare it for new arrivals. In addition, cashiers shall remove room rack slips from room racks to indicate departure. Lastly, these very rack slips of departed guests shall be filed in a cardboard box to serve as a guest history record

Semi-automated Systems

This very system is less common in small and middle size hotels. For, these very hotels, financially wise, might not afford the huge investments associated with the installation of different hardware and software. The main advantage of this very system over manual system is that various reports can automatically be generated. However, the major disadvantages associated with this system are various complexities of operating and controlling devices due to the fact that these equipment are not integrated with other systems and are subject to frequent maintenance problems.

Pre-arrival activities: At this very stage, guests can either call a national reservation network or directly contact the hotel. Moreover, reservation clerks can prepare pre-registration records, guest folios, and information rack slips.

Arrival activities: At this very stage, already reserved guests shall verify their pre-registration forms and have only to sign it. On the other hand, walk-ins shall complete a multiple copy registration record from the beginning.

Occupancy activities: At the occupancy stage, in order to track the different guest charge expenditures and all other possible guest transactions, hotels get an intensive use of various kinds of vouchers. Moreover, the most widely used equipment, under this very stage, is the mechanical cash registers and front office posting machines. Lastly, under this very stage, night auditor shall continuously resolve any discrepancy in guest accounts and efficiently reconcile guest folios.

Departure activities: At this very stage, cashiers shall relay room status information to the housekeeping department. Moreover, they should place registration records of departed guests in property's guest history files.

Fully Automated Systems

Pre-arrival activities: Under this stage, the reservation department is equipped with a software package, which is interfaced and connected with one or more central reservation office(s). Moreover, the reservation department can automatically generate letters of confirmation, produce requests for guest deposits and handle pre-registration activities for all types of guests and generate daily expected arrival lists, occupancy and revenue forecast list.

Arrival activities: At this stage, various reservation records can be transferred to front office department. Moreover, hotels might be equipped with an on-line credit authorisation terminals for timely Credit Card Approval, self check-in/check-out terminals. Lastly, all guest charges and payments are saved in electronic guest folios. As far as walk-ins are concerned, all registration activities should be initiated from the very beginning.

Occupancy activities: Under this very stage, guest purchases at different revenue outlets are electronically transferred and posted to appropriate guest accounts. Moreover, the front office department can run and process continuous trial balances and, therefore, eliminate the tedious work for the Night Auditor.

Departure activities: At this very stage, cashiers can automatically produce bills to be sent to various guests with direct billing privileges and create electronic guest history records.

FRONT OFFICE FORMS

At different stages of the guest cycle different forms are used depending on which operating system a hotel chooses. Below are some of the common forms used:

- Pre-arrival activities:
  - Reservation record or a reservation file
  - Letter of confirmation
  - Reservation rack and reservation rack slips
- Arrival activities:
  - Registration card (or record) or registration file
  - Room rack and room rack slips
- Occupancy activities:
  - *Guest folio*: shall be of duplicate forms and pre-numbered for cross-indexing control purposes
  - *Vouchers*: support documents detailing facts of a transaction, but does not replace the source document (i.e. the invoice). Examples of vouchers might include charge vouchers, allowance vouchers, paid-out voucher, and correction vouchers.
  - Information rack slips
- Departure activities:
  - Credit card vouchers
  - Cash vouchers
  - Personal check vouchers
  - Transfer vouchers
  - Guest history records

Functional Organisation

Whatsoever system and setting the hotel might use, it should reflect easy access to the equipment, forms, and supplies necessary. Moreover, the setting shall reflect position flexibility. Moreover, nowadays trend shows that traditional mail, message, and key racks are unnecessary at the Front Desk. Rather, they shall be stored in drawers or slots located under or away from the Front Desk. For, this would ensure security and safety of guests.

Front Desk designed alternatives:

— *Circular or semi-circular structure*: this very structure provides an effective service to more guests and appears more modern and innovative but since guests will approach the Front Desk from all angles, more staff is needed.

— *Traditional straight desk*: Under this very design, fewer staff is needed, but fewer guests can be served at the same time.

— *Deskless environment*: Under this design, there is no Front Desk at all. This is usually replaced by a hostess, or steward welcoming the guest, seating him or her on a chair/sofa, and conduct registration activities there while, for example, having a cocktail or a drink.

Front Office Equipment

Front office equipments are:

— Room rack

— Mail, message, and key racks

— Reservation racks

— Information racks

— Folio trays or folio buckets

— Account posting machine

— Voucher racks
— Cash registers
— Telephone equipment

Front Office Responsibilities

The work of a receptionist involves spending a lot of time dealing with guest enquiries of all descriptions. The ability to answer guest enquiries accurately and promptly is the key to good customer service. While it may not be possible to know all the answers, to all questions, all the time, there are steps you can take to ensure that each guest enquiry is dealt with satisfactorily.

Types of Enquiry

The type of enquiry you can expect to get on reception usually falls into three categories:

— *Reservation*: to deal with enquiries about reservations either over the telephone or in person, the receptionist must have on hand up-to-the-minute information of room status, the advance reservation chart, and the hotel directory and room rates/tariffs.

— *Information for the guest*: guests have come to expect reception staff to have all sorts of information at their fingertips. Enquiries can range from the cost of sending a postcard to Europe, to car rental facilities, to information on places of interest in the locality.

— *Information regarding guests:* enquiries about guests should be handled with caution and discretion. All guests are entitled to a measure of privacy and protection and any person requesting information about a guest, for example, the name and room number of a resident, should be referred to a supervisor or manager.

Receptionists are right if they believe that the customer expects them to know everything. Of course you cannot know everything, but it should be in your power to satisfy the guest's need, whatever the nature of the enquiry. As this is the service that is most likely to be in demand from reception or the information desk, you should build up your knowledge, particularly of the most frequently asked questions. These may include information on:

— the hotel facilities and services

— the locality—geographic location

— the locality—places of interest

— local services, e.g. transport, places of worship, airline offices, etc.

— entertainment—restaurants, theatre, etc

— additionally, foreign visitors may request information on local customs, cultural issues and language.

So while it may not be possible for the receptionist to have the answers to all questions, it is important to know where to get the answer and how. Every effort should be made to assist the guest with his enquiry. To do so promptly and accurately will require you having access to a range of information directories. You should have:

— a list of all the facilities and services in the hotel, with details such as opening times

— a list of names of members of staff, their job titles and telephone extensions

— details of what is happening from day-to-day throughout the hotel

— a good idea of what goes on in the locality so that you can inform guests looking for details of church services, entertainment and so on

— good reference sources to hand, such as local papers (for entertainment, shopping), telephone and trade directories, relevant street maps and so on

— timetables of local transport services

— tourist guide book of the region

Having the information on hand is of no use unless you know how to use the reference material you have. Make sure you find out how to use the reference books in the hotel to get the information you need—know how to use the index system, read timetables and interpret the postal tariffs. Adopt a simple general procedure to deal with standard enquiries:

— Greet the customer with a smile.

— Listen carefully to find out the requirements.

— Make a note of the relevant details if necessary.

— To avoid misunderstandings, repeat the main points back to the customer. Take special care if the enquiry is complicated, or the person has difficulty hearing.

— Ask further questions if you still are unclear.

— Deal with the enquiry immediately.

If the enquiry is for information

— Offer the options: "There are a lot of restaurants available around here, Sir. "Describe some of the options available.

— Recommend a course of action, for example, ".May I suggest you try our Italian restaurant on the ground level?"

— Offer to do the legwork "I'll just check for you Sir."

— Confirm what has been arranged, if applicable: "That's a table for four at 8 p.m. this evening."

— Finish the exchange on a positive now: "I hope you enjoy your meal."

If the enquiry is for service

Many requests or enquiries are received which do not

involve information, the guest wishes to have, for example, extra towels. Requests for assistance of this kind could be received by telephone or in person. The basic principles of dealing with a general enquiry remain the same with the inclusion of two important steps:

— Record or log the requests in the reception log box. Note the room number, request details, time request were received, action taken, e.g. reported to housekeeping, your initials. If any follow-up action is taken this should be recorded in a similar way.

— Notify the appropriate department, e.g. housekeeping if the request is for extra towels, maintenance if the air-conditioner is not working and so on.

You should always try and deal with a guest enquiry yourself as it is very annoying for the guest if he has to ask several different staff members the same question. However there will be times when you cannot answer the enquiry and will have to direct the guest elsewhere. You should know what type of enquiries it is better not to try to answer but to pass on to the appropriate person. Some examples of these may include:

— What special discounts can be given to a group booking—refer to the front office manager or another senior manager

— Whether the hotel can accommodate a wedding on a particular day- refer to the banqueting manager

— Can the receptionist book an airline seat—refer to the local travel agent

The important points to remember when referring enquiries elsewhere are:

— Know who it should be referred to

— Explain to the guest why be you are referring it

— Do so promptly

Mail and Message Handling

When handling mail and messages it is important to process them promptly and efficiently. This is good customer relations practice where the principles of speed, accuracy and professionalism are all key to "getting the job done" to the highest possible standard. The range of mail and messages you are likely to be dealing with are:

— *Incoming mail*: Received via the postal system, mail may arrive for various departments in the hotel, hotel guests and staff. With the arrival of new technology it is now possible to receive "letters" by Facsimile (the fax machine) or via the computer terminal, which is known as electronic mail or e-mail.

— *Outgoing mail*: Letters and packages for posting.

— *Messages*: Telephone and personal messages for your own and other departments in the hotel and hotel guests.

Mail handling procedure

It is necessary to have a procedure for receiving, recording and distributing all types of incoming mail both for guests and the hotel to ensure that the right message gets to the right person with the minimum delay. A simple and efficient procedure would involve:

— Time/date stamp all mail as soon as is received.

— Record in the mail register (a book to record all mail received and sent).

— Sort into appropriate batches—internal and guest.

— Distribute promptly.

Guest mail dealing

Guest mail may fall into four categories and therefore it

is important to know how to handle each type efficiently. The following procedures are suggested:

— Mail for guests in residence
  — Sort alphabetically.
  — Check against the alphabetical guest list and write the room number on the envelope.
  — Place in the appropriate pigeonhole in the letter rack. Large envelopes, packages, and registered mail will need to be stored in a separate place.
  — Notification may be sent to the guest to tell him that mail has arrived, for example, if the hotel has a telephone message light system this might be activated.
  — Alternatively, the hotel may operate a delivery system where standard mail is delivered to the guest room by the porter/bellboy.
  — A notification memo is placed in the pigeonhole in the letter rack asking the guest to collect it if a registered letter or package is received at the reception or information desk.

— *Mail for departed guests*: Many guests will leave a forwarding address, filling in a mail forwarding form. These are kept on file for a specified length of time. Once the expiration date passes, the cards should be removed. Any mail arriving after that date, or if no forwarding address was left, is returned to sender via the post office.

— *Mail for future guests*: Mail for guests yet to arrive is sorted into alphabetical order and kept to one side. The advance reservation list is checked for the guest's arrival date, a note made in the hotel diary that mail is being held, and on the appropriate date it is placed in the letter rack. Hotels with a computer system can check the guest records and leave a message on the computer for the guest at check-in.

— *Mail for which no record of a guest can be found*: This mail should be held over for a specified number of days and checked daily against the arrivals list in case a guest arrives who did not have a reservation or there was a misspelling in the guest name originally. If after the specified number of days the name can still not be found then the mail is returned to sender via the post office.

Special delivery services

Registered mail and special delivery services, for example DHL, must be signed for by the person accepting delivery and in turn must be signed for by the guest on collection. The recommended procedure for handling deliveries of this sort is:

— Enter into a logbook with date, time of arrival, and receipt number

— Place under lock and key or in a safe

— A notification memo is placed in the letter rack or the message light is switched on asking the guest to collect.

— The logbook is signed by the guest to confirm that they have taken delivery

However, you should always check the hotel policy and procedure regarding this and follow the guidelines accordingly.

Dealing with outgoing mail

If reception is responsible for dealing with any outgoing mail then a procedure is necessary to ensure that this mail is dispatched with the minimum delay. A standard procedure might be:

— Set a deadline for receipt of mail to be mailed that day.

— Make regular collections from the various departments throughout the day.

— Sort and weigh to ensure the correct postage is affixed.

— Post office receipts for registered mail should be attached in a special book kept for that purpose.

Front Office Accounting

The front office accounting system shall be customised and tailored to track each hotel's needs. Therefore, no two hotels have exactly the same front office accounting systems. Generally Accepted Accounting Principles (GAAP) are the following:

— *Unit of Measurement*: Companies operating in a specific country shall use that country's local currency as a unit of measurement.

— *Historical Cost*: The principle of historical cost states that the value of merchandise or services obtained through business transactions should be recorded in terms of actual costs, not current market values.

— *Going Concern*: The principle of going concern (also known as continuity of the business unit) requires financial statement to be prepared under the assumption that the business will continue indefinitely and thus carry out its commitments. Normally, a business is assumed to be a going concern unless there is objective evidence to the contrary.

— *Conservatism*: The principle of conservatism guides the decisions of accountants in areas that involve estimates and other areas that may call for professional judgement. Therefore, the principle of conservatism provides accountants with a practical alternative for situations that involve doubt. In these very situations, the solution or method shall be the one that does not overstate assets or income.

— *Objectivity*: This very principle states that all business transactions must be supported by objective evidence proving that the transactions did in fact occur.

— *Realisation*: Under the realisation principle, revenues resulting from business transactions are recorded only when a sale has been made and earned, when a hotel receives cash from a guest served in the dining room, for example.

— *Matching*: The matching principle states that all expenses must be recorded in the same accounting period as the revenue that they helped to generate. When expenses are matched with the revenue they helped to produce, external and internal users of financial statements can make better judgements about the financial position and operating performance of the hospitality business. There are two accounting methods for determining when to record results of a business transaction: cash accounting and accrual accounting.

— *Consistency*: The generally accepted accounting principle of consistency states that, once an accounting method has been adopted, it should be followed consistently from period to period. This way, accounting information can be comparable.

Accounting Terminologies

Some accounting terminologies used frequently in the front office department are given below:

Accounts: An Account is a form on which financial data are accumulated, summarised and brought to its ending balance. Moreover, all accounts shall have two entries referred to as Debit (dr) (or charges) versus Credit (cr) (or payments). The most widely used representation of accounts is the T-Account, which summarises debit entries on the left-hand side and credit entries on the right-hand side.

Hotels operating under the manual system get use of journal forms to account for different front office accounting transactions. As far as front office accounting is concerned, there are two major types of accounts widely used:

— Guest accounts describe all charges and payments of guests who are already registered at the hotel.

— Non-guest (house or city) accounts: describe all charges and payments of non-guests. To illustrate, a potential guest sending a certain deposit to guarantee a reservation is a non-guest. Moreover, charges and payments of guests who checkout with any method of payment other than cash, shall be opened a non-guest account. Lastly, visitors and employees with charge privileges shall be opened non-guest accounts.

Folios: A folio is a statement of all transactions (i.e. debits & credits) affecting the balance of a single account. At Checkout, any guest folio should be balanced to 0 through full cash payment, credit card transfer, personal check transfer, special programme transfer, and direct billing transfer.

The correct way of maintaining folios starts with proper posting, which is the process of recording transactions on a folio (i.e. proper folio, proper location and proper amount). Under the manual, semi automated and fully automated systems, folios are called hand-written folios, machine-posted folios, and computer-based electronic folios respectively. Moreover, all folios shall have a unique serial number for internal control and storing purposes. In the front office department, there are four common types of folios used:

— *Guest folios*: accounts assigned to individual persons or guestrooms

— *Master Folios*: accounts assigned to more than one person or guest room; usually reserved for guest groups

— *Non-Guest (or semi-permanent) folios*: accounts assigned to non-guest businesses or agencies with hotel charge purchase privileges

— *Employee Folios*: accounts assigned to employees with charge purchase privileges

Apart from the above mentioned common folios, front office department get use of some other types of folios such as A-type, B-type, C-type, D-type, and E-type folios.

Vouchers: Vouchers depict the details of the transaction information gathered at the source of transaction and is, hence, a supporting documents used only for internal control purposes. Below are some of the commonly used vouchers in the hospitality industry:

— Cash vouchers

— Credit card vouchers

— Charge vouchers

— Transfer vouchers

— Paid-out vouchers

— Correction vouchers

— Allowance vouchers

Points of sale [POS]: A point of sale is the location at which goods or services are purchased; sometimes called a revenue center. Moreover, due to technology breakthrough, some non-traditional point of sales emerged such as in-room movie and in-room vending service systems. Since charges are usually incurred at remote points of sale, and guest and non-guest folios are maintained at the front office department, posting of different guest and non-guest charges shall be performed. An electronic transfer ensures this, under the fully automated system. Under manual and semi automated systems posting shall be done by a physical submission of different vouchers to the front office department.

When posting charges, the following items shall be considered:

— Amount of the charge

— Name of the point of sales outlet

— Room number & name of the guest

— Brief description of the charge

— Guest signature & employee identification

Ledgers: The front office ledger is the collection of front office account folios, which usually include guest ledgers (i.e. charges and payments of all guests staying at the hotel). At any moment in time, the account receivable includes the addition of guest ledger and non-guest ledger (or city ledger) which refers to charges and payments of all non-guests.

Creation of Guest Accounts

All guest folios shall be created during the pre-arrival or arrival stage of the guest cycle. Moreover, folios might be either placed in front desk folio tray [i.e. posting tray, folio well, or bucket] or stored as an electronic guest folios in fully automated systems. As far as walk-ins are concerned, all their guest folios are created at the arrival stage!

Record keeping systems:

— *Non- automated systems*: Ensured through a series of columns listing individual debit and credit entries accumulated during the occupancy stage after which and establishment of an ending outstanding balance is needed.

— *Semi-automated systems*: Under this very system, all guest transactions should be printed sequentially on a machine-posted folio. Later, the front office clerk needs to come up with the folio outstanding balance. It is extremely important here to mention that, under this very system, each account's previous balance shall be re-entered each time a transaction is posted to the folio.

— *Fully-automated systems*: All guest charges are automatically posted to an electronic folio

Guest charge privileges: Potential guests who would like to have guest charge privileges shall present an imprint of an acceptable credit card or direct billing authorisation at registration. Failing to do so, guests would have to pay, in full, all their charges through cash, hence called Paid-in-Advance [PIA] guests and have, hence, have no post status.

Credit monitoring: In order to monitor and control charge privileges, the front office clerk should check whether the total net purchases are less than the minimum of floor Limit (i.e.: credit card company's limit) and house limit (i.e. hotel's limit). At least, each day, lists of guests with high risk or high balance accounts shall be communicated to all point of sale outlets. This is vital since, failing to do so, will let point of sales outlets continue giving charge privileges to a point that eventually the credit card company refuses to pay the amount of money exceeding its limit. This will cause very serious financial losses to the hotel.

Tracking transactions

Under the manual and semi-automated systems, tracking transactions is ensured through an intensive use of vouchers. On the other hand, Under fully automated systems, tracking transactions is ensured through on-line electronic transfer of transactional information from remote points of sale to the front office main frame terminal.

In accounting, a transaction is an exchange of goods and services for cash or a promise to pay. Under this very assumption, "nothing happens until a transaction occurs". This means that front office clerks shall first of all have a transaction, its supporting documents to be able later to debit or credit certain accounts. In hotels transactions might have the form of:

— *Cash payment*: In this very transaction, front office clerks shall post cash payment as a credit in the guest folio. Moreover, cash vouchers shall be used as a transaction-supporting document.

— *Charge purchase*: Charge purchases represent deferred payment transactions that increase the outstanding balance of a folio account. In this transaction type, front office clerks shall use charge vouchers as a transaction-supporting document.

— *Account correction*: Account correction is used to resolve a posting error in a folio detected at the day the error is made (i.e. before the closing of the business day). In this transaction, front office clerks shall use correction vouchers as a transaction-supporting document.

— *Account allowance*: Account allowances occur because of two reasons:

  — Either as compensation of poor service, or as rebates for coupon discounts. That way, guest outstanding balance decreases.

  — As to correct a posting error detected after the closing of the business day.

For both reasons, front office clerks shall prepare an allowance voucher as a transaction supporting document.

— Current transfer

— Cash advance

Internal control

In the hotel industry, the main purpose of internal control is to track transaction documentation, verify account entries and account balances, and to identify vulnerabilities in the accounting system. The keyword to internal control is auditing, which is the process of verifying front office accounting records for accuracy and completeness. Below are some forms that are of extreme importance to internally control, one of the most vital assets in the hotel (i.e. cash):

— *Front office cash sheet*: The front office cash sheet lists each cash receipt or disbursement in order to reconcile cash on hand at the end of a cashier's shift with the documented transaction that occurred during the same shift.

— *Cash, house banks or petty cash*: Petty cash is the amount of cash assigned to a cashier so that he/she can handle the various transactions that occur in a particular work shift. At the beginning of each shift, all cashiers must sign their cash banks and at the end of the shift, shall deposit all cash, checks, and other negotiable instruments in the general cashier's safe deposit box. Moreover, at the end of each shift, cashiers should watch out for cash discrepancies (i.e. any difference between front office cash sheet and the actual amounts in their cash drawers).

Cash discrepancies might have the form of cash overages, shortages, or due backs. Lastly, cashiers might come up with the net cash receipt, which is:

Amount of all cash, checks, and other negotiable instruments in cashier's drawer—amount of the initial cash bank + all paid outs

— *Audit control*: Along with the fact that hotels might employ internal control auditors, at least once in a year, (especially for hotels traded in the stock market) to get use of external certified public accountants responsible for approving hotel's accounts.

Internal control for food and beverage sales

Guest Check (also called Server's Checks): This initiates the Food & Beverage order taken from the guest, and represents the invoice given to the guest.

— Guest checks should be pre-numbered, tinted and have duplicates. Moreover, it shall be kept in locked storage, in numerical order.

— Used checks, unused checks versus void checks!

— Post to dinner, the server must price and total the guest check (applicable for manual systems), unless the point-of-sale equipment can automatically perform the addition.

— Later, the cashier receives payment or makes the guest sign his/her guest check and deposits everything to the cashier.

— At the end of the shift, the cashier's cash drawer and supporting documents are accounted for (i.e. cash, credit card vouchers, food charges, and any miscellaneous paid-outs). Later, they are reconciled against cash register reading using a daily cashier's report

— Beverage sales in a lounge, a bar presents a harder job for internal control

— Some basic internal control procedures for beverage sales are listed as follows:

— Require the bartender to ring each sale as it is made

— Require the bartender to insert each paid check into a locked box

— The cash register drawer shall never remain open even for a small period of time

— Servers are not allowed to first pay the bartender in cash and collect later from customers

— Bartenders should not be allowed to take register readings or reconcile their own cash at the end of their shifts

Guest charge privileges are allocated to guests who have provided an imprint of a valid credit card or were given a direct billing privilege at registration. In this case, all guest charges are recorded as debits in their respective guest, or master folios.

Accounts Settlement

One of the responsibilities of front office clerks is to settle guest accounts, which means the eventual collection of payment for outstanding account balances (i.e. bringing account balances to 0]. This is usually ensured either by full cash payment, transfer to an approved credit card, personal check, special programme, or direct billing account. Checkout and settlement describe the activities associated with the final stage of the guest cycle (i.e. departure).

The major activities, which are conducted at departure, include:

— Resolving outstanding guest account balances

— Updating room status information

— Creating guest history records

Departure Procedures: At checkout, front office clerks shall:

— Check for mails, messages, and faxes
— Check for safe deposit box, or in-room safe keys
— Post all outstanding charges
— Verify account information
— Inquire about additional recent charges
— Present the guest folio for guest signature
— Verify the method of payment
— Process the account payment (i.e. zeroing out the account)
— Update the room status

Account Aging

Account aging refers to the method(s) of tracking past due accounts based on the dates the charges were incurred. To illustrate, credit card payment accounts usually have ages of maximum one month. However, some other non-guest accounts (ex. late charges, disputed bills, bad checks and skippers accounts) might have ages measured in months, and even years. Below, is the terminology associated with each account age:

— Less than 30 days accounts—Current Accounts
— More than 30 days accounts—Overdue Accounts
— Older than 90 days accounts—Delinquent Accounts

Guidelines for Cashiers

— The opening machine totals for paid and paid-out must be the same figures that appear on the previous shift's cash report as the closing machine totals for paid and paid-out

— At the close of the shift, the cashier should subtotal paid and paid-out for the current shift, and record the closing figures in the machine's totals column

— If at any stage, cashier accidentally miss-keys any transaction, adjustments can be made to the machine

— Net cash received = cash paid-in (closing)—cash paid-in (beginning)

— Net cash paid-out = cash paid-out (closing)—cash paid-out (beginning)

— Net cash sum of cashier's shift = net cash received—net cash paid-out

— The cashier should extract the net cash sum from the cash drawer, and secure the money in the general cashier's safe deposit box until deposited in the Bank

— At the end of any shift, the cash drawer should contain exactly the same amount as it did when the cashier opened his/her shift.

— If any cash overage or shortage occur, the cashier must recheck the cash report and search all the transaction records for possible miss-keyed entries

Hotel Expense Accounting

In the accounting terminology, expense is an income statement account representing the cost of items consumed in the process of generating revenue or that expires due to the passage of time. Expense cannot be mixed with expenditure. For, Expenditure represents the purchase amount of a certain asset. In the hotel industry, expenses are divided into two main categories:

Direct expenses

These are the expenses that vary with the level of production. For example, in the Food and Beverage department, the Cost of Food Sales is a direct expense. For, the more dishes we serve, the more cost of Food Sales the Hotel incurs. Moreover, in the Telephone Department, the Cost of Calls is a direct expense. For, the more we connect guests to whatever destination wanted, the more cost of calls the hotel incurs. At this very stage a bracket would be opened to explain that there is a primordial difference between revenue generator departments.

In fact, revenue generator departments are classified into two: Service Type departments versus merchandising departments. Service type departments are revenue generators making money from solely providing services (Ex. Rooms Division department). On the other hand, merchandising departments ensure revenue by getting use of certain raw material, processing it, and than sell the final product. Therefore, only merchandising departments have a direct expense called Cost of Sales.

Indirect expenses

These are the expenses that do not vary with the level of production, or variable costs that can not be feasibly distributed to various Financial Reporting Centers. In the hotel industry, indirect expenses are, hence, divided into two different categories:

Fixed Charges: Examples might include rent, insurance, property taxes, and interest expense. For, these very expenses are incurred for the benefit of the hotel as a whole not for the benefit of each single department. To illustrate, if a hotel insures itself against fire, theft and burglary, and one day some valuable equipment has been stolen, from any department whatsoever, the insurance company will indemnify the hotel.

Undistributed Expenses: Examples might include electricity, energy, and water expenses. For, usually the hotel receives a total energy bill to be paid. In the old days, some hotels went for allocating this amount according to certain factors. However, this practice proved to be misleading, since it might under-allocate energy expenses for some departments and over-allocate it for others. Nowadays, most of the hotels decide not to allocate such expenses any more. Rather, hotels report such expenses in separate schedules.

At this stage, departments of a typical hotel would be listed along with their various related direct expenses. Later, examples of fixed charges and undistributed expenses would be discussed. Last, a bracket would be opened to discuss one of the most important Direct Expenses in any hotel, which is Payroll and Related Expenses. For, hotels being described as labour intensive companies devote a big percentage of their financial resources to such an expense.

Typical hotel departments

Rooms Division Department: It is the place where guests receive several kinds of services ranging from reservation, registration, to checkout and settlement of their accounts. This department typically compromises a Rooms Division manager, an assistant manager(s), registration clerks, cashiers, mail and information clerk, and uniform service personnel. The various types of Rooms Division department direct expenses include:

— *Commissions expenses*: This account includes payments by the hotel to authorised agents that bring room business to the hotel. Usually at the end of each month, hotels sit with these agents in order to reconcile their monthly sales figures and authorise commission payment (usually in the form of a percentage of room revenue)

— *Reservation expenses*: This expense account represents any payment to various agents contracting to bring potential room revenue business to the hotel. These agents might have the form of Central Reservation Offices (Whether affiliate or non-affiliate), Intersell agencies.

— *Contract cleaning expenses*: This expense account represents payment to contracting outside cleaning agencies. Some hotels (especially small and middle size hotels) might opt for contract cleaning because of its attractive financial implications. If this is the case, these hotels might not be forced to have a housekeeping department, or might keep housekeeping staff to minimum. Such expenses should be determined in light of the contract signed between both parties (i.e. the hotel from one side and the cleaning company from the other.)

— *Laundry and dry cleaning expenses*: This cost applies to outside laundry and dry cleaning costs for the Rooms Division department. In most of the cases, such contracts are signed to benefit more than one revenue generator. In this case, the rooms division department shall report the laundry and dry cleaning expenses related only to the Rooms Division department.

– *Guest transportation expenses*: These expenses include the cost of transporting guests from and to the hotel via various means of transportation (ex: Mini-buses, limousines.). If the guest transportation's volume business, staff, and costs are significantly high, then a separate department might be established.

— *Linen expenses*: This specific expense account includes the allocation of a portion of linen expenditure for a specific period of time. This practice goes along with one of the accounting principles: the matching principle. Some sub-accounts of linen expense might be:

— Towels expenses
— Blankets expenses
— Facecloth expenses
— heets expenses
— Pillow expenses

— *Guest supplies expenses*: This account includes the various guest supplies provided free of charge to guests in their rooms. Some sub-accounts of guest supplies expenses might include:

— Newspaper expenses
— Guest stationary expenses
— Shoe cloth expenses
— Coffee expenses
— Writing supplies expenses
— Toilet requisites expenses
— Flowers expenses
— Hangers expenses
— Matches expenses
— Ice expenses
— Candy expenses

— *Cleaning supplies expenses*: Such an account includes the cost of Rooms Division's cleaning supplies. Some sub-accounts of guest supplies expenses might include:

— Brooms expenses
— Soaps and polishes expenses
— Cleaning cloths expenses
— Mops expenses
— Cleaning chemicals expenses
— Dusters expenses

— Brushes expenses
— Insecticides expenses
— Dustpans expenses
— Pail expenses
— Disinfectants expenses
— Cleaning accessories expense

— *Printing and stationary expenses*: This expense account includes printed formats, office supplies, printed manuals and guidelines for the use of the Rooms Division employees. Some sub-accounts of printing and stationary expenses might include:

— Binders expenses
— Floor plans expenses
— Pencils and Pens expenses
— Vouchers expenses
— Rack card expenses
— Reports expenses
— Desk pad expenses
— Envelopes expenses
— Ink expenses
— Folio expenses

— *Uniforms expenses*: This expense account includes the allocation of a portion of uniforms asset (if the hotel purchases uniforms) for a certain period of time along with the expense of repairing, and cleaning them. If the hotel rents uniforms rather than purchasing them, then the uniform expense shall include the renting cost, usually predetermined in light of the contract linking the hotel and the uniform renting company.

Food & Beverage Department: This department is responsible for the preparation and service of food and beverage to guests. It compromises the kitchen, restaurants, bars, and any premise in which Food and Beverage is served.

Telephone Department: This department is responsible to handle guest communication. This might be insured through connecting guests to desired locations, whether in-house, local or long distance calls. Moreover, this department is usually composed of a chief operator, supervisors, operators, and messengers. Last, with the automation revolution affecting right now most hotels, it became possible to separate calls of guests and communication handled by hotel employees, therefore, making it possible to have the telephone department as a minor revenue generating department. For, prior to automation, the separation of cost of calls was not possible and hence the telephone department might show frequently a loss since telephone direct costs are overstated.

Administrative & General Department: Actually looking at any hotel organisation chart, Administrative and General Department (A&G) does not exist. It is however a financial reporting centers including executives of the Hotel and other employees involved with executive and financial activities (ex: Accounting personnel, resident Manager, Accounts Receivable clerks, Night Auditors). Moreover, if there is staff in the hotel not included in departments due to low business volume not justifying the establishment of a department, they might be included under the A& G department (ex. Data Processing Staff, Transportation Staff, and Personnel Staff).

Marketing Department: This department is composed of a marketing manager, marketing assistant managers responsible for sales, convention, public relations, and advertising functions, along with marketing personnel. This department is a cost center that indirectly supports revenue generators in their sole aim of generating hotel revenue. This can be insured, for example, through large group reservations, hence maximising room revenue, or buffet, conference, and catering opportunities brought by this very department hence maximising room revenue, F& B revenue, and the hotel revenue as a whole.

Property, Operation and Maintenance (POM): Concerned with the appearance and physical condition of the building, the repair and maintenance of equipment, and rubbish removal. Some positions of this department might include POM manager, POM assistant manager(s), electricians, plumbers, gardeners, painters, and interior design specialists.

Data Processing Department: This special department might be established in hotels operating under the fully automated system. Moreover, such hotels should have significant investment in computer equipment and staff to justify the establishment of a single department. If these conditions do not exist, than the Data Processing functions would be financially grouped under administrative & general department.

Human Resources Department: Similar to data processing department, if the dollar amount and staff incurred for employees' hiring, screening, interviewing, selecting, recruiting, and Training is significant, than a human resources department may be established. Otherwise, human resources functions would be financially grouped under administrative & general department

Guest Transportation Department: If the dollar amount and Number of Staff employed in the transportation of Guests is significant, a separate department might be established. Otherwise, guest transportation staff would be grouped under rooms division department.

Financial reporting center

A financial reporting center is an area of responsibility

for which separate cost information must be collected, might be classified as revenue centers, support centers, and other financial reporting centers

Revenue Centers—Generate revenue through sales of Products and/or services to guests

— Rooms

— Food and Beverage

— Telephone

— Gift Shops

— Garage and Parking

— Other Operated Departments

— Rentals and other Income

Support Centers—those departments that have minimal guest contact and do not produce Sales. Yet, they do provide services to revenue centers, which, in turn, provide services to guests

— Administrative & General

— Marketing

— Property Operation and Maintenance

— Data Processing

— Human Resources

Other Financial Reporting Centers—include Energy Costs and Fixed Charges (Rent Expense, Property Taxes, Insurance Expense, Interest Expense, Depreciation and Amortisation Expenses)

FRONT OFFICE RECORDS

The major two front office records that are stored at departure are guest history records (which are stored alphabetically) and guest folios (stored numerically)

Guest History Records

Guest history records are collections of personal & financial data about guests who have stayed at the hotel. Maintaining guest history records helps the hotel better understand its clientele and determine guest trends when they develop. Moreover, these very records might serve as a source of mailing list or to identify guest characteristics that are important to strategic marketing. In addition, they serve as to develop and place advertisements that appeal to the types of clientele the hotel attempts to attract. Finally guest history records points out the need for a new, supplementary, or enhanced services.

Moreover, even though guest history records are stored in the front office department, they are handed to marketing department, whenever needed. In fact, marketing department might get use of guest history records as to create a programme to reward frequent guests with a free stay after a certain number of visits, or as an indicator to watch out for future repeat guest reservations in order to increase the hotel's repeat business market share. Guests tend to remember the friendliness, convenience, and special services that distinguish one property from another. This is called competitive advantage.

Night Audit

The major functions of the night audit is to:

— Verify posted entries to guest and non-guest accounts

— Balance all front office accounts

— Resolve room status and rate discrepancies

— Monitor guest credit limits

— Produce operational and managerial reports

The night audit requires attention to accounting detail, procedural controls, and guest credit restrictions. In this sense, the night auditor shall track room revenues, occupancy percentages, and other standard operating statistics. He/she shall, also, prepare a daily summary of cash, check, and credit card activities that occurred in the front office department on a daily basis. In night auditing, end of the business day is a vital time for the auditor. As far as the closing of business day is concerned, management shall determine the end of day, which is the time after which the night audit can prepare his/her daily Reports. This end of day is usually the time where the majority of outlets close or no more have frequent activity.

The night auditor shall always compare the data conveyed in different folios against points of sales outlets daily reports, housekeeping room status report. This is called cross-referencing, and is a vital procedure in the internal control. After comparing, the night auditor should come up with the guest, non-guest, and departmental accounts. This total should match the daily POS totals (i.e. in balance). If not, then the auditor is said to be out-of-balance, and the night auditor shall substantially review all account statements, vouchers, support documents, and departmental source of documentation in order to bring the audit to balance.

The night audit shall compare all credit limits of guests and non-guests accounts with credit card floor limits, hotel's house limit, guest's status and reputation. If high balance accounts are detected, the night auditor shall note and report this to management the following day. Under the manual, a daily transcript and a supplementary transcript are used to track daily transactions of guest and non-guest accounts respectively. Hotels operating under semi-automated systems use D-Cards for the same purpose.

Non-automated system: under this very system, 4 forms are widely used, which are:

— Daily and supplementary transcripts

— Guest and non-Guest folios

— Front office cash sheets

Semi-automated system: The audit of guest and non-guest accounts is ensured mostly through mechanical or electronic posting machines. The most important form obtained under this very system is the D Card.

Fully-automated system: This very system is the best compared to manual and semi-automated systems. In fact, this system can be interfaced with point of sale terminals, call accounting systems, and other revenue centers for quick, accurate and automatic postings to electronic guest and non-guest account folios. This very fact enables the night auditor to concentrate more on auditing transactions and analysing front office activities.

Night Audit Process: The night audit process focuses on two areas:

— Discovery and correction of front office accounting errors ensured through the cross-referencing process.

— Creation of accounting and managerial reports including audit balance, average rate, occupancy percentage, usage of package plans and other marketing programmes, and the number of group rooms and complementary rooms occupied.

Front Office Communication

The voluble speaker monopolises the conversation without giving anyone else a chance to do any thing but to wait for a chance that never seems to come. There is a simple way by which one who is inclined to run-on can refrain himself from being a pest or a pest a bore: stop and think.

Communication on the Telephone

The telephone has virtually replaced all other forms of communication and with the frequency of it's use, has come the frequency of it's abuse. One can be held captive on the telephone as easily as in person by a garrulous friend or associate.

Personal Calls: When you talk on the telephone, whether in your home or in an office, the quality of your voice and your ability to express yourself clearly and concisely are of utmost importance. The person at the other end of the line obviously cannot see your facial expressions or gestures, and the impression received depends totally on your voice. Speak clearly and distinctly, with the same inflections one would use in a face-to-face conversation. If you must put the telephone down during the conversation, do it gently, and when you hang up, do not slam the receiver down. The person at the other end may still have the phone close to his ear, and the sudden sharp bang can be quite deafening.

Invitations: Don't let too young a child answer the telephone. A lot of the caller's time is wasted trying to make the child understand the message and relay it back to the right person. Don't hang up before letting the phone ring at least six times. Nothing is more irritating than to rush down form the attic or the bathtub to answer and to find that the caller has hung up.

Tips for Good Conversationalists

— Show interest in what other people are doing, how they are doing and where they are heading.

— Are able to make a fast switch, from business to world politics are from ecological concern top a new opera being performed.

— Know how to tailor their topics to the interest of the people they are addressing. Don't interrupt. It is extremely rude to stop someone in the middle of a discourse, even if he has been dragging on interminably. Wait for a propitious moment, and then break into the conversation, launching another topic.

— Speak from experience and knowledge and not careless conjecture. Look people straight in the eye when talking to them. Eye contact is important in any situation. If you don't look directly at the person you are talking to, it could mean that you hiding something, or looking for someone more important to talk do. Refrain from correcting in public another person's facts, grammar or pronunciation. Real friends help by pointing out in private, repeated errors that may make a colleague or friend look inarticulate or uneducated.

— Know how to question a stranger in a friendly, rather than a prying manner.

— Know when to talk business and when not to. People who can only talk about office matters are usually unmitigated bores. A good conversationalist really contributes to business discussion with peers, associates and clients, but also really contributes to discussions with people not associated with his business life.

— Don't burst someone's ballooning from of other people. If some one is passionately defending a point of view, it is indefensibly reduce to disagree disagreeably. You can always respond negatively without animosity.

— Address everyone within the group, not just one or two people. It is rude to have the floor and then single out someone to talk to, instead of the group that happens to be present.

It's exclusionary. A good conversationalist catches the eye of each person in the group ona rotating basis while talking, so that every one feels like a partner in the conversation.Know how to make a shy person feel part of the group. If he notices someone off to the side, without anyone to speak to, He will ask that person a question and bring him into the conversation by introducing him and asking his opinion on some matter.

Have a sense of humor. Without it there is no hope of a good conversation or a good rapport.

Dining in Restaurants

Reservations

When choking on food cough it out onto a napkin and place it on the plate, or if need be for a prolonged cough, excuse yourself from the table.

Coughing, Sneezing or Blowing your noise - It is not necessary to leave the table to perform any of these. In case the bout is prolonged excuse yourself form the table. Never use the napkin for this purpose. In case you do not have a handkerchief, go to the nearest bathroom.

Stones, bugs, hair etc. in food—There is no remedy to this than to quietly remove it. If it doesn't upset you, continue with your meal, otherwise, leave the food aside without calling attention to it and embarrassing your host. But if you are in a restaurant, inform the waiter and get a replacement. Spills-in case of a spill, neatly clean it up with a clean spoon or the tip of a knife. In case of a stain, dab a little water on it with the corner of the napkin.

Some Dining Don'ts

— Don't encircle the plate with one hand while eating with the other

— Don't push back the plate after you have finished eating
— Don't put liquid in your mouth, if it's already full
— Don't wipe off the tableware in the restaurant
— Don't crook your finger when picking up your cup
— Don't wave round your fork with food in it.
— Don't cut up your entire meal before you start
— Don't pile up accompaniments on top of the meat on your fork
— Make reservations in one name only. When you call to make a reservation be sure to give in all the details about the group. Also mentions special preference if any. In case you are going to be delayed or are canceling your reservation be sure to call up and inform.

When waiting for people at a restaurant;

If you are the first to arrive at a restaurant wait for the next person to arrive before you seat yourself. Always inform the head waiter that you are expecting a person request that he do shown to the table on arrival. It is proper to order one's drinks while one is waiting. While being seated all women precede men. However a host always leads the way to the table. He should in fact prior top to everyone's arrival make sure of the seating of his guests if possible must be catered to. While paying the bill never display the total, and quietly put the money into the folder.

Ordering cocktails and wines

Ask all the guests what they would like to drink and in case any one doesn't drink always offer a soft drink. Wine should preferably be ordered after the food order has been placed. Choose a wine that goes well with food ordered. If you do not recognise the wine labels it is always proper to ask the wine waiter's suggestion on the choice of wine.

Ordering food

There is nothing wrong with sticking to the old custom of the man ordering for the woman. But in case the waiter asks a lady for her order directly, she should not insult by relaying the reply through her male escort. Always show some consideration for the host's wallet while ordering, unless you know that he is very well off. At a restaurant table never comb your hair or run your hands through your hair. At the most what a lady can do, is to powder her nose or apply a little lipstick at the end of a meal. Family and friends, even thought they are more important to us in our lives.

Young children

All youngsters should be taught from their childhood that there are certain rules that are to be obeyed. Obedience to a "no" is perhaps the earliest lesson one must learn. Fair play among children is really good sportsmanship. Teach children the practice of kindness, taking turns and sharing. Do not let them get into the habit of interrupting. Teach them courtesies like please and thank you they should also be taught how to greet people. Another important lesson to be given early is table manners.

Older children

Just they have been taught respect your privacy, learn to respect theirs. Insists on good clean grooming, no matter what the latest fashion is. They should be taught the art of being a good host or a hostess. Teach them telephone manners and should set certain reasonable limits for them to receive and make calls.

Husbands and wives

Neither a husband nor a wife should make a social contrary to what is popularly believed, it is permissible to taste your partners food, if done unobtrusively. At the end of the meal if here is a lot of food that has been wasted there is nothing in asking the waiter to pack it up for you to take it home.

Should be treated with utmost respect and one should give them all the love and affection that they deserve. At the same time parents and in-laws should learn to respect the privacy and the decisions of their children and must no interfere in their lives.

Elevator Etiquette

Everyone at the front of a crowded elevator car should automatically get off, when the doors open, even if they are not their destination floor. The people behind cannot possibly emerge with ease if the people in front do not exit to give them enough room to move. If everyone on the car is going to get off at the same floor, then the people in front should get off smartly and to the side, again to make it easier for those following behind. Traditionally it was customary for gentlemen to perform every kind of contortion necessary to allow ladies behind them to leave the elevator car first.

The best way to call the waiter would be to raise your hand so that you attract his attention. If you don't manage to do so you can call out softly "waiter" or you could ask a waiter standing nearby, to call your waiter. While paying a check the total should never be disclosed and the payment should be made quietly. In case there has been a mistake, get the waiter's attention top it quietly and never create a scene. When splitting the check it is best to ask for separate checks if the group is small but in case the group is large, then the person who has been acting as the spokesperson should take enough amount of money from everyone to cover the amount for the food as well as the tip.

Inter Relationships

Often we reserve our best behavior for company and often for strangers, giving less than our best to our. Engagement without consulting each other. Of all the advice one could give a bride or the groom, perhaps the best world be to use the words "we", "our". Even a husband and wife should respect each other's privacy and should not pry into each others mail.

5

Housekeeping Management

The housekeeping categories used by the housekeeping department usually include: housekeeping salaries and wages, payroll taxes and benefits, and other expenses. Salaries and wages include those of the entire housekeeping department; payroll taxes and benefits include the operator's share of additional costs related to payroll; the category of other expenses encompasses any other cost incurred by the housekeeping department that is not payroll-related. The buying function in lodging chains is often centralised. Items like soap, linen, mattresses, pillows, furniture, and fixtures are procured by the company's purchasing department and shipped to the different units on request.

Purchasing in large independent properties is done by the purchasing agent, who is a specialised buyer in charge of procuring products for all departments in the property. Smaller properties often allow the department heads to purchase goods for their respective areas of responsibility. In any case, it should be the job of the executive housekeeper to always pretest and approve all items used in the housekeeping department and decide the quantities and the specifications of the products to be bought. It should not be the job of the purchasing agent, or any other person for that matter, to purchase material and supplies without the consent of the executive housekeeper. It is also important to solicit the input of janitors, section housekeepers, housepersons, and laundry personnel on the appropriate characteristics of the items that in the end are to be used by them.

All merchandise purchased should have precise specifications, which are descriptions of the products' quality and factors that should reflect precisely the performance needs for each particular institution. Specifications should be stated clearly, giving the information needed to assure proper identification. For instance, a luxury resort does probably require the best bed linen money can buy, while a small, inexpensive motel may just need bed linen of fair quality. Before buying a product, prices should be obtained from at least three different vendors. Product price and vendor dependability and service should be reviewed once or twice every three months. Purchasing decisions should be made based not only on price but on quality, suitability, and storage availability as well.

The executive housekeeper must control the function of purchasing by defining clearly what is to be procured, who will be in charge of the buying, what specifications are to be considered, and what quantities will be needed. The person in charge of purchasing must consistently provide the needed quantities of products in housekeeping inventories. Although in some cases purchasing is done by the corporate office or by the property's purchasing agent, the executive housekeeper is ultimately responsible for the cost and results of what is purchased.

For some products, linen for instance, pars need to be established; for others, for example soaps and paper products, maximum and minimum quantities are set up. Pars can be defined as the number of required on-hand items to perform housekeeping operations. In the case of linens, for instance, the optimum number of pars is 4. This means that ideally the property should have on hand one set of sheets and pillowcases set up in the guestroom beds at any given time, another set being laundered, an additional set ready to go in floor closets and room attendant carts, and one final set on reserve. For guest and cleaning supplies, the maximum quantity is the greatest number of units that should be in stock at any given time, while the minimum quantity refers to the fewest number of units.

For example, the maximum and minimum number of cases of soap could be 35 and 25 respectively. That means that if at any given time the soap inventory is above 35, the product is overstocked. On the other hand, if the number of cases falls below 25, additional supplies must be ordered. This system eliminates the risk of overstocking or of running out of products. The receiving function of goods ordered must also be controlled. Unless adequate inspection and receiving procedures are used, the best purchasing system may fail because it is at this point that determination must be made of whether or not the products meet the specifications and quantities of the order previously placed.

Failing to inspect the merchandise adequately may result in higher costs, lower quality, theft, and fraud. On receiving a shipment, the goods should be compared with those listed on the receiving sheet or purchase order to verify the correctness of the delivery. If the goods meet the prearranged requirements, they are accepted by signing the invoice or delivery memo. If the products do not meet inspection requirements, they should be refused and a notation indicating the reasons for refusing the delivery made. The function of storing merchandise must also be controlled adequately. Access to storerooms must be limited to authorised personnel only. The storeroom should be locked off -hours and a record should be kept of the person entering it and of the merchandise taken. Valuable items like towels and some guest supplies should be stored in an area that remains locked at all times.

The storage area should be designed to hold the specific products stored in it; bottom shelving levels should be at least 10 inches off the floor to ensure adequate ventilation and to allow for cleaning underneath. A rotation system should be established by which oldest stock is placed in front and issued first. In large properties, housekeeping items may be stored in the main storeroom. In this case, the housekeeping department will need to fill a requisition form to request products.

Floor closet storage should also be locked at all times and access limited to the section housekeepers, housepersons, or supervisors in charge of the area. To account for the cost of housekeeping operating assets used, physical inventories are conducted regularly, in most cases monthly. Linens, uniforms, and cleaning and guest supplies inventories are taken by counting all items on hand and listing them on a physical inventory form. Laundry chemicals may be included in the cleaning supplies category or counted separately for better control. The purpose of taking physical inventories is to find out what amount of items for each category is on hand and to work out its current market value.

Physical inventories are difficult to conduct as all items that need to be accounted for must be counted one by one. In the case of linens, for instance, linens are found in guestrooms, laundry room, linen room, floor closets, room attendant carts, etc. To keep tight control on valuable items, for example imported chocolates for special guests, a perpetual inventory system may be implemented. Executive housekeepers must administer and maintain their proprieties' fixed assets classified as Furniture, Fixtures and Equipment (FF&E), Software, and Department Equipment. Although new establishments are usually handed over to the management team equipped with allitems needed for operation, the executive housekeeper is directly involved in the replacement, refurbishing, and upkeep of most fixed asset items in the property. For this reason, executive housekeepers must have appropriate knowledge of the assets that are under their control.

Regardless of their type of service, lodging properties must maintain interior design consistency standards throughout the building. Whether a property has been classified as economy, mid-market, or luxury, its guestroom and public area design, colour patterns, fabric and upholstery quality, and overall appearance must befit the category they represent. Doing piecemeal refurbishing or renovating must always be avoided. Colours, for instance, must be complementary. In general, blue is a complement of orange, green of red, and yellow of violet. Using several light tints and shades of the same colour makes rooms seem larger, while full-intensity hues tend to make the room seem compact. Adjoining walls should be painted the same colour to provide a sense of continuity.

Executive housekeepers are generally responsible for the refurbishing and upkeep of the furniture in guestroom, public, and employee areas. Furniture should be solidly built, easy to maintain, functional, and attractive. It is not advisable to purchase pieces of furniture directly from a catalogue; instead, the executive housekeeper should carefully examine samples to ensure that the products have been built to withstand repeated rough use. All furniture tops should be plastic-laminated or finished with water-repellent polyurethane to avoid scratches, rings, and stains caused by abusive treatment and spilled liquids.

Desk chairs should have padded backs to provide comfort to guests and prevent wood from hitting desktops. Furniture dotted with glides or casters will prevent carpet damage when pushed or pulled around the room. Luggage racks are better if built-in and fitted with wall-protecting panels, as there is a greater likelihood that the luggage will bump against and deteriorate walls when detached racks are used. Desks should be large enough to accommodate a desktop computer and a fax machine.

TV/VCR units should be an actual piece of furniture, rather than simply a conventional metal stand, and should be fitted with 180-degree swivels so that guests can see the screen from anywhere in the room. Case furniture such as chests of drawers, credensas, armoires, desks, and bureaus also should be purchased with durability in mind. Drawers should be equipped with nylon ball bearings and slide glides so that they don't jam when opening and closing. In general, guestrooms should provide a warm residential look; for instance, love seats and armchairs can replace the standard chairs so often found in hotel rooms. Upholstery fibers may be natural, synthetic, or plastic.

Natural fabrics, such as cotton, linen, silk, and wool, are rich looking and long wearing but expensive and delicate to maintain because they stain easily. Synthetic fibers are less expensive and easy to clean but they are less elegant and more likely to generate static electricity. Often, upholstered materials are a blend of natural and synthetic fabrics. The greatest advantage of upholstery plastic materials such as vinyl is that they can be easily cleaned by just wiping with a soapy cloth; however, they generally have a duller appearance than natural or blended materials.

Upholstery fabrics should be strong enough to withstand repeated shampooing. Treating fabrics With soil-retardant sprays can decrease the need for dry-cleaning the material. It is also important that upholstery fabrics be treated with flame-retardant finishes. Before putting upholstered furniture fabrics into use, they should be pretested to ascertain the best way to clean the pieces without causing shrinkage or discoloration. Some fabrics can be cleaned with solvent, others can be cleaned with water and detergent, and some only allow for vacuuming. In general, synthetic fabrics such as nylon and plastics such as vinyl are the most stain-resistant and easy-to-clean upholstery materials. Beds are the central attraction in guestrooms and often a big selling point for travellers when choosing a lodging property. When asked to pay an average of $70.00 per night per room, guests expect to receive a clean, well-maintained sleeping area and a comfortable bed.

In commercial operations, beds consist of a frame to support the springs and mattresses and unattached headboards. Bed frames usually consist of metal bars with legs attached to each corner or of a metal or wood platform. The main advantage of platform frames is that room attendants don't have to vacuum underneath the box frame, thus saving time when cleaning the room. Headboards are mounted on the wall and should match the general design of the room's furniture. It is important to know the composition of the bed structure of each property in order to figure out the maximum member of people that the property can house.

Knowing the different types of beds and how many guests can stay in the rooms will help executive housekeepers plan for bed and bathroom linen and supplies. Another type of sleeping equipment is the mobile bed. Families on vacation and travelling high school or college groups often require additional sleeping accommodations in guestrooms. The rollaway, or bed on wheels, consists of a folding frame with an attached bed spring body. The mattress in rollaways must be made of latex foam or have very light, flexible innersprings so that they too can fold with the frame. Because rollaways are unable to provide a comfortable surface to hold the weight of an adult person, they should be recommended only for children or young people to avoid legitimate complaints about the property's not providing adequate accommodation.

Cribs are also essential to have in order to accommodate infants or young children. While cribs should be collapsible to save storage space, their extension mechanisms should be kept in good working order to prevent the crib from collapsing when being used. Dual-purpose sleeping equipment is common in guestrooms. These pieces of furniture provide both seating space and extra sleeping capacity, eliminating the need to roll in a mobile bed on short notice. Sofas, couches, chair-beds, and in-wall beds are the most common dual-purpose pieces of furniture found in lodging properties. Sofas, couches and chair-beds convert into beds by removing the cushions and pulling out the folding frame and mattress or by dropping the back to the level of the seat. In-wall beds, also called Murphy beds, are concealed in the wall behind a panel, giving the room the appearance of a studio or parlour rather than a bedroom.

Surveys of favourite guest amenities conducted regularly by hospitality magazines consistently show that guests put comfortable mattresses at the top of the list, second only to cleanliness. Most mattresses used in lodging operations are of the innerspring type; they have metal coils that support the weight of the sleepers while conforming to their body contours. The strength and number of coils determine the mattress firmness, which may range from medium to super firm. Heavy-gauge steel wire coils are best, allowing for weights to flex down a specific area without disturbing the space surrounding the pressure points. This allows for two persons of different weights to lie side by side and each get different levels of buoyancy.

The firmness of the mattress is determined by the gauge of steel used, the number of turns of each coil, and the way the coils are attached to the mattress frame. Preferably, the springs should be encased in fabric pockets to provide independent coil action, rather than being attached to each other with wire or hooks. Good mattresses have sufficient padding to cushion the springs beneath and provide a smooth surface. The padding should be nonallergenic and comply with the government flame-spread regulation, which states that a lighted cigarette should not be able to ignite the insulation.

Water-filled mattresses (waterbeds) became quite popular with the public when they were first used in the 1960s, but they soon proved to be inconvenient with lodging operators because they often leaked and because the water had to be heated, which became costly. Although today's waterbeds are efficiently built with individually filled cells that do not need to be heated because of an insulating foam layer, there doesn't seem to be a great demand for them from lodging guests. Lodging properties, however, should have a few waterbeds to fulfil the request of interested travellers. Guestrooms and lodging property lobbies are also furnished with accessories such as mirrors, decorations, pictures, and lights, to complement the furniture.

For instance, strategically placed mirrors can give small rooms an illusion of depth; serene motifs in paintings will provide a feeling of tranquillity; triple magnification make-up mirrors and wall-mounted hair dryers in bathrooms are a welcome amenity; a well-stocked mahogany bookcase in the lobby will provide a homey feeling to guests who enjoy reading. Beautiful carpeting can enhance the appearance of lodging properties and make a lasting impression on guests. On the other hand, discoloured, worn, or dirty carpets are usually sources of guest complaints. The first step in selecting the right carpet is to match its colour, texture, and pattern with the design of the area where it is to be installed.

Then, other factors need to be considered, such as determining the anticipated level of wear and tear caused by the intensity of traffic, the location of the carpet, and the budget allocated for it. When heavy traffic is expected, carpets should feature strong resistance to abrasion, as well as texture retention and anti-soiling and staining characteristics. The location of the carpet should determine specifications such as enhanced colourfastness, antimicrobial protection, resistance to snags, and resilience under rolling loads.

Besides durability and stain resistance, carpets in lodging properties should be capable of withstanding repeated cleaning treatment. Before purchasing carpet, be sure you fully understand the warranty coverage offered by the manufacturer or installer. Warranties for commercial carpets should include protection for wear and tear, colourfastness (fading from sunlight and atmospheric contaminants), tuft bind deterioration, static charges, backing strength, ravelling of seams and edges, and any other manufacturing defects.

Executive housekeepers should have sufficient knowledge of carpet construction to ensure that the right carpet is selected for each area in the property. There are three main elements in the composition of carpets: the pile, or face; the backing, or material to which the pile is secured; and the padding, or cushion on which the carpet rests. Most commercial carpets are tufted, that is, the yam is threaded through the backing material to form loops. The backing material usually is woven jute or polypropylene with a layer of adhesive latex extended over the material to anchor the tufts. Knitted carpets are made by interlacing together the pile yam and the backing.

The process of embedding the pile fibers electrostatically into a layer of adhesive material applied to the backing is called flocking. Weaving is the old-fashioned way of making carpets using conventional looms. The yarns are interlaced together to form the pile and the backing. As with linen, the yarns woven lengthwise are called the warp and the yarns going across are the wefts. The process of making carpets by compacting the fibers and the backing by mechanically punching them together is called needle punching. Improper lighting in rooms may discourage guests from staying in a particular establishment.

Guests, particularly business travellers, expect to find adequate lighting to be able to work over flat surfaces such as tables and desks, or to read in bed or sitting on a couch or armchair. Lights of adjustable intensity should be placed strategically so that guests can arrange their preferences to suit their needs; for example, subdued lighting for relaxation or bright lighting for working or entertaining friends. Having three-way lamps or lights activated by rheostats give guests the option to set the mood of the room to their liking. Floor lamps are not recommended in guestrooms because they can be easily knocked over and they create tripping hazards. Desk lamps should have the on-off switches at the base to reduce the risk of guests burning their fingers on the light bulb or upsetting the shade's balance when reaching around to locate the switch.

One advantage of fluorescent lights is that they use less energy and last longer than regular bulbs. In all cases, sufficient wattage must be provided in lamps that guests will use for reading or working purposes. Long gone are the days when hoteliers could sell rooms equipped with a minimum of basic features. Today's business traveller is putting a new spin on the concept of guestroom equipment. Lodging chains that cater to corporate clientele offer in-room or satellite office support services including computers and fax and copy machines. Guestrooms are often equipped with multi-line telephones complete with voice mail and PC compatibility; some hotels even provide cellular phones and 24-hour access to translators and information in other languages.

Refrigerators and microwave ovens are quite common in suite hotels, and coffee-makers, together with selections of coffee and tea blends, are now available in the rooms of most properties. Wide-screen television sets and high-quality clock radios are a must in four- and five-diamond properties, as are in-room safes. In-room strongboxes are seen as a last-ditch defence for the guests' personal belongings, including items as large as lap-top computers. The locking systems of in-room safes range from ordinary keys to programmable push-buttons, magnetic-lock devices, and the guest's credit card. Some microprocessor safes automatically lock for 30 minutes after four false attempts to open them. Besides being a great convenience for guests who don't want to line up for safety deposit boxes, in-room safes are effective against thieves and even employees who may use stolen keys to burglarise rooms.

Valuables can be stored by guests themselves and remain secure during trips to the pool, jogging around the block, or going out to dinner. Some safes have built-in memory, which enables the front office personnel to read the date and time of the most recent safe openings and closings. This can provide convincing evidence in case of a loss claim against the property. Some up-scale lodging properties, particularly resorts and first class hotels, offer minibars in their guestrooms and suites.

Stocked with beverages and snacks, minibars can be profitable because guests are often tempted to have a last drink before going to bed or first thing in the morning. Fully automated minibars can electronically sense when an item is removed, sending the corresponding charge to the guest's room account. Non-automated units must rely on the honesty of the guest to notify the front desk just before checking out if goods have been consumed. Depreciable fixed assets that are not furniture or equipment, such as bedspreads, mattress covers, blankets, pillows, and window coverings may be categorised under the classification of software.

As with mattresses, bedspreads should be purchased with the qualities of durability, comfort, maintenance, and fire safety in mind. Bedspreads are an important component in the decor of guestrooms and should complement the motif, colour, and design of the room. Fabrics made of 100 percent polyester offer excellent resistance to fading, staining, shrinking, and wrinkling.

Polycottons, a blend of polyester cotton, are less expensive than fabrics made of 100 percent polyester, but their life span is shorter, they have fewer fire-retardant qualities, and they fade more easily. While the normal recycling life span of a good bedspread should be at least 5 years, polycotton bedspreads only last from 2 to 3 years. Other factors to consider when specifying bedspreads are their fill and seaming. Fill is one of the key elements that determines the appearance of bedspreads. The number of ounces of fill per square yard should be 7 or more. Non-compressed fills are better than mechanically packed fills because of their ability to spring back to its original 'loft is greater.

Wide, seamless bedspreads are preferred to those constructed with seams because they don't come apart as easily. Bedspreads can be large enough to reach to the floor or just to cover the mattress. In this case a pleated cloth skirting called a dust ruffle may be placed between the mattress and the box spring to extend around the sides and foot of the bed. Washable bedspreads should be purchased with the guarantee that they will not shrink, fade, or wrinkle. Par levels for bedspreads should be one plus 10 percent to allow for washing and replacement.

The purpose of blankets is to act as insulators. A heavy blanket does not necessarily keep the warmth of the body from escaping through it. On the other hand, a material (even if it is light) that is tightly woven will retain body heat. However, all blankets should be porous enough to allow any moisture buildup under them to escape to the surrounding air. Wool is a delicate natural fiber that is very warm but that requires extreme care when laundered.

Cotton, on the other hand, washes easily but it is a poor insulator and shrinks up to 15 percent if not purchased preshrunk. Synthetic fibers such as acrylics and polyester, if properly constructed, are suitable to commercial operations. Acrylic fibers are warmer than polyester but not as strong. Because guests may fall asleep while smoking in bed, blankets should be fire retardant. The size of the blanket should be large enough to cover the length and width of the mattress and have some additional inches for tucking.

All mattresses should be fitted with moisture-proof covers at all times to prevent staining. Vinyl plastic covers are impermeable and can be washed like any other fabric. Their use is recommended for cribs or small cots for young children and hospital beds. Felt pads made of moisture-proof, flame-retardant, 100 per cent polyester resist shrinkage and are quite durable.

Most commercial pillows axe filled with synthetic fiber, mainly polyester. Synthetic pillows are quite common in commercial properties because they are inexpensive, easy to launder, and nonallergenic. When purchasing pillows, it is important to make sure that the fill is of good quality so that it springs back into shape easily; lumpy, heavier fills are an indication of inferior grade. The synthetic covering of the pillow must be fire retardant and stain proof and able to withstand frequent washings. Pillows with natural fills such as down and feathers are very expensive, particularly goose down.

Lodging properties should stock a few natural-fill pillows to meet the occasional request for them. Because of the price, down and feather pillows should be provided to guests on a loan basis, that is, a record should be kept in the housekeeping department of the room number where the pillows were delivered and then should be recovered after the guest's checkout. The first consideration for selecting wall coverings is that they match the general decor of the room; the second, and just as important, consideration is their durability and ease of maintenance. The two most common forms of wall coverings are paint and vinyl. The paint used to finish walls should be easy to wash with soapy water and of very good quality so that the surface doesn't require repainting after a short period of time.

Vinyl wall coverings are available in several thicknesses to suit the area to be covered; for instance, walls covered with thin layers are vulnerable to bumps from baggage and carts and should be used only to cover no-traffic areas. Heavier vinyl can withstand heavy impacts and can be used over surfaces susceptible to abrasion. Although far more expensive than paint, vinyl wall coverings generally pay for themselves because they require very little maintenance. Vinyl coverings are made by laminating the material to cotton or polycotton backings and are glued to walls using an adhesive paste. To prevent mildew from loosening the vinyl from the adhesive, the glue should contain a mildewcide. Fabric wall coverings can provide rooms and hallways with a luxurious, elegant look but they should be avoided in commercial operations because of the difficulty of cleaning or replacing them when soiled. Wallpaper should be used only if it is stain and water-resistant and allows for damp cleaning with soap and sponge.

Windows in offices, lobbies, and employee areas are usually fitted with vinyl blinds. Because of their susceptibility to fading, fabrics used for curtains must be resistant to direct sunlight. As curtains attract dust and odours, they require frequent washings and dry cleaning; for this reason, it is advisable to purchase good-quality, vinyl-coated fabrics that can retain their shape and colour for long periods of time. Curtains should be flame retardant to comply with local fire departments specifications. Drapery can be simple or quite ornate. Valances, and shirred or pinch-pleated fabrics, can add elegance and warmth to rooms, although they will require more cleaning time to keep them dust free.

In all cases, the curtain rods and cords must be sturdy to avoid damage; having batons instead of cords may reduce the chance of breakage. The housekeeping department needs major pieces of equipment to clean guest, public, and employee areas and to transport clean and soiled linen, trash, and supplies. In all cases, the department equipment used in housekeeping should be of heavy-duty quality, able to withstand rough and continuous use. Often, purveyors of chemical supplies also carry a complete line of equipment. In some cases, manufacturers have their own representatives who will describe the machines and demonstrate their performance.

Perhaps the most significant piece of housekeeping equipment is the housekeeping cart. Usually, one cart is assigned to the cleaner of each section of guestrooms and one to each janitor. The cart should be large enough and have enough shelves to carry a full complement of supplies needed in each working shift in order to avoid unnecessary trips to the linen room for additional supplies. Although sturdy, the cart must be light and maneuverable enough to be pushed by one person from door to door and from floor to floor, including pushing it into and out of service elevators. The cart should be contoured with rubber bumpers to protect walls and wall corners and have casters with brakes of superior quality.

Some carts can be purchased with side panels that can be locked in order to prevent linen and guest amenities from being exposed to whomever walks past them, thus eliminating theft. If fitted with laundry and trash bags, these should be made of heavy-duty material to withstand hard use. Plastic baskets or caddies containing guest amenities and cleaning supplies are generally placed on the top shelf of carts. Several types of vacuum cleaners are used by housekeeping. One requirement common to all of them is that they be heavy-duty and powerful enough to provide efficient, one-pass cleaning.

The typical vacuum cleaner used in guestroom carpet cleaning is upright, with one or two motors. The dual-motor type has one motor to drive the beater brush and another to provide the suction. Some useful characteristics of commercial vacuums are as follows: having collector cups or zipper receptacles instead of paper bags (some models can be messy and difficult to empty, in which case it is better to use disposable bags), long electric cable, wraparound bumpers, secondary filters to protect the vacuum motor, adjustable brush settings, three-position handles, and self-lubricating brushes.

Some vacuums are incorporated into the housekeeping cart. This arrangement, however, may cause some difficulties. Because the hoses must be long enough to reach all corners of the room, suction power may be reduced. And since the vacuum must be operated in hallways, the noise permeates throughout the area. Also, because the machine is attached to the cart, repairs and maintenance are more difficult to perform on site than in the engineering shop. Large-area vacuums are used in hallways and lobbies that contain extensive areas of carpeting.

The three major purposes of chemicals used in the housekeeping department are to remove dirt, to destroy harmful microorganisms, and to preserve and beautify furniture, fixtures, and surfaces. Chemical cleaners are manufactured to remove soils from surfaces through chemical action. The stronger the chemical is, the better effect it will have on getting the job done. The strength of cleaning chemicals is measured on the pH scale. pH is the symbol for the logarithm of the reciprocal of hydrogen ion concentration in gram atoms per liter. Cleaning chemicals that have been enhanced with alkalis or acids to strengthen their cleaning powers can be dangerous to humans and often cannot be used on certain surfaces.

A neutral cleaner can be used for all types of jobs but its cleaning power is limited. The executive housekeeper should have adequate knowledge of the department's needs to select cleaning chemicals appropriate for each type of cleaning job to be performed regularly in the housekeeping department. Generally speaking, high-alkaline cleaners are effective degreasers while acidic cleaners are good for fighting lime and rust, which are always found in urinals and toilets. Another name for cleaners is detergents.

Detergents act chemically to emulsify dirt, holding it in suspension so it can be removed away from the surface. Synthetic detergents are easy to rinse off and often have excellent cleaning, deodorizing, and germicidal characteristics. Most cleaning detergents are made from mineral oils. All-purpose cleaners have neutral pH-balanced formulas for general-purpose cleaning jobs. They usually are synthetic detergents, often vegetable oil based, of which pine oil is very popular because of its pleasant scent and strong deodorizing power. All-purpose cleaners may have corrosion inhibitors to protect metal surfaces.

Single-purpose cleaners are heavy-duty cleaners used for specific cleaning jobs. Abrasive cleaners are cleaning powders or pastes combined with silica for tough cleaning jobs. These cleaners will scratch soft surfaces like fiberglass or porcelain. Gentler cleansers made with nonscratching calcite instead of silica greatly reduce their abrasive action.

Degreasers are highly effective cleaners, often biodegradable, that remove grease, tar, ink, food deposits, smoke film, fats and other grimy soils. Degreasers can be highly effective on concrete floors. It is important to remember that some products advertised as degreasers may be toxic and therefore not suitable for use on kitchen surfaces.

Although most all-purpose cleaners can be used as deodorizers, stronger chemicals are needed to counteract stale odours. Deodorizers can be purchased as mists, wall and urinal blocks, cup and wick, and aerosols. Glass cleaners are ammonia- and alcohol-based products that clean and provide a protective coating to glass surfaces. Glass treated with good-quality glass cleaners resist fogging caused by moisture and temperature changes and in some manner repel dust, dirt, fingerprints, and smudges. Most glass cleaners can also be used as multipurpose cleaners on chrome, stainless steel, enamel, formica, ceramic tile, and other washable surfaces.

Another purpose of housekeeping supplies is to beautify surfaces and fixtures. Furniture polishes are liquid waxes or oils or silicone-based sprays designed to protect and give shine to wood, leather, vinyl, metal, and plastic surfaces. When pigments are added to liquid furniture polish, the product helps cover nicks and scratches in wood furniture, panelling, and floors.

Staffing a Housekeeping Operations

There are several activities involved in staffing a housekeeping operation. Executive housekeepers must select and interview employees, participate in an orientation programme, train newly hired employees, and develop employees for future growth. Each region has its own demographic situations that affect the availability of suitable employees for involvement in housekeeping or environmental service operations. For example, in one area, an exceptionally high response rate from people seeking food service work may occur and a low response rate from people seeking housekeeping positions may occur.

In another area, the reverse may be true, and people interested in housekeeping work may far outnumber those interested in food service. Advertising campaigns that will reach these employees are the best method of locating suitable people. Major classified ads associated with mass hirings will specify the need for food service personnel, front desk clerks, food servers, housekeeping personnel, and maintenance people. Such ads may yield surprising results. If aliens are hired, the department manager must take great care to ensure that they are legal residents of this country and that their green cards are valid.

More than one hotel department manager has had an entire staff swept away by the Department of Immigration after hiring people who were illegal aliens. Such unfortunate action has required the immediate assistance of all available employees to fill in. Whether you are involved in a mass hiring or in the recruiting of a single employee, a systematic and courteous procedure for processing applicants is essential. For example, in the opening of the Los Angeles Airport Marriott, 11,000 applicants were processed to fill approximately 850 positions in a period of about two weeks. The magnitude of such an operation required a near assembly-line technique, but a personable and positive experience for the applicants still had to be maintained. The efficient handling of lines of employees, courteous attendance, personal concern for employee desires, and reference to suitable departments for those unfamiliar with what the hotel or hospital has to offer all become earmarks for how the company will treat its employees.

The key to proper handling of applicants is the use of a control system whereby employees are conducted through the steps of application, prescreening, and if qualified, reference to a department for interview. Even though an employee may desire involvement in one classification of work, he or she may be hired for employment in a different department. Also, employees might not be aware of the possibilities available in a particular department at the time of application or may be unable to locate in desired departments at the time of mass hirings.

Employees who perform well should therefore be given the opportunity to transfer to other departments when the opportunities arise. According to laws regulated by federal and state Fair Employment Practices Agencies (FEPA), no person may be denied the opportunity to submit application for employment for a position of his or her choosing. Not only is the law strict on this point, but companies in any way benefiting from interstate commerce may not discriminate in the hiring of people based on race, colour, national origin, or religious preference.

Informal Orientation Programme

Too often, a new employee is told where the work area and restroom are, given a cursory explanation of the job, then put to work. It is not uncommon to find managers putting employees to work who have not even been processed into the organisation, an unfortunate situation that is usually discovered on payday when there is no paycheck for the new employee. Such blatant disregard for the concerns of the employee can only lead to a poor perception of the company. A planned orientation programme will eliminate this type of activity and will bring the employee into the company with personal concern and with a greater possibility for a successful relationship. A good orientation programme is usually made up of four phases: employee acquisition, receipt of an employee's handbook, tour of the facility, and an orientation meeting.

Employee Acquisition: Once a person is accepted for employment, the applicant is told to report for work at a given time and place, and that place should be the personnel department. Pre-employment procedures can take as much as one-half day, and department managers eager to start new employees to work should allow time for a proper employee acquisition into the organisation. At this time it should be ensured that the application is complete and any additional information pertaining to employment history that may be necessary to obtain the necessary work permits and credentials is on hand.

Usually the security department records the entry of a new employee into the staff and provides instructions regarding use of employee entrances, removing parcels from the premises, and employee parking areas. Application for work permits, and drug testing, will be scheduled where applicable. All documents required by the hotel's health and welfare insurer should be completed, and instructions should be given about immediately reporting accidents, no matter how slight, to supervisors.

Familiarisation of Facilities: Upon completion of the acquisition phase, a facility tour should be conducted for one or all new employees. For new facilities, access to the property should be gained within about one week before opening, and many new employees can be taken on a tour simultaneously. It is possible for employees to work in the hotel housekeeping department for years and never to have visited the showroom, dining rooms, ballrooms, or even the executive office areas.

A tour of the complete facility melds employees into the total organisation, and a complete informative tour should never be neglected. For ongoing operations, after acquisition, the new employee may be turned over to a department supervisor, who becomes the tour director. An appreciation of the total involvement of each employee is strengthened when a facilities tour is complete and thorough.

Employee Orientation Meeting

Employee orientation meetings that are scheduled too soon fail to answer many questions that will develop within the first two weeks of employment. The meeting should be held in a comfortable setting, with refreshments provided. It is usually conducted by the director of human resources and is attended by as many of the facility managers as possible. Most certainly, the general manager or hospital administration members of the executive committee, the security director, and the new employees' department heads should attend. Each of these managers should have an opportunity to welcome the new employees and give them a chance to associate names with faces. All managers and new employees should wear name tags.

In orientation meetings, a brief history of the company and company goals should be presented. Although the new employee will be gaining confidence and security in the position as training ends and work is actually performed, informal orientation may continue for quite some time. The formal orientation, however, ends with the orientation meeting. Finally, it should be remembered that good orientation procedures lead to worker satisfaction and help quiet the anxieties and fears that a new employee may have.

Need Effective Training

Such ability will depend in part on past experiences, but

more commonly it can be credited to the type and quality of training offered. Employees, regardless of past experiences, always need some degree of training before starting a new job. Small institutions may try to avoid training by hiring people who are already trained in the general functions with which they will be involved. However, most institutions recognise the need for training that is specifically oriented toward the new experience, and will have a documented training programme.

Some employers of housekeeping personnel find it easier to train completely unskilled and untrained personnel. In such cases, bad or undesirable practices do not have to be trained out of an employee. Previous experience and education should, however, be analysed and considered in the training of each new employee in order that efficiencies in training can be recognised. If an understanding of department standards and policies can be demonstrated by a new employee, that portion of training may be shortened or modified. However, skill and ability must be demonstrated before training can be altered.

First training of a new employee actually starts with a continuation of department orientation. When a new employee is turned over to the housekeeping or environmental services department, orientation usually continues by familiarising the employee with department rules and regulations. Many housekeeping departments have their own department employee handbooks.

Training may be defined as those activities that are designed to help an employee begin performing tasks for which he or she is hired or to help the employee improve performance in a job already assigned. The purpose of training is to enable an employee to begin an assigned job or to improve upon techniques already in use. In hotel or hospital housekeeping operations, there are three basic areas in which training activity should take place: skills, attitudes, and knowledge.

Employees need guidance in their attitudes about the work that must be done. They need to be guided in their thinking about rooms that may present a unique problem in cleaning. Attitudes among section housekeepers need to be such that, occasionally, when rooms require extra effort to be brought back to standard, it is viewed as being a part of rendering service to the guest who paid to enjoy the room. The rooms are there to be enjoyed. Positive relationships with various agencies and people also need to be developed.

The most important task of the trainer is to prepare new employees to meet standards. With this aim in mind, sequence of performance in cleaning a guestroom is most important in order that efficiency in accomplishing day-to-day tasks may be developed. In addition, the best method of accomplishing a task should be presented to the new trainee.

New equipment may require new attitudes about work habits. Employee behaviour while on the job that is seen as an indicator for additional training may be divided into two categories: events that the manager witnesses and events that the manager is told about by the employees. Events that the manager witnesses that indicate a need for training are frequent employee absence, considerable spoilage of products, carelessness, a high rate of accidents, and resisting direction by supervisors. Events that the manager might be told about that indicate a need for training are that something doesn't work right, something is dangerous to work with, something is making work harder.

Although training is vital for any organisation to function at top efficiency, it is expensive. The money and man-hours expended must therefore be worth the investment. There must be a balance between the dollars spent training employees and the benefits of productivity and high-efficiency performance. A simple method of determining the need for training is to measure performance of workers: Find out what is going on at present on the job, and match this performance with what should be happening.

The difference, if any, describes how much training is needed. If the employee could not do the job even if his or her life depended on the outcome, there is a deficiency of knowledge (DK). If the employee could have done the job if his or her life depended on the outcome, but did not, there is a deficiency of execution (DE). If either deficiency of knowledge or deficiency of execution exists, training must be conducted. The approach or the method of training may differ, however. Deficiencies of knowledge can be corrected by training the employee to do the job, then observing and correcting as necessary until the task is proficiently performed.

Methods of Training

Each method has its own advantages and disadvantages, which must be weighed in the light of benefits to be gained. Some methods are more expensive than others but are also more effective in terms of time required for comprehension and proficiency that must be developed. Several useful methods of training housekeeping personnel are listed and discussed.

On-the-Job Training: Using on-the-job training (OJT), a technique in which "learning by doing" is the advantage, the instructor demonstrates the procedure and then watches the students perform it. With this technique, one instructor can handle several students. In housekeeping operations, the instructor is usually a GRA who is doing the instructing in the rooms that have been assigned for cleaning that day. The OJT method is not operationally productive until the student is proficient enough in the training tasks to absorb part of the operational load.

Simulation training: With simulation training, a model room (unrented) is set up and used to train several employees. Whereas OJT requires progress toward daily production of ready rooms, simulation requires that the model room not be rented. In addition, the trainer is not productive in cleaning ready rooms. The advantages of simulation training are that it allows the training process to be stopped, discussed, and repeated if necessary. Simulation is an excellent method, provided the trainer's time is paid for out of training funds, and clean room production is not necessary during the workday.

Coach-Pupil method: The coach-pupil method is similar to OJT except that each instructor has only one student (a one-to-one relationship). This method is desired, provided that there are enough qualified instructors to have several training units in progress at the same time.

Lectures: The lecture method reaches the largest number of students per instructor. Practically all training programmes use this type of instruction for certain segments. Unfortunately, the lecture method can be the dullest training technique, and therefore requires instructors who are gifted in presentation capabilities. In addition, space for lectures may be difficult to obtain and may require special facilities.

Conferences: The conference method of instruction is often referred to as workshop training. This technique involves a group of students who formulate ideas, do problem solving, and report on projects. The conference or workshop technique is excellent for supervisory training.

Demonstrations: When new products or equipment are being introduced, demonstrations are excellent. Many demonstrations may be conducted by vendors and purveyors as a part of the sale of equipment and products. Difficulties may arise when language barriers exist. It is also important that no more information be presented than can be absorbed in a reasonable period of time; otherwise misunderstandings may arise.

Whereas training begins after orientation of an employee who is hired to do a specific job, upon introduction of new equipment, or upon observation and communication with employees indicating a need for training, development begins with the identification of a specific employee who has shown potential for advancement. Training for promotion or to improve potential is in fact development and must always include a much neglected type of training -supervisory training. Many forms of developmental training may be given on the property; other forms might include sending candidates to schools and seminars.

Developmental training is associated primarily with supervisors and managerial development and may encompass many types of experiences. Development of individuals within the organisation looks to future potential and promotion of employees. Specifically, those employees who demonstrate leadership potential should be developed through supervisory training for advancement to positions of greater responsibility. Unfortunately, many outstanding workers have their performance rewarded by promotion but are given no development training. The excellent section housekeeper who is advanced to the position of senior housekeeper without the benefit of supervisory training is quickly seen to be unhappy and frustrated and may possibly become a loss to the department.

EFFECTIVE HOUSEKEEPING

In the department of the cook, the housekeeper does not

generally much interfere, yet it is necessary that she should possess a good knowledge of the culinary art, as, in many instances, it may be requisite for her to take the superintendence of the kitchen. As a rule, it may be stated, that the housekeeper, in those establishments where there is no house steward or man cook, undertakes the preparation of the confectionary, attends to the preserving and pickling of fruits and vegetables; and, in a general way, to the more difficult branches of the art of cookery.

On the contrary, if the cook be not so clever an adept in her art, then it will be requisite for the housekeeper to give more of her attention to the business of the kitchen, than in the former case. It will be one of the duties of the housekeeper to attend to the marketing, in the absence of either a house steward or man cook. The daily duties of a housekeeper are regulated, in a great measure, by the extent of the establishment she superintends.After breakfast, which, in large establishments, she will take in the "housekeeper's room" with the lady's-maid, butler, and valet, and where they will be waited on by the still-room maid, she will, on various days set apart for each purpose, carefully examine the household linen, with a view to its being repaired, or to a further quantity being put in hand to be made.

The housekeeper's room is generally made use of by the lady's-maid, butler, and valet, who take there their breakfast, tea, and supper. The lady's-maid will also use this apartment as a sitting-room, when not engaged with her lady, or with some other duties, which would call her elsewhere. In different establishments, according to their size and the rank of the family, different rules of course prevail.

For instance, in the mansions of those of very high rank, and where there is a house steward, there are two distinct tables kept, one in the steward's room for the principal members of the household, the other in the servants' hall, for the other domestics. At the steward's dinner-table, the steward and housekeeper preside; and here, also, are present the lady's-maid, butler, valet, and head gardener. After dinner, the housekeeper, having seen that all the members of the establishment have regularly returned to their various duties, and that all the departments of the household are in proper working order, will have many important matters claiming her attention.

There may also be the dessert to arrange, ice-creams to make; and all these employments call for no ordinary degree of care, taste, and attention. The still-room was formerly much more in vogue than at present; for in days of "auld lang syne," the still was in constant requisition for the supply of sweet-flavoured waters for the purposes of cookery, scents and aromatic substances used in the preparation of the toilet, and cordials in cases of accidents and illness. There are some establishments, however, in which distillation is still carried on, and in these, the still-room maid has her old duties to perform.

In a general way, however, this domestic is immediately concerned with the housekeeper. For the latter she lights the fire, dusts her room, prepares the breakfast-table, and waits at the different meals taken in the housekeeper's room. A still-room maid may learn a very great deal of useful knowledge from her intimate connection with the housekeeper, and if she be active and intelligent, may soon fit herself for a better position in the household. In the evening, the housekeeper will often busy herself with the necessary preparations for the next day's duties. Numberless small, but still important arrangements, will have to be made, so that everything may move smoothly.

In a physical point of view, a housekeeper should be healthy and strong, and be particularly clean in her person, and her hands, although they may show a degree of roughness, from the nature of some of her employments, yet should have a nice inviting appearance. In her dealings with the various tradesmen, and in her behaviour to the domestics under her, the demeanour and conduct of the housekeeper should be such as, in neither case, to diminish, by an undue familiarity, her authority or influence. As, in the winter months, servants have much more to do, in consequence of the necessity there is to attend to the number of fires throughout the household, not much more than the ordinary every-day work can be attempted.

The spring is the usual period set apart for house-cleaning, and removing all the dust and dirt, which will necessarily, with the best of housewives, accumulate during the winter months, from the smoke of the coal, oil, gas, etc. This season is also well adapted for washing and bleaching linen, etc., as, the weather, not being then too hot for the exertions necessary in washing counterpanes, blankets, and heavy things in general, the work is better and more easily done than in the intense heats of July, which month some recommend for these purposes.

Winter curtains should be taken down, and replaced by the summer white ones; and furs and woollen cloths also carefully laid by. The former should be well shaken and brushed, and then pinned upon paper or linen, with camphor to preserve them from the moths. Furs, etc., will be preserved in the same way. Included, under the general description of house-cleaning, must be understood, turning out all the nooks and corners of drawers, cupboards, lumber-rooms, lofts, etc., with a view of getting rid of all unnecessary articles, which only create dirt and attract vermin; sweeping of chimneys, taking up carpets, painting and whitewashing the kitchen and offices, papering rooms, when needed, and, generally speaking, the house putting on, with the approaching summer, a bright appearance, and a new face, in unison with nature.

Oranges now should be preserved, and orange wine made. The summer will be found, as mentioned above, in consequence of the diminution of labour for the domestics, the best period for examining and repairing household linen, and for "putting to rights" all those articles which have received a large share of wear and tear during the dark winter days. In direct reference to this matter, that sheets should be turned "sides to middle" before they are allowed to get very thin. Otherwise, patching, which is uneconomical from the time it consumes, and is unsightly in point of appearance, will have to be resorted to.

Executive Housekeepers

Executive housekeepers inspect rooms for cleanliness and check on other housekeeping tasks to make sure that workers are following proper procedures. They make sure that the work of the housekeeping department falls within the established standards of quality for the hotel. In some establishments executive housekeepers supervise the staff who set up rooms for conventions, banquets, exhibits, and other programmes. Executive housekeepers may be in charge of ordering housekeeping supplies and equipment. They may help in the selection and purchase of new furniture.

Some executive housekeepers work with interior decorators to develop new decorating schemes for rooms and public areas. The housekeeping staff tells the executive housekeeper about damage and equipment that needs repair. Executive housekeepers conduct their own inspections and make recommendations on the relocation of equipment and the use of space. They also develop procedures on how to inform the engineering/ maintenance department when its services are needed. They keep records on personnel, payroll, expenses, and housekeeping activities. They keep management informed about repair work, improvements, personnel difficulties, and expenditures. They submit a yearly budget for review and approval.

In small or medium-sized hotels and motels executive housekeepers may share cleaning chores with the staff. Executive housekeepers who work in small institutions may also be in charge of other operations such as maintenance and ordering food. Housekeepers in hospitals make sure that patients have safe, clean rooms. They follow strict procedures for cleanliness and sanitation to prevent the spread of infection and disease. They develop education programmes for the staff and teach them how to handle contaminated wastes safely. They teach them safety techniques and the correct way to use supplies and equipment.

Staff development is important, and executive housekeepers make sure staff education programmes are ongoing. As a rule, working conditions are very good. Executive housekeepers work in clean, attractive, comfortable buildings. Although they usually have their own office, they spend a good part of their time in other parts of the establishment. They may be on their feet most of the day.

Housekeepers in resort hotels or motels may work longer hours during the tourist season. Executive housekeepers who live in the hotel have regular hours, but they may be on call at any time. Executive housekeepers in hospitals, schools, and other institutions usually work forty hours a week. Salaries depend on the experience and education of the housekeeper and the size and location of the establishment that employs them. According to the Bureau of Labor Statistics, in 2000, executive housekeepers averaged $27,830 a year. Salaries ranged from $7.80 to $20.60 an hour, or $16,220 to $42,850 a year.

Some hotels may offer executive housekeepers and their families room and board and use of hotel services. Other benefits are paid vacations, sick leave, hospital insurance, and tuition assistance for continuing education. At one time the job of executive housekeeper went to the person in the housekeeping department with the most experience or seniority. Today, many executive housekeepers have a college degree or have taken advanced courses in business and management.

Executive housekeepers will have better employment opportunities if they have at least a two-year college degree or have taken some advanced courses in hospitality. They should have a basic knowledge of accounting to keep records and to prepare budgets and reports. A knowledge of labor laws and safety regulations is important. Executive housekeepers may also find it helpful to study sociology, psychology, economics, personnel management and human relations, and communications. Purchasing, interior design, maintenance and inventory control, basic computer skills, and rules and procedures for sanitation and health may be beneficial. Universities, community colleges, and vocational schools offer programmes that prepare students for institutional housekeeping. These schools may also offer continuing education courses for those already in the field.

Many executive housekeepers belong to the International Executive Housekeepers Association (IEHA). IEHA is a professional organisation with over 6,000 members who work in commercial, institutional, or industrial settings. The International Executive Housekeepers Association has established educational standards for the profession and sponsors certificate and college degree programmes. IEHA also offers numerous self-study courses. Executive housekeepers may also belong to the American Hotel & Lodging Association (AH&LA). AH&LA is a professional organisation with over 13,000 property members who work in the hotel and lodging industry.

Executive housekeepers should be able to communicate well with management, staff, the public, and suppliers. Occupations can be adapted for workers with disabilities. Persons should contact their school or employment counselors, their state office of vocational rehabilitation, or their state department of labor to explore fully their individual needs and requirements as well as the requirements of the occupation. Executive housekeepers work in hotels, motels, condominiums, and clubs. Others work in hospitals, nursing homes, and health-care centers. Some work on college campuses or in schools.

Many of the best jobs are in large cities and their suburbs. A growing number of resort hotels and motels in less populated places also offer excellent opportunities. According to the Bureau of Labor Statistics, the number of jobs for executive housekeepers is expected to increase about as fast as the average for all occupations. The hospitality industry is enjoying moderate growth in the twenty-first century. Some developers are building new hotels and resorts. These establishments may create opportunities for executive housekeepers who are new to the field.

Most jobs will open as workers retire or find work in other occupations. Some large establishments require prospective executive housekeepers to have a college degree in hotel and restaurant management. Others may hire experienced workers who have taken courses in the field. Job seekers may start as floor supervisors, executive assistants, or assistant heads of housekeeping departments. They learn housekeeping procedures and policies and gain experience managing a staff. In time they may take over the management of the housekeeping department during the late afternoon or evening shift.

Smaller hotels and motels may hire executive housekeepers who lack a formal education in the hospitality field but have worked their way up through the ranks. However, even in these small institutions, the trend has been to look for candidates who have taken some hospitality or business courses. Job seekers may find opportunities at newly built hotels, resorts, hospitals, nursing homes, or other establishments. The International Executive Housekeepers Association maintains a referral service for job seekers and for employers looking for candidates. Since executive housekeepers already hold the top position in their profession, further advancement may be limited.

6

Managing Food and Beverage Operations

Food and Beverage Management companies often manage both housing and food and beverage operations for clients. In such cases, an area or regional director assumes broader responsibility for the overall management account and the director of food and beverage operations works with him or her in a support capacity. During the 1990s, food and beverage department profits grew at an 8.3 percent compound annual pace. This compares to a 5.1 percent growth rate for full-service rooms department profits during the same period. In addition, beverage in hotel vernacular refers to the sale of alcoholic beverages. Prior to the 1970s, most hotels considered food and beverage as a necessary evil in order to attract guests to rent rooms.

The exceptions were some urban properties that truly attempted to draw local patrons, and resorts that positioned their restaurants as an integral part of the guest experience. For those hotels not emphasising food and beverage, their main goals were to keep the kitchen clean and not lose too much money. As limited-service hotel development began to flourish in the 1970s, hoteliers realised that you can still attract leisure and commercial travelers without having an on-site, three meal a day restaurant.

During the 1980 and 1990s, the majority of new hotels constructed did not contain food and beverage facilities. Concurrently, the owners of those hotels that remained in the full-service segment dictated that their properties could no longer afford to operate a department that lost money, and/or did not serve any strategic purpose. The result has been a polarisation regarding food and beverage service within the industry. On the one hand you have lodging facilities that have either eliminated their restaurants and lounges, limited the hours of operation, or solely offer complimentary food and beverage service. Alternatively, hotels that continue to offer full food and beverage services have aggressively operated their departments in order to make money and complement the market position of the property. Methods to accomplish these goals have included the leasing of restaurants and lounges to outside operators, bringing in celebrity chefs, or heavy investment in menu development and décor.

Each year from 1990 through 1997, the annual growth rate for rooms revenue at full-service hotels surpassed the same measurement for food and beverage. However, in 1998, this trend reversed. In 1998, a drop in occupancy, combined with a slow down in the growth of room rates. During the same year, food and beverage revenues grew 7.5 percent, the third consecutive year of growth in food and beverage revenue in excess of 6.0 percent. Historically, the growth in beverage revenues has lagged behind the growth in food revenues. From 1980 through 1999, food sales grew at a compound annual rate of 4.1 percent. This compares to an average compound annual growth rate of 1.1 percent for beverage sales during the same period.

During the eighties and nineties, food revenues grew each and every year. Beverage revenue, however, posted annual declines in sales volume during eight of those years. This fluctuation shows the sensitivity of alcoholic beverages sales to social patterns, as well as internal marketing efforts. Changes in social behaviour might also explain the recent surge in food and beverage revenues. The rental of guest rooms will continue to have the greatest impact on bottom line dollars. However, management has proven that given the proper level of attention and support, the food and beverage department of a hotel can be an attractive component of the product, as well as a profit center unto itself.

Hotel Food and Beverage

The attitude of hotel owners and operators towards food and beverage is one of two extremes; make a serious go of it, or limit your operations to meet the minimal needs of your guests. The days of chain-mandated, bland, break-even restaurants and lounges are history. A quick look at current hotel development reports shows the diversity of the food and beverage operations at hotels these days. The vast majority of new hotels have no F&B facilities at all. On the other end of the spectrum, the "fastest-growing" segment is upscale operations with multiple food and beverage outlets and large banquet facilities. Even those properties that fall into the traditional mid-market, full-service category are either limiting their menus, or closing down during certain meal periods.

In 1994, hotels in the highest quartile averaged food and beverage revenues 6.4 times those in the lowest quartile. This multiple grew to 8.2 in 1999. These statistics clearly show that hotels emphasising food and beverage operations have been very successful in growing their revenues. Conversely, those properties that have made the decision to limit their food and beverage service have simply gone into a maintenance mode. While the growth of combined F&B revenue has matched total hotel revenue growth, a closer examination finds significant growth in food sales, while beverage income has slid in importance. From 1994 through 1999, food revenues for the subject sample grew 7.2 percent, 0.8 percentage point greater than the growth rate for all hotel revenues.

Branding and Repositioning

Hotel guests generally enjoy the convenience of F&B outlets, hut when given the chance, they frequently choose a known brand off the premises, leaving a hotel for nearby restaurant chains. In the process, they take much-desired dining dollars with them. As customers become more brand—aware, competition for F&B business continues to grow in importance for many hotels. From the hotel's perspective, a joint venture or outsourcing arrangement can provide a combination of restaurant skills and brand strength, often supported by national advertising. Hotels adding branded restaurants have reported improved F&B volume, including room service sales, as well as an attendant increase in occupancy and average rate.

In a period of hospitality industry consolidation, branded restaurants may become a point of differentiation among hotel properties. Restaurant companies, of course, also stand to gain from this flurry of alliances. In today's market, many companies are being forced to look outside traditional development options and to consider new types of locations. Given these benefits, it is surprising there is not more outsourcing of food and beverage in the hotel industry.

During the early 1990s, businesses faced the difficult task of assessing procedural strengths and weaknesses to trim fat and streamline processes. Outsourcing non-critical activities allowed companies to extend their organisational core competencies. The hospitality and leisure industry was no exception to this trend. During the past few years, hotels have been called on to assess their core competencies, while attempting to shed responsibility for non-core activities. Core competencies can be defined as those unique disciplines that confer competitive advantage, motivating customers to buy a company's goods and services over those of a competitor.

As this decade comes to a close, businesses are further dividing the non-core segment into two categories: "essential non-core" and "non-essential non-core." Those activities that are both non-core and non-essential are being shut down. Processes that are essential, but "non-core," become prime candidates for outsourcing. Providing quality rooms and guest services remains a hotel's primary function. The F&B function, however, commands attention because of its importance to guest satisfaction and brand management.

Many hoteliers, however, make the mistake of thinking that it takes the same competencies to operate a restaurant as it does to run a hotel. In actual fact, the restaurant business requires a different set of skills, including more attention to detail, than rooms management. By reengineering F&B operations, hotel management has the opportunity to redirect energies from the restaurant business and focus efforts on enhancing hotel operations and profitability and, potentially, shareholder value.

Management Styles

It is important to look at both the local and corporate management styles of both the hotelier and restaurateur, Incompatibility of the two styles could result in a rocky relationship and tumultuous times. In order to avoid this friction, some hotels have found it advantageous to appoint the general manager of the restaurant to the hotel's executive team, thereby creating a sense of responsibility and belonging and enhancing relationships throughout the organisation. Quality standards and monitoring mechanisms should be detailed to ensure that the restaurant is operated at a standard that is acceptable and complementary to that of the hotel. Additionally, hours of restaurant operation, including room service, are critical specifications. As breakfast is typically a money—generating activity, and frequently not one that restaurant chain operators are accustomed to serving, many hoteliers prefer to maintain responsibility for this meal.

However, concessions affecting profitability occasionally need to be made in order to solidify a working relationship. A successful outsourcing relationship involves first and foremost trust and cohesion between the two partners. Of course, operational terms must be clearly detailed and make economic sense for both parties. While the requirements of a restaurant chain may be more stringent and costly than those of an independent restaurant operator, the basic tenets of a trusting partnership, complementary levels of quality, compatible clientele and a location with sufficient demand to justify a restaurant operation are all necessary. Successful implementation of an F&B outsourcing partnership can result in enhanced brand recognition and profitability for both the hotelier and the restaurateur.

Outsourcing Partnerships

Outsourcing partnerships typically bring together organisations with diverse capabilities. Understanding what each side of the equation requires to succeed is essential. This important guideline applies whether a hotel owner is considering outsourcing all or part of its F&B operations to a restaurant chain, or merely outsourcing its coffee shop to a local restaurateur. Historically, restaurant chains have been strict about the demographics and economic indicators in a market before committing to a location. And until recently, there was no shortage of suitable sites.

Prime demographic indicators include a mix of office space, upper-middle class residences, and upscale apartments with higher-income professionals looking for an element of fun. If a potential restaurant site was not viewed as a "home run" location, a restaurateur would typically pass on a development opportunity. Due to increased competition and a limited number of prime sites, restaurant companies have found they must go further afield than in the past, breaking traditional biases about what locations work.

Until recently, hotels have been reluctant to outsource their F&B operations—or single restaurants. Traditionally, hotel management viewed F&B operations as a low margin or unprofitable service required to enhance guest satisfaction. As such, F&B profitability was always examined with a mentality of "minimising a loss." As a way to rationalise an unprofitable track record, hotel management often convinced itself that there was insufficient demand for profitable F&B operations. In addition, as hotels emerged from the last recession and downturn in hotel profitability, emphasis was placed on the renovation of guestrooms, lobbies and banquet space over F&B outlets.

Based on historical trends, renovation priority has consistently been given to profit-generating guestrooms over unprofitable food and beverage operations. Additionally, hotels opting to create a new concept or introduce an existing, branded concept may find start-up costs to he exorbitant. Estimated costs of upgrading a food and beverage outlet to a chain's specified standards range from $500,000 to $1.5 million, depending on the extent of renovation and equipment purchases required.

Of course, outsourcing operations to a local restaurateur would likely cost far less. The hotel, however, would not benefit from the brand recognition associated with a larger, more established name in the marketplace.

Lastly, hotel management companies earning fees based on gross revenue may be reluctant to reduce the base on which their management fee is calculated. This may prompt hotel owners and managers to reassess their management position. Frequently the parties agree to either renegotiate revenue-based fee percentages or include revenues earned by third-party F&B operators in the management fee calculations. Despite the issues associated with outsourcing of food and beverage operations, there are compelling reasons for hotels to consider this option. Brand strength and competitive positioning for the hotel property are among the most important.

Competition

No outsourcing arrangement will work, unless there is market demand. Competitive analysis should include restaurants in neighboring hotels, as well as stand-alone restaurants in the area. Profitability issues and pricing a new outlet also must be considered in the market context. Many hotels find that the brand name restaurant buys recognition in the customer 5 mind and creates a draw for business. The partnered restaurant sets the hotel apart from other hotels in the area and segment by providing a strong competitive and marketing advantage.

Marketing

The hotelier and restaurateur must establish responsibility for marketing of the new concept. Frequently hotels agree to advertise the operator in the guestrooms, although the outlet typically absorbs the cost of signage in the rooms and throughout the hotel. Additionally, the restaurateur typically assumes responsibility and accountability for all external advertising.

Guest Expectations

The goal of outsourcing F&B operations is to enhance profitability by increasing internal as well as external traffic, without losing the current customer base. It is essential to consider guest reaction to the change in F&B concept. If a negative reaction is anticipated, a hotelier risks losing its customer base and thus future earning potential to the competition.

Structuring an Outsourcing Partnership

Leasing: A hotel leases a room or section of the hotel, preferably with self-contained back-of-the-house areas in exchange for a flat fee and/or a percentage of sales. Statistics are not available for this type of transaction, as leasing deals vary depending on the area of space being leased, the brand being introduced into the market, the location of the hotel and agreements that may have been established by a head office. The hotel benefits by receiving a guaranteed rent, plus a revenue "top-up" each month. The landlord, however, loses control of F&B operations. Management must agree to let someone else run the show.

Franchising: This option suits a hotel seeking to change a restaurant concept without investing in an internal and potentially untested concept. The hotel buys an established brand and system for a fee. The process begins with an upfront payment—a buy-in to the right to operate a better known and more profitable concept. Frequently, the franchisor requires the hotel to make an additional payment for a capital investment, requiring a purchase of specified equipment.

Under the franchising terms, the hotel pays the franchisor a royalty fee, usually based on a percentage of sales, for the privilege of using the name and resources. Throughout the relationship, it is the franchisees responsibility to ensure that hotel staff is adequately trained to assure quality consistent with other branded sites.

Joint Venture: This is a variant of franchising and contracting. The hotelier creates a strategic alliance with a known, successful restaurateur. The two parties create a separate financial company, which is appointed as the lessee of the restaurant. The new organisation, the restaurant lessee., then outsources the F&B operations to the restaurateur. Typically the hotel provides the capital expenditures and the restaurateur brings intellectual property and expertise. The two parties share the successes and the related profits.

Proprietary Brands: Hotel chains can create a proprietary brand, introducing the concept into all of its properties. This approach appeals to guests who enjoy consistency throughout a hotel chain. However, it is difficult to gain wider customer identity outside of the hotel properties.

Foodservice Design

Each stage in the design process are described below.

— *Masterplanning*: This is the first step in the process, where you establish what your project should consist of, and if it should exist at all. The main objectives of this phase are justification of the project and exploration of potential design solutions.

— *Programming*: Once you have determined that the project is at least worth exploring, a narrative should be developed that will describe the scope of the project as well as its various "components," such as the individual areas within a single facility, or facilities that comprise a greater complex. This narrative will often include required adjacencies (areas that must be located one another), desired sizing, and any special requirements or considerations. The programme communicates the owner's desires and requirements to the design team in written form.

— *Concept Design*: This is often the first time that the effort includes any form of graphic communication. The conceptual design is the first attempt to translate the written programme into graphic form. It will typically consist of Bubble Diagrams, which identify the anticipated location and size of each area in the programme. It may also consist of renderings that highlight the exterior, entry, or other key design elements of the project.

— *Schematic Design*: This phase in the design process builds on the Concept phase through the development of Block/Schematic Drawings, geared to identify elements such as walls, counters, and key pieces of furniture or equipment. These drawings focus on defining the footprint of the space, but do not contain a great deal of detail within these "blocks."

— *Design Development*: At the end of this stage, the general floor plan is typically locked in and the detail within each space must be defined and developed. Whereas a bar's locations and dimensions might have been identified in the Schematic Phase, it is in Design Development where the individual pieces of equipment are selected and incorporated into the design. At the end of this phase, it should be expected that all walls, furniture, fixtures, and equipment will have been included on the drawings and clearly identified. While it is not necessary to know the manufacturer of an individual piece of equipment in our bar, it is important to know what equipment is required, as well as the required dimensions and configuration.

— *Construction Documents*: Also called Working Drawings, this stage consists primarily of the mechanical, electrical, and plumbing (MEP) coordination required to make the building function. The "systems" within a building are very similar to those which exist in the body when you think about it—Structural (skeleton), Mechanical (breathing), Electrical (basis of cell communication and activity), plumbing (well, you should be able to figure that one out yourself), etc. This phase requires a significant amount of coordination between a large number of disciplines. It is an extremely important aspect of the design process, as a mistake in this stage can be very costly.

— *Specifications*: Once the Construction Documents are completed, written specifications are developed to convey all of the information to the construction team. These specifications include details on the manufacturer, model number, and any required options for everything from the door hardware to the paint, and the flooring materials to the foodservice equipment. These specifications are then used by the construction team to gather pricing from General Contractors and their sub-contractors.

Food Service Ware Washing

Regardless of the size or type of a foodservice facility, a three-compartment sink will be required. The three compartments are for Washing, Rinsing, and Sanitising the wares (dishes, flatware, pots, pans, etc.)—in that order. Now, some jurisdictions do require four-compartment sinks where the fourth compartment is a separate dumping and scrapping compartment. Many of you may be surprised to learn, however, that a dish machine is completely optional. Knowing that we are required to sanitise all soiled wares, it is important to note that there are two methods of sanitisation that may be used. The first is by temperature, and is referred to throughout the industry as the high-temp method. The high temperature method requires a final rinse by water that is at a temperature of 180 degrees Fahrenheit. At this temperature, the water will kill any remaining micro-organisms.

Test strips and temperature gauges (if on a dish machine) may be used to confirm that the required temperature has been reached. The second method for sanitising is chemical, which relies on a chemical solution to kill off any remaining harmful biological elements. Some of the chemicals that may be used include chlorine, iodine, and quaternary ammonium compounds, referred to as quats. Both of these methods of sanitising, high-temperature and chemical, are acceptable by the health department and can be used in either a three compartment sink or a dish machine.

With both the high-temperature and chemical options available, you may be wondering which is better. The high-temperature solution is best to use in dish machines, where possible, as it does not rely upon the proper mixture of chemicals to be effective. If the chemical solution ratio is off just a bit, its effectiveness in killing micro-organisms will be reduced or even eliminated, thereby providing a false sense of security to the operator. The high-temperature machines do a better job of removing certain residues (such as food or lipstick) than the low temperature machines. Also, the 180 degree final rinse causes the water to bead off more quickly, reducing the drying time and the space required to allow the items to dry. It should be noted, however, that the infrastructure for a high-temperature dish machine is far greater than that of a chemical machine due to the requirement of a condensate hood—a hood system designed to remove heat and moisture from the room.

Use of a high-temperature machine without a condensate hood can lead to mold problems, and is typically restricted by local building authorities. It is this additional cost that often causes operators to choose chemical machines, despite the superior performance of the high-temperature units. When it comes to three-compartment sinks, the chemical method is most commonly used. Though the high-temperature method can be used in a three compartment sink as well, it requires an additional heater (increased cost) and employees to submerge their hands in 180 degree water (inconvenience and safety concerns).

Food and Beverage Profits

There are many reasons why hotel Food and Beverage profits are not what we would like them to be. Foremost among them is usually the fact that revenues are not as high as they might be. The lack of separate identity and entrances for outlets has a negative impact but for the most part hoteliers aren't the street fighting promoters our free standing restaurant counterparts are.

Think about how you'd spend your finite promotional dollars if you had a choice between promoting the hotel in its entirety or just a profitable restaurant outlet. Clearly it makes more sense to advertise the hotel and its services or to have the sales staff either build commercial room demand or pursue group room bookings. These items have profit margins in excess of 75—80%. A hotel's Food and Beverage department is an exception if profit exceeds 20%. In both cases as hoteliers must admit, administrative, marketing, maintenance and utilities expenses are not deductions from these margins.

Unlike our restaurant counterparts who must bear all these expenses directly we shuffle them off as Unallocated Expenses. In the end it makes sense because most hotel Food and Beverage revenues are driven by the Rooms Department's level of activity and the buildings and operational structures are not such that some expenses can be isolated cost effectively. These are not all new things, everything but the menu plan and outlet market plan should be in your hotel's annual business plan, so preparing a mini-plan for each Food and Beverage outlet should not be a monumental task.

Standard hotel procedures must include services, attitudes and amenities that are very appealing to the hotel's guests. Services are kind of obvious but attitudes are a little tougher. Rather than exclusively hiring experienced servers look for people with a positive, cheerful outgoing attitude that either have experience or are trainable. Your servers must enjoy their patrons, thank them for coming, ask them if they will be in tomorrow, how their room is, etc. In short they must care. It will help the food and Beverage outlets and the hotel in general. Amenities are a more exciting and creative issue.

7

Hotel Sales Organisation and Operations

There are sales people who come to the industry with no previous experience in hotels and are highly successful – outperforming their colleagues who may have been in hotel sales for many years. Usually but not always these are people who have come from commission sales of some sort. It is not necessarily the fact that other industries have better training programs, it is not just the sense of urgency that comes with having to create an income every month, it also has to do with the habits that they must develop in order to successfully pay the mortgage and eat.

There are some of the habits that distinguish the 'awesome' sales person from the 'average' one. They are given below.

1. *Daily disciplines.* Successful sales people take their goals, revenue, prospecting, calls etc. and break them down into monthly, weekly, daily activities. They have a good idea of their call to closing ratio, that is, how many calls, telephone or e-contacts, they need to make to close a contract. They know how many prospects they need to locate in a day and a week to meet their prospecting goals. They practice 'daily disciplines' every day.

2. *Prioritise activities.* Not all activities, calls, traces, etc, are created equal. Prioritised sales people call on those prospects most likely to produce revenue before they do the trace calls to say 'hello' to existing accounts – they prioritise their calls.
3. *Think revenue not just rooms.* The successful sales person pays attention to the property's revenue management strategy and understands that the name of the game is revenue – not rooms. The revenue management strategy informs their prospecting activities.
4. *Whales and tunas.* Successful sales people know that they need a mix of both large and small groups and accounts to meet their revenue goals and to balance out the group calendar. Some sales people only want to pursue the big 'glamour' accounts. The problem with that is it takes much longer to land them than the smaller, less flashy, tunas. If the whale doesn't close within the timeframe of the sales persons goals, the sales person may not be there when the whale account eventually signs the contract.
5. *'Intra-preneurs'.* Successful sales people treat their market or their territory like a business – their business. They function as intraprenuers within the organisation. That makes them think creative and allows them to think out of the box in addressing issues within the organisations on their client's behalf.
6. *Personal SWOT analysis.* Successful sales people evaluate their strengths in order to leverage it in to more business and maybe even a better position for themselves. They are also honest about the areas where they could use some training and/or support and actively ask for it or seek out opportunities to get the training they need. They seek out opportunities in their market area and never underestimate the potential threats of competitors.

7. *Sense of urgency*. Successful sales people have a sense of urgency about working their plan because they know that if they fall too far behind it will be very difficult to catch up. They stay late when they have to and ask to leave early when they are caught up. Their sense of urgency is focused and directed not just a sense of urgency about activity, any activity. They choose their association memberships and functions carefully so that they only participate in those likely to be a source of business.

New Strategies in Hotels Sales

The threats of terrorism and war is taking an already elevated level of security to new heights. Public buildings, office towers and military installations are increasingly difficult to access. Hotels, especially large destination and gateway properties, are aware of the potential risks to guests and have their own security issues.

The temptation on the part of hoteliers may be similar to that following September 11. Immediately following that event most businesses, including hotels and hotel companies, went into a temporary state of paralysis. Business travel came to a screeching halt and hoteliers' first reaction was to look for ways to reduce expenses. However, this time expenses have already been cut to the bone in many cases.

There are some hotels and hotel companies that included the marketing and sales function in their expense revisions. While there was often a great deal of 'flab' in these budgeted expenses, the smart companies measured their cuts against productivity and many have sought to provide enhanced training opportunities for their sales staff to enable them to cope with the new economic realty.

When we look at the travel trends following September 11, we see that corporations have pared down their business travel. Association and trade show attendance has been negatively impacted by the economy. The market segments that were once the backbone of hotel revenues can no longer be assumed to support property budgets.

Couple that increased level of security with the urgent need on the part of hotels to develop new business, a new approach to prospecting for new business has to be developed. A mainstay of 'backyard' marketing used to be to make cold calls on every commercial building within a certain radius. This simply will no longer work in major metropolitan areas. Access will be denied very quickly to those without appointments. Alternative markets take more time, skill and creativity to develop.

How then to ensure that a hotel is squeezing every bit of business out of their local markets? The following are but a few ideas and certainly not exhaustive.

1. *Develop and maintain a directory of businesses and associations in your market.* If you have compiled a a report in the past, you have a head start. If not, there are many business directories that you can buy. However, remember that once these directories are published, they are going out of date. Be sure to check the publication date so that you are not buying more directory information than you need. Go for a drive and walk into buildings. Write down the list of business and organisations on the inside directory so that you have an up to date list.
2. *Research which industry sectors are outperforming the market.* There is still corporate business out there, you will need to discover which industry sectors are thriving in this economy and go after them.
3. *Cross-reference the sector list against the directory. This will tell you the prospects in your market that in all likelihood are doing well and can pay your rate.* The

professional associations that serve these sectors are also likely to have strong attendance. For example, the pharmaceutical and medical supply sectors are performing reasonably well. Apart from the obvious, calling any pharmaceutical companies in your market, visit your local hospital and ask the purchasing department who their suppliers are and can you get a list or offer them a rate for those suppliers coming into town.

4. *Explore alternative markets.* Why we dump the market on the newest sales manager or the sales assistant. More than ever, this market requires a lot of creative 'digging' to uncover groups that you may have never considered before.

These are just a very few of the things that hotels can do to redirect their sales efforts for new business development. Communicating with and qualifying these new leads also requires a different strategy than what has always been done before.

Direct Sales

Today, hotels are faced with the challenge of delivering profits in an ever-changing environment of declining revenues and profitability. Independently owned and operated hotels have the added challenge of limited marketing resources. As a result, owners and managers of independent properties, now, more than ever, have to ensure that each marketing expense is justified and that it produces the best return on investment. Direct sales is the most controllable and quantifiable element. In order to achieve maximum production, it is critical to:

— Hire, train, and expertly direct the best sales people.

— Implement systems to ensure optimal productivity and individual accountability.

— Develop and maintain action plans and goals which are targeted, specific, and proactive.

Success in today's market is accomplished by a different game plan than when demand was at its peak. Therefore, in order to ensure effectiveness, it is useful to start with several key concepts:

Skills are required in any other profession and in any other department in the hotel in order to perform the job. Many times, we look to hire a sales person with a "rolodex" without considering his/her ability to sell, i.e., identifying business for the property and moving that business from another hotel. Client contacts can quickly come and go, resulting in an obsolete rolodex, but effective sales skills will result in constant business and on-going client relationships.

Expert sales skills can produce business despite product deficiencies, rate structure, or market conditions. Since most owners and operators do not have perfect properties, it is even more critical to ensure that each sales person is highly skilled to generate business and to deal with client objections and problems effectively. A dedication to expert sales skills is the best insurance for market share and profitability.

Direct Sales is responsible for maximising rate and occupancy. Who would argue with that statement? But without properly structuring and organising the sales department, and without establishing all elements of the rooms business, rate and occupancy will more often than not be compromised. By understanding market segmentation and supply/demand dynamics, the sales effort can be maximised by focusing on impacting business for gap periods, not during peak periods which require no effort or resources to fill.

The hotel, as part of its planning and over-all strategy, must determine what segments of the market will produce the best mix of business on a daily basis and translate that information into sales action plans and sales goals. Working with and understanding each market segment will determine those segments for which direct sales is responsible. A detailed plan or rooms budget will provide the basis for an effective sales plan.

One responsibility of direct sales is to create an account base by prospecting for new business and maintaining existing business. Production of this quantified business will fluctuate so it is important that new accounts are opened and non-producing ones are closed, ensuring that targeted goals are continuously reached.

Incentive programs are a great way to motivate and get better results. But in order to ensure that all bookings represent the hotel's best financial interest, it is important to incorporate the cycle of demand periods. Otherwise, the incentive program is ineffective if sales people can achieve their individual goals at the expense of the hotel's revenue potential.

Above-average leadership will produce above-average results. All world-class athletes recognise the importance of leadership and coaching in order to achieve top performances. Therefore, to ensure maximum results, effective sales and marketing leadership is required. At the hotel level, a leader is one who understands the big picture and can plan and organise as well as understand and implement the details to consistently accomplish the goals, despite market conditions. In small boutique hotels, there may not be a director of sales. In that case, leadership is still important and can be fulfilled by a general manager, a corporate sales person, or an outside sales specialist.

Sales plans are devised after a well thought-out marketing plan is established. Sales accountability is important to ensure results. As part of the planning, it is important for hotel leadership to establish and maintain systems and procedures to monitor productivity of each sales person on an on-going and timely basis.

Setting goals and keeping score is important. We all know that a golf game and a tennis match are much more interesting when we keep score; and we all perform better when our competitive juices are challenged. Even the Weight Watchers Program has determined that weight loss is more effective with the weekly "weigh-in" to measure the results of the individual's efforts.

To maximise the sales person's performance, it is important to establish specific and meaningful goals, broken down on a monthly and weekly basis; and to establish a culture where the actual performance vs. goals is critical for job performance. Set goals which include activities to produce booked and consumed business as well as booking and consumed rooms goals. On-going and consistent monitoring and evaluation will foster performance and will quickly help identify non-performers.

Performance-based Sales Compensation Strategies

Most hospitality sales professionals earn a straight salary with a small to moderate incentive compensation program. Commissions or bonuses do not make up a large percentage of their overall compensation package. Good salespeople perform better when given a reward for their performance. The rewards for those who rise to the challenge should be commensurate with their efforts and unfortunately, incentiveless packages encourage mediocrity. Shifting to more aggressive incentive strategies will challenge your sales staff to perform at a higher level, resulting in increased revenues for both the property and the sales team.

Every employee, regardless of title, feels that they should be rewarded justly for the amount of work they put into a job. A compensation plan that offers employees the opportunity to control their level of income in relation to their level of effort creates a highly productive workforce. James Coumbe, a sales representative from Del Lago Resort sums it up nicely. "The beauty of a performance based incentive plan is that if one works hard enough, one can surpass the market average. That's what's great about being in sales, you have a direct impact upon your income based on the amount of energy and commitment you are willing to put in. You produce, you get paid. Under a straight base or a limited incentive plan, your control of your income dwindles, which may lead to complacency affecting the bottom-line of the property but not that of an individual sales person."

Financial compensation is the most widely used means of motivating employees. Whether compensation equates to commissions, bonuses, paid vacations, gifts, stock options, etc., incentives play a major role in the sales team's motivational environment.

If your property already has a plan that is not garnering the results you are looking for, first examine your original objectives. Is it possible that your existing plan was not designed to meet your objectives to begin with? Then ask yourself if your plan is competitive with what other properties are offering and do you have buy-in from your sales team? After those questions have been answered it may be apparent that your plan needs some adjusting, but doesn't necessarily require a complete overhaul.

Designing a plan that meets the needs of both management and the sales team requires a series of compromises. In order to keep employees motivated, an effective plan must balance the benefits of a guaranteed steady income with the power of incentive income. If you set the base salary too high, you may encourage complacency. If you set the base salary too low, then your sales team may begin to worry about how to meet living expenses during off-seasons.

As all business is not created equal, different types of bookings result in higher realised revenues for the property therefore a good compensation plan should be structured to pay out accordingly. One way is to create a value rating system in which business booked with a greater return to the property results in higher commissions paid. Examples of variables to consider include need periods, patterns, rate, etc.

The goal is to maximise occupancy levels based upon the unique needs of the individual property. This hierarchical structure motivates employees to seek out the type of business that is most profitable for the company. It should also be noted that a good plan is also flexible because what works for one property may not work at the next. The idea is to create a plan that can change as conditions warrant, without having to change the basic plan itself.

For a plan to be successful, it must be well received. Hence employee buy-in can often make or break the best compensation plans. Collective ownership ensures acceptance, fosters teamwork rather than competition, and contributes to a strongly motivational atmosphere. Additionally, a good plan must be simple for the sales team to understand and the property to administer. "Fairness can be ensured by striving to base the plan on measurable factors that are controllable by the sales team," explains Management of a Sales Force authors.

An attractive compensation plan is an extremely powerful recruiting tool. Strong plans help build dream sales teams by attracting the caliber of employees desired. Above average performers seek out companies at which they can excel. Additionally, a strong plan assists in strengthening tenure. Under a performance based compensation program, there is a significant difference in the total incomes of the top performers since they understand that if they sell more, they can earn more. If they feel that their earning potential is greatest at your property, that's where they'll stay. Upon implementing alternative incentive programs, properties will quickly discover which employees have the skills necessary to be effective salespeople. Top performers will be excited about the opportunity to increase their earning potential. Marginal and poor performers will naturally be much less enthusiastic about the change.

Revenue Recovery

Many general managers and directors of sales establish sales goals for their sales teams that are not being met. They cannot seem to get their sales people to develop new business and close it, despite the resources that management is making available to them. There is no doubt that it is tough out there but the strong sales people will not only succeed but regard this as an opportunity to prove something to themselves and their management. Sales people with the 'right stuff' want to know how to develop their skills. The others spend their time figuring out why these things won't and can't work.

The skill set that made sales people successful during the boom years is not necessarily the skill set that will help them succeed during the tough times. When all that was required was to answer the phone, follow-up and book the business, the expectations were different. As a respected business associate put it so well, "What we had were farmers who harvested the field, what we need now are hunters to locate and close in on new business."

Not everyone is capable of making the transition from 'farmer' to 'hunter'. Some will pick up the tools of the new skill set and embrace the transition; others will simply not be capable of doing that. The onus is on management to ascertain who in their department will make the cut and how to hire those who have it in them to become hunters. It all goes back to having the right people in the right positions if you want to succeed. In other words, it all boils down to the point of hire. General Managers who assumed their positions during the mid-nineties often don't know what to look for in a potential candidate. Experience in the past is not necessarily a predictor of success in this economy.

Here are a few steps that managers can take and tools that you can use to make the best possible hiring decisions. They are not infallible but can be predictors of success for hiring good sales people:

1. *Personality inventories*: Decide the specific traits that you are looking for in a successful sales person who can work well in your organisation.
2. *Questions to ask*. Give careful thought to the questions that you are going to ask a candidate. These should include specific questions regarding successes and challenges. "What was the most difficult selling situation you have encountered and how did you handle it?" Solicit the input of your staff and other successful sales people into the development of your list of questions. Make sure that you ask the same questions to all potential candidates so you have a basis for comparison and write down the answers.
3. *Involve others in the process*. Have other department heads interview the potential candidate as well as someone in your sales department with whom this candidate will have to work. Record their input in the interview file. This also puts the interview process into perspective and allows some objectivity.
4. *Never make a decision based on one interview*. No matter how desperate you are to fill a position, take your

time. Call them back for at least a second if not a third interview. This gives you an idea of whether or not they have more than one suit. It also allows you time to think and view them over a period of time. The 'aura' that they may have projected on the first interview may not be as glowing the third time that you see them. Let them know your time frame for making this decision.

5. *Make the expectations for the position perfectly clear.* Do not underestimate the difficulty of the position or the market. Let them know what you expect in terms of booking activity, call goals and follow-up. Give them an incentive to run for and how you will schedule regular reviews to evaluate their skills and progress. Also, outline the potential consequences of not achieving their objectives.

While the above are not the only things to consider, it is a good guideline to use in the interview process. Once you have hired a candidate, treat them well and give them the tools to do their job. Provide training and an orientation program to acquaint them with the property's operation.

Effectiveness of Sales Departments

When demand is high and the issue is one of managing the yield, sales departments can become confused as to the goals and management is often less than clear on tying yield management goals to sales production goals and incentives. Sales people, sensitive as they are, become discouraged by what they perceive as mixed messages on rate versus occupancy.

There are three distinct areas that can assist management in measuring sales effectiveness:

— Defining the areas to be evaluated;

— Monitoring sales performance in relation to the above areas and

— Designing incentives to reflect Management's goals for the property.

Training of Sales People

The current employment climate in the hotel industry has put severe limitations on the ability of hotels to recruit and retain sales people with sales experience and/or a background in hotels. In many cases, we are promoting from within, usually the front desk, or relying on intuition that untried recruits are trainable. This situation is even more apparent in the limited to moderate service sectors, that is, non-convention hotels reliant on their local markets to generate the majority of their demand.

Compounding the situation in the limited and moderate service sectors are decreasing occupancies in both the limited service and all suite sectors for 1999. This makes an effective sales effort more critical at a time when flat revenues limit the resources a property or management company has to retain qualified sales and marketing professionals.

In the current climate, we are dealing with sales people often with no experience, whose longevity with the property is relatively brief, often only nine to eighteen months. With little training and a steep learning curve, it becomes the 'deep end of the pool' training. That is, we throw them into the deep end of the pool and wait on the side. If they float, we figure they will make it. The other side of the coin is that with such a short average duration on the job, many companies are reluctant to spend the dollars sending them to training.

With a high degree of turnover and a shortage of recruits, sales positions, both at the property and corporate levels are left open for long periods of time. Any sales momentum is lost and clients have difficulty being serviced. In addition, many 'experienced' sales people were never taught the basic steps of the sales process or how to completely penetrate their markets. Those whose experience has been in the years between 1992-98, the 'boom' years, were primarily managing the yield from increased demand prior to the entry of new hotel product into their respective markets and may have little experience in generating demand from market penetration and additional revenue from existing accounts.

Understanding what new sales people are looking for from an employment situation is crucial to maximising both longevity and training. Studies show that they are not there for the money alone, and we all know that the salaries in the hotel sales field have not kept pace with the rest of the marketplace. On the one hand, they want to feel part of a team, that their input and opinions are solicited and valued but on the other, they want to know what's in it for them, in terms of rewards for performance and career potential.

8

Financial Control

Once an individual with the requisite expertise was identified and the family/personal issues were resolved, the company developed a package to ensure the individual was not adversely affected financially by the assignment. The individual's basic pay was augmented with additional entitlements or allowances to cover the following:

— Cost of living (COLA);

— Expatriate premium;

— Housing;

— Education (for individuals with families);

— Home leave;

— Professional tax advice; Tax protection/tax equalisation.

When possible and practical, an individual generally continues to pay contributions to social security, pension schemes, and life and medical coverage in the home country. As a result, if the individual is transferred to a country or area with a high cost of living or a more costly taxation regime, providing a remuneration package can prove to be very expensive. The Balance Sheet approach is relatively easy to understand, reduces suspicion that the executive is being disadvantaged, and by virtue of the fact that the executive is well remunerated, aids mobility. In addition, however, it can be:

— Expensive for the employer;
— Focused on the net benefit to the employee rather than driving down costs for the employer;
— Probably outdated as employers move to a global approach.

Tax Equalisation/Protection

To ensure that the employee is not financially worse off, tax equalisation and protection schemes are often adopted. In a tax equalisation scheme, a hypothetical amount of home country tax is calculated on the usual elements of compensation. The employer withholds the hypothetical tax while paying the actual tax liabilities to the employee's home and host countries.

There is often an extra cost associated with this payment of an employee's tax liability by the employer, as this generally creates further taxable income, and therefore there is a tax on tax or 'gross up' effect. At the end of the year the final hypothetical tax liability is calculated and any under-, or over-payment of hypothetical tax is paid by, or reimbursed to, the employee. Consequently, the executive who has been transferred is no better or worse off than before the assignment. Any benefits arising from tax planning within these schemes are benefits to the company.

With a tax protection scheme the employee is responsible for actual tax and social security liabilities in both the home and overseas countries. These liabilities are then compared to the liability that would have risen had the assignment not taken place and any additional tax costs are reimbursed on a grossed-up basis. As a result, the employee cannot be worse off, but may receive a tax windfall if the actual costs are lower than they would have been in the employee's home country.

Net Pay Schemes

Net pay schemes are also a common feature of such assignments. Hypothetical tax and social security is calculated dependent upon an individual's salary, family size and other factors. The individual's pay, net of this amount, is guaranteed. The employer then assumes responsibility for all actual tax liabilities which are paid on a grossed-up basis. Usually net pay is also augmented by allowances for the individual. An advantage of this method is that no year-end reconciliation is needed as the net pay is guaranteed beforehand.

Pre-Assignment Planning

Tax protection or equalisation in a high tax environment can be very expensive for the employer. Planning an assignment, therefore, is crucial to reducing the associated costs as far as possible. Much can be done to limit the impact of taxes, including:

- Taking advantage of potential tax treaty exemptions. This may require consideration of the number of days spent in the foreign country, and who should be the employer or who should bear the employee's costs.
- Qualifying as a non-resident in years of arrival and departure, and consequently being taxed at a lower rate or not taxed at all. Timing here can be crucial.
- Maximising advantages of graduated tax rates.
- Delivering related allowances as cost effectively as possible. For example, home country social security costs may be saved if a portion of the allowance is paid by the employer as a direct payment to a third party for services such as housing. This is in contrast to providing a cash allowance to the employee, which would be subject to social security contributions.

— Using opportunities such as separate employment arrangements and special premiums for work outside the foreign country.

Pension

Pensions are another important area for consideration to ensure that pension contributions/coverage are not disrupted. For a short-term assignment an employee generally would continue contributing to his or her home country scheme. However, this may not necessarily be the most tax efficient planning for an individual on a longer term assignment, who possibly may not return to the home country. A solution adopted in the hotel sector involves establishing a worldwide unapproved plan to prevent employees accumulating limited pension entitlements in several locations. In this case, the benefits of maintaining one single fund outweigh the reduced tax efficiency.

Globalisation and Localisation

Globalisation puts considerable pressure on human resource personnel to re-evaluate the traditional methods of providing for executive assignments and to develop innovative new packages suitable for the globalised economy. This represents an increased challenge to human resource personnel during a time when head counts for support functions are under scrutiny.

In addition to the traditional expatriate moving to a specific assignment country and back, typically with a specific technical skill, there is a new breed of mobile executive who has no home country, but rather moves from location to location with career progression a primary motivator. For the latter, a single rigid policy covering different types of employees will be ineffective, and a more flexible, global policy is required.

Expatriate assignments also are becoming longer-term because of changes in the business environment. Such expatriates may have adapted to the host country way of life, and as the employer has made the up-front investment in transferring the individual overseas, a solution needs to be identified to phase the individual onto local terms and conditions. The key to a successful transition will be the presentation of the reasons and methodology of the transition policy to the individual in a way which is easily understood and accepted.

It is likely that the Balance Sheet approach will soon be outdated as a general method for dealing with international transfers. Despite its popularity, fairness of treatment and logical approach, it is becoming too expensive for the employer to assume tax protection/ equalisation. Furthermore, using general assumptions to calculate the allowances for transferred individuals is often not the most appropriate way to determine benefits. It does not provide an incentive to drive down costs; perhaps most importantly, it lacks the flexibility required in today's global economy to enable the package to be tailored to meet individual circumstance and requirements.

The move to a global policy for international transfers requires a fundamental re-evaluation of the compensation and benefits approach. Pay and benefits will need to be re-engineered, with a system to differentiate high performance individuals and which reduces the importance placed on the pure money aspects of the pay and benefits package. This is not, however, going to be all bad news for the mobile executive; to date, this individual may not have extracted maximum value out of the assignment package.

The future will see the introduction of more flexible packages of benefits to meet the personal objectives of the individual. Rather than having fixed housing and schooling allowances, for example, an overall price might be put on the remuneration package so the individual can choose how that package is made up and used. In essence, the individual will be able to pick from a menu of benefits and design the package which is most appropriate to specific needs and aspirations. This menu, of course, must have tax considerations incorporated into the design so that the concept of gain sharing can be used to obtain the employee's buy-in and assistance in developing the benefits which will be offered. Such an approach would be weighted for different assignment locations to take account of local cost differentials.

Public Market Financing

As the relationships between operating and real estate interests in the international hotel industry continue to consolidate, the labour and capital intensities of the industry have come into sharp focus. While there is plenty to be concerned about regarding the labour side of the equation productivity, education, training, job fulfilment and the impact of technology come to mind - there remains a major challenge on the capital side. In a world where there is a general shortage of capital, hospitality companies must now work much harder in the global competition for money. And as the industry begins to recover in many countries from the excesses of the 1980s, the search is on for new solutions to the capital dilemma.

Accentuating the dilemma is the fad that the losses of the early 1990s and the associated declines in property values have scared away many of the industry's traditional private capital providers. And they do not appear to be returning anytime soon. So it is not surprising that in some markets around the world there is strong interest in public financial markets as a place to seek capital, even though they tend to present some very unique challenges.

Securitisation of hotel property and corporate financing has been a popular item in capital markets in the United States during the last several years and looks set to become a permanent feature on the financing landscape. Elsewhere around the world, the use of public markets to fund the international hotel industry is spotty at best.

Real Estate Investment Trusts

For many years, the U.S. hotel industry benefited from the largesse of private institutional capital, primarily the insurance industry, savings institutions and commercial banks to fund property expansion and acquisition. With these resources no longer as available, the industry has been forced to turn to alternative sources such as the public market and has had to adjust to a new set of rules.

As 1994 came to a close, Securitisation of hotel property and mortgages in the United States was a very hot topic. Real Estate Investment Trusts or REITs (which distribute earnings from real estate, free of corporate taxes) had become high fliers in the stock market. Having finally dealt with the structuring challenges that are unique to REITs and previously made hotel REIT formations problematic, a series of issues came to market in late 1993. These tended to be relatively small issues but they delivered some of the best stock performance in the REIT sector, with investor interest driven largely by the turnaround in the U.S. hotel industry that continues to this day. Following these initial successes, secondary offerings came to market during 1994 and the general enthusiasm was palpable. But with interest rate escalations throughout the year, the fervor began to fade and by late 1994, the market had retreated. Uncertainty concerning the outlook for hotel REITs was widespread with the conventional wisdom being that it would be a while before we would see any resurgence of interest.

Well, what a difference a year can make. This past year finally turned out to be a significant one for public market financing of the U.S. hotel industry. There was a renewed interest in REITs late in 1995 signaled by the successful launch of the largest hotel REIT yet - the $305 million Patriot American issue involving a portfolio of 20 hotels. And earlier in the year, Starwood Capital successfully recapitalised Hotel Investors Trust, a "grandfathered" REIT that had been operating for years with a unique paired share structure that allows the REIT to manage as well as own property - something other REITs are not allowed to do. As these large hotel REITs have come to market, there appears to be an appreciation for size that translates into more favourable pricing. This suggests that small capitalisation REITs may not see as much popularity as heretofore when they essentially had the market to themselves.

REITs both large and small are but examples, however, in a large public financial marketplace that is increasingly serving the capital needs of the U.S. hotel industry. During the last four years, approximately $4 billion of capital has been raised for publicly traded hotel companies and $1 billion for hotel REITs - split evenly between debt and equity. And the pace quickened in 1995 with a steadily rising stock market. Hotel industry financings were up by one-third over the prior year at approximately $2 billion.

Following the fall-off in the REIT market late in 1994, the market for new hotel REITs had been slow in returning. But with the success of the large Patriot American deal, the market seems ready for more. Interest rates, however, have a big impact on the REIT market, so future activity will be sensitive to interest rate volatility on the basis of a stable interest environment, however, it is estimated that hotel REITs might represent as much as billion in 19%. Easier to predict than volume is the style or structure of future hotel REIT financings. They are likely to be large and well-covered by Wall Street's research analysts - an essential element if an issue is to gain any respectability and following.

Hotel REITs have also tended to be all equity offerings with lines of credit to fund expansion - but these lines can run out quickly following an active property acquisition program. Future hotel REITs will therefore need to develop capital structures that present blends of debt and equity in an effort to reduce the weighted cost of capital and provide for better balance as the capital base is expanded.

Since quality sponsorship is so critical to success in public markets, it also appears likely that we will see fewer Initial Public Offerings (especially during a period of consolidation) and more secondary offerings involving the return to market of well-established hotel companies with a proven track record. No matter how much enthusiasm exists for the industry's positive economic situation, there is little doubt the focus in the future will be on management and its ability to deliver through the next cycle.

C Corporations

In addition to the return of hotel REITs last year, there was also a resurgence of activity involving "C" Corporations - traditionally structured companies that have historically been the main players in the public market, A series of new C-corp issues attracted a great deal of institutional investor interest, something that is not always as prevalent on the REIT side of the market. Some small C- corp issues also showed very strong growth stories as the hotel market has turned around. This has attracted a lot of new investors, which is clearly healthy in broadening the base of investor support for the industry.

An interesting trend is the growing acceptance of hotel real estate as part of a public company's balance sheet. Notwithstanding the tendency for the stock market to focus on short-term earnings, some of the recent hotel C corp issues have suggested that hotel property ownership can be appreciated, particularly if it delivers operating leverage in a period of rising occupancy. Of course this appreciation can disappear quickly in a downturn when the leverage works in reverse and delivers losses very quickly.

The public market tends to value a growth story. Working against this concept in the REIT arena is the requirement of the tax code that 95 percent of a REIT's earnings be distributed out to the investors each year. As a consequence, for those companies trying to build franchise value through customer relationships and in need of a constant source of reinvestment capital, the REIT structure is not generally a suitable vehicle. But for those with large real estate portfolios, judicious use of the REIT format for "off balance sheet" property financing can produce a satisfactory outcome. The lease format used by hotel REITs to address the tax laws' prohibition of involvement in the management of the property, tends to secure a long-term involvement with the property - something that is of particular value in a market where traditional property owner/manager relationships have become far more tenuous and unpredictable.

In the context of the hospitality industry at large, it is worth mentioning the gaming industry's involvement with public market financing. Gaming companies have long been involved with the public markets as a result of not being able to tap into private institutional sources of money. Without the respectability that it has today, gaming companies originally had to operate in the high-yield market. And as the gaming sector grew and the earnings escalated with new jurisdictions, a compelling story for gaming stocks has developed in recent years.

More recently we have seen the setbacks of poor press, some negative votes against new jurisdictions and one or two high-profile bankruptcies. This can quickly dampen the enthusiasm, and so it remains to be seen as to what the longer-term public market environment will be like for gaming companies. For those with experienced management, a well established franchise and customer following, and a position in established jurisdictions, there should be few difficulties.

Public Market

In evaluating whether to take a hospitality company to the public market for the first time, it is worth reviewing some simple fundamentals to determine if a company has what it takes to make it through the rigorous initial public offering process. Look for the following: the nature and energy level of the management team, stability of earnings, a solid outlook for growth and a focused story and business concept. Other issues to be contended with include the extent of existing leverage, the current owner's objectives and pricing expectations and the need for debt versus equity and their relative costs.

Otherwise successful companies also must recognise that taking a company public for the first time will probably mean facing a discount in value to account for the unknown. The counter-vailing view is that public market investors driven by the hype surrounding a bull market may value a high-profile hospitality company significantly in excess of what the private market might judge the stock to be worth - the herd mentality one might say. Timing is, of course, everything.

As Wall Street becomes more involved in hotel property financing, it is not surprising that the rating agencies have begun to play a role. Ratings have tended to be associated with the packaging of small hotel mortgages into Real Estate Mortgage Investment Conduits or "REMICs." Such conduits tranche the capital into various risk levels that carry a range of ratings and are priced accordingly. REMICs were expected to play a big role in hotel financing especially as these programs were supported by some of the country's largest franchisors as a service to their franchisees. But they turned out to be relatively expensive for borrowers of small amounts. As the industry turned around, there was more competition from local banks willing to finally take a closer look at their neighborhood borrowers who had been ignored since the real estate collapse in 1991.

As the rating agencies look at hotel debt issues, the factors of importance include portfolio diversification, the adequacy of management fees, the presence of satisfactory replacement reserves and the structure. Whether rating agencies can play a role in encouraging an expanded role for public market financing of the hotel sector remains to be seen. The early signs are that they are interested in understanding the business and appear willing to participate.

And yet even if there is a willingness on the part of the rating agency community to play a role, it must be recognised that at its heart, the public market is far more fickle than the private market. Sentiments of sup port and enthusiasm for an industry can evaporate quickly if there are unexpected setbacks. Conventional wisdom at the moment, however, seems to suggest that the U.S. hotel industry's fundamentals are positive and the upward trend in profitability should continue for at least two more years. Demand for hotel rooms, however, tracks extremely closely with the underlying change in Gross Domestic Product. So as goes the economy, thus will follow the hotel industry. And if the economy falters, expect to see some major interruption in the otherwise rosy outlook for hotel stocks and debt issues.

But even if the industry continues on its present positive track, we should not assume that the public markets will provide all of the answers to the liquidity crisis for the industry. Considering the overall size of hotel financing needs in the United States, which we estimate at $8 billion annually, the public markets account for only a modest portion of the need at approximately 15 percent.

Because of the hotel industry's fragmented structure, its real estate orientation and its general reputation as part real estate/part business, we have not seen as many publicly quoted hotel companies as one might expect in an industry of its size. This hopefully will change in future years as the hospitality industry gains further respectability and hotel corporations enlarged through the process of consolidation seek broader access to public capital.

Consolidation can also have a counterpoint, however, and in the U.S. hotel and gaming industries this means de-consolidation. Two companies are of particular note in having split or attempted to split their gaming and hotel operations - Promus and Hilton. Marriott Corporation split for different reasons in an attempt to separate their real estate from their operational activities.

Finally Sheraton Hotels, a stalwart of the U.S. hospitality scene, is now part of a split-up by parent ITT of its varied businesses into three groupings. The first, ITT Destinations, is the consolidation of its hospitality, gaming, sports and entertainment businesses. The public market reactions to these reconstitutions of hospitality companies have by-and-large been favourable, suggesting that it pays to continuously look "outside the organisational box" when trying to create shareholder value.

As hotel groups become larger and operate on a truly global basis, we are likely to see simultaneous hotel company listings in key financial markets around the world such as New York, London and Tokyo. One of the advantages of such international public market exposure relates to the quest that many hospitality companies have for global brand presence. Customer focus deriving from a brand strategy can quite reasonably tie into shareholder relationships on a global scale. It is just a matter of time.

World Finance Markets

Chris Evans, director of corporate finance-hospitality and leisure in the firm's London office, reports that London's public market has not historically been of major significance in the financing of development, or of mergers and acquisition activity in the hospitality and leisure sectors in the United Kingdom.

In the past, many lenders and institutional and individual investors have viewed the hospitality industry somewhat suspiciously, and have preferred to provide corporate debt to hotel companies or to purchase shares in quoted hotel companies to spread sector risk as widely as possible. This preference has meant that the industry has been characterised by relatively unsophisticated financings.

The ownership structure of the industry in the United Kingdom has also been of influence in this regard. Hotels tend to be owner-operated and, with relatively few exceptions, the major hotel owning and operating companies are subsidiaries of conglomerates. Where capital has been required for development and M&A activity at such companies, it has normally been provided by the parent company since, generally speaking, corporate debt at such a level is rather less expensive than project or deal-specific debt.

Furthermore, in the United Kingdom there are relatively few independent hotel management companies operating hotels under franchises from the major international brands. In the United States such independent companies have been great users of public market capital. Those which do exist in the United Kingdom are small - in most instances operating two or three hotels.

Development and acquisitions activity at such companies tend to be financed on a project-by-project basis with security provided by the asset to be financed plus, in many cases, additional company or personal guarantees. The one major exception to this general rule is the Whitbread Hotel Group (formerly Scott's Hotels), which owns and operates 13 hotels under franchise agreements with Marriott International. Whitbread Hotels Group, however, is a relatively small subsidiary of Whitbread PLC the brewing company, and funds for the £185 million acquisition of the 13 Scott's hotels were provided by the parent company. Special share issues, however, have been used among the relatively few quoted "pure" hotel companies - particularly during the late 1980s. Oueen's Moat Houses financed a series of corporate and individual hotel property acquisitions via rights issues.

Turning to the future in the United Kingdom, given the capital intensive nature of the industry, we have observed an increasing interest among both the major conglomerates and the independent hotel owned management companies in innovative financing methods - particularly in off-balance sheet financing. We believe that this interest will extend in the future to public capital markets. As recovery in the sector in the U.K. continues apace, we foresee a much wider interest among both providers and users of such capital.

In Australia, Phil Kasselis, Director of Hospitality Consulting in the firm's Sydney office, reports that the Australian Stock Exchange has 16 listed companies in a Tourism and Leisure Index. The TL Index was established in 1994 with over half the index made up of casino stocks. The index outperformed the market by a factor of 3:1 in 1995, confirming the enthusiasm investors have for the fast developing gaming industry and the fundamentals of the hotel sector, where demand growth continues to outstrip supply and should continue to do so for the next several years and probably up to the year 2000 when Sydney hosts the Olympics.

In the Australian property funds, where hotels as an asset class are generally under-represented, we should see an increase in the allocation of capital to this sector as profits return and the hotel industry outlook remains positive. Casino operators, hotel owners and hotel management companies will also expand their presence in the public financial markets, finding it a cheaper and easier way to raise capital than traditional bank debt. Large institutions are also likely to increase their involvement with publicly listed hospitality companies.

Public/Private Partnerships

Public entities have at their disposal a wide array of programs and financial vehicles that can assist in making a hotel project feasible and thus contribute to an area's overall economic well-being. The potential to access lower-cost financing, tap redevelopment incentives, structure favorable land lease terms, secure site improvements and other alternatives should not be overlooked by hotel developers when development projects have a clear link to public interests.

Public financing of private hotel investment is not new in the United States. The Small Business Administration (SBA), for example, has financed the development of smaller hotels since the mid 1950s. In the past four years, loans provided by the SBA for hotels were approximately three percent of total SBA loans, and the average size was $560,000.

Most commonly, however, public financing and other incentives to promote hospitality investment in the United States have arisen at the local level in development of convention headquarters hotels, which are essential to the success of these large meeting and trade show facilities. Conventions are big business in the United States with more than 800,000 national meetings held annually, much of that market dominated by corporate bookings. Collectively, these conventions attracted some 55 million attendees in 1993.

The more than 500 public and private convention and meeting centers in the United States, in fact, typically form a linchpin in the economic development strategies of local and regional governments. Convention center development and expansion have been components of local economic development strategies since the mid-1980s and continue to rise. Three new centers opened in the last 18 months at locations in Charlotte, North Carolina; Mobile, Alabama; and outside Washington, D.C. And a 1994 Tradeshow Week survey indicated that more than 60 percent of U.S. convention centers were considering expansion — versus only 31 percent in 1993. Planned expansions of exhibition space in convention centers are expected to generate 58.8 million square feet as of 1994, climbing to 64 million by 1999.

The interdependent economics of convention centers and the hotels that serve them create opportunities for public/private partnerships of benefit to government entities and private investors. The evolution of public/private partnerships to support development of convention headquarters hotels, as a result, offer an excellent foundation for examining how public sector financing and other incentives can support private hotel investment.

Most cities require a convention headquarters hotel to market their convention center successfully. Yet many mid- to upper-tier cities often lack sufficient hotel inventory that can be specifically committed to this purpose. Conversely, room nights generated from a convention center are often insufficient to exclusively support a convention headquarters hotel serving the meetings and trade shows so important to local economies. Further complicating the problem, convention headquarters hotels often incur higher than typical development costs due to the amount and quality of public areas required. The result — a need for public/private partnerships to support the economic feasibility of a convention headquarters hotel. This hotel, in turn, will support the public investment made in a convention center, as well as generating other local economic benefits.

These public/private partnerships have therefore become increasingly critical as convention center facilities have proliferated in the United States. They also evidence the range of options available to the public sector to support private hotel development. While these types of incentives most often may be used to support convention hotels, they may also be important tools for other types of hotel projects in which there is a strong relationship between public interests and private investment.

Nearly 65 percent of U.S. convention centers are owned by cities, counties, states or other types of government authorities. Major convention cities, such as New York or Las Vegas, generally have had sufficient hotel supply in appropriate locations to support the needs generated by meeting and trade show participants. For many other municipalities, however, new hotel development can be critical to competing for the middle- to upper-tier convention market. Convention facilities in these cities may be located in areas peripheral to hotel concentrations. In addition, existing hotel operators are often reluctant to commit the room inventory required to serve convention delegates — typically offered in package deals at lower room rates — while simultaneously reducing rooms available to serve guests that make up their core business.

The basic economics in hotel development and operations pose additional challenges. Convention-oriented hotels are typically 10 to 20 percent more expensive to develop than a comparable size, group-oriented hotel. At the same time, room rates for a convention hotel's core market segment may run 20 to 30 percent below comparable business hotels due to discount package deals negotiated for delegates as part of convention attendance.

To remain successful, a convention center must attract annual national bookings in the range of 25 to 30 events that have a minimum of 2,500 participants each. These bookings, however, on average support occupancies of only 30 to 35 percent in terms of total room nights. As a result of these factors, convention center hotel properties must either achieve higher average occupancies, develop other sources of business or realise higher room rates attributable to non-convention guests to succeed.

Convention hotels can often attract alternative sources of revenue, including sponsoring convention and meeting trade separate from a convention center. Sources of business may include smaller group business, commercial activity, and wholesale and tour operator business. Nevertheless, the hotel is in most cases fundamentally dependent on the convention center for its core business. To entice new development, local government entities must often work jointly with hotel developers to overcome the obstacles that tend to make these hotels more costly to develop and less profitable to operate.

These issues raise critical questions. What tools can government bring to bear to attract private hotel investment by improving their economics? How can a hotel developer work with local governments to close the economics gap and make development feasible?

Initiatives prior to the 1986 Tax Reform Act pointed the way to creative forms of public/private partnerships serving the interests of convention centers and their headquarters hotels. The City of Miami, for example, provided an array of incentives to attract hotel development in support of the James I. Knight Center. The city acquired land, provided a 45-year lease with attractive terms and furnished off-site improvements, as well as site utilities. The hotel additionally was awarded the food & beverage concession for the convention center, and real estate property taxes were abated during construction.

The incentives provided by the City of Toledo at Seagate Center is another case in point. A $7.4 million Urban Development Action Grant was loaned to the developer through the Convention Bureau at attractive rates and terms. Tax increment financing was used to support public improvements, while real estate taxes were abated. In addition, the hotel was supplied with convention center-owned parking at prevailing market rates.

More recent public/private partnership successes include the Westin Hotel venture in Providence, Rhode Island, which involved a $290 million bond issue, that covered the convention center, hotel and parking. A Sheraton Hotel at the Jefferson Center in Birmingham, Alabama, involved a $148 million low-interest bond offering, guaranteed by JCA and supported by city and county occupational taxes.

Not all public/private partnerships come together, despite concerted efforts on the part of both private developers and public entities. In Tampa, studies indicated a strong need for a convention hotel to support the city's new convention center. A city commission approved a proposed 900-room Marriott hotel, estimated to cost more than $140 million or more, and to be owned by a private 'not for profit' corporation. Public financing for the hotel, however, was rejected by the Tampa City Council last year. A special task force spent six months analysing two options and is presently formulating recommendations.

The dilemma faced in Los Angeles also is a case in point. A major expansion of the Los Angeles Convention Center was completed late last year, increasing total meeting space to more than 600,000 square feet. Historically, however, the center has hosted only about 20 conventions annually, and competition from other Western cities — including San Francisco, San Diego, Anaheim, Long Beach, Seattle, Portland and Las Vegas — has become more intense. The Los Angeles

Convention and Visitors Bureau has contended that a convention hotel within walking distance is required to make the city more competitive for attracting large conventions. Yet the downtown Los Angeles hotel market has been weak since the onset of the recession early in this decade, a condition which has been further exacerbated by the Los Angeles riots in 1992 and the Northridge earthquake.

Generally, public contributions that can drive development of a hotel may include land at favorable lease terms, off-street parking facilities, construction/use rights of public space and marketing support. Hotel developers may also be granted the convention center's food and beverage service concession. This ancillary revenue can be an important step to offset the lower room rates often associated with delegate business. Among the contributions made by the hotel developer are equity funding, the track record of team members, a superior product development plan, and strong management and marketing.

In addition, the public and private entities must have controls in place to ensure that relationship objectives are maintained. A convention headquarters hotel, for example, must commit room nights to the convention center, even at the cost of displacing higher rated business. Conversely, the convention center must book events, which generate room nights, perhaps foregoing higher revenue-generating consumer shows that tend to be oriented to a local audience.

Private/Public Techniques

A range of successful private/public techniques are available to further these partnerships:

Site control

Land values in urban or resort environments are generally very high with these costs typically representing a significant component of hotel development. Government participation is often essential, either by writing down the market value of a property or purchasing a property to lease to a hotel owner on a long-term basis at an economic cost.

Miami Beach's experience is instructive. The city in 1992 expanded its existing convention center located near City Hall, a location remote from Miami Beach's highly developed existing hotels. No new major hotels have been developed in 27 years. Studies commissioned by the city addressed several pivotal issues. It was determined that none of the existing hotels — clustered primarily at some distance along the coastline— would or could continuously sell room nights to major national conventions that desire to book the city's convention center. Additionally, major hotel developers would be unlikely to develop a new hotel away from the beach area without significant incentives.

Low-cost financing

In the past five years, new full-service hotels have been

extremely difficult to finance. Convention hotels, furthermore, are generally regarded as being of even higher risk — a result of the uncertainty related to occupancies and above-average development costs. As a result, public financing can be the key element in making a convention center hotel feasible.

Again, a number of options are available to the public sector. While tax- exempt public bond issues are subject to 'private purpose' limitations, there are techniques which can blend in public funding to privately owned and operated hotel ventures. These include financing and leasing back the 'public' areas of a hotel (or a parking, etc.) facility. Public revenues from hotel taxes or real property taxes may be designated for the facility through non-tax exempt issues. In addition, cities, counties and other government entities may offer certain operating guarantees, such as payment of debt service, for a specified period of time. Miami Beach, for example, agreed to issue $52 million in bonds as its share of land and construction of the $158 million convention hotel.

In some cases cities have made equity investments in convention hotels. The municipality may become the junior equity partner in the hotel with 'first-in' risk capital, and 'last-out' return. In a broad policy sense, the city's rate of return is potentially greatly enhanced by an improved local economy, higher visitation and associated tax revenues.

Other Incentives

Local governments also have incentive options that will have significant impact on the economies of building a convention headquarters hotel. These include incorporating public spaces and amenities, such as joint parking or meeting facilities to reduce the overall cost of the convention hotel. Municipalities may also provide property tax abatements, as well as redevelopment zone benefits such as expedited permitting and access to other public funding sources.

From a development and operational standpoint, there are a number of challenges facing hotel companies as they consider convention headquarters hotels. In addition, many deals have failed because a city has insufficient resources to close a transaction, or lacks an understanding of the resources it can bring to bear in support of these developments.

More than a standard Request for Proposal (RFP) to attract a quality developer is often needed. The public sector must understand what types of incentives it has available to drive a project — and the best way to frame the RFP process. And it will clearly require specialised expertise to ensure that financial incentive structures make the most of available opportunities and that the expectations are realistic.

In setting parameters for competitive bidding on these projects, municipalities or other public jurisdictions need to be specific about certain factors, such as the hotel size, design, quality of facilities and amenities, and management. But rather than defining the competition in a rigid envelope, it is more important to ensure that respondents customise a proposal that meets the city's criteria and defined needs, and includes financial structures crafted to match the public resources available. Clearly defined procedures for evaluation of proposals are also crucial.

Hotel development can generate a significant stream of economic benefits for a community including support for a tourism industry, job creation and an expanded tax base. Public incentives to support private hotel investment, as a result, can become a decisive component required to assure that public economic development goals are achieved.

9

Strategic Management of Human Resources

Labour Management

The scale of employment in tourism world-wide is large and estimates are provided below. The sector is relatively labour intensive and often provides employment opportunities both in regions which may otherwise struggle to find employment and for sectors of the labour market with particular needs (such as women, and those seeking part time or seasonal positions).

In addition, the World Travel & Tourism Council (WTTC) identify tourism as the largest employer in many countries, both developed and developing, with a growing realization on the part of governments of the importance and significance of tourism employment. Tourism is a growth industry in most countries (with, in many cases low investment per job), whereas most other industries, apart from information technology, will provide fewer jobs. Yet, despite the importance of human resource issues in tourism, knowledge of the scale and structure of employment in the tourism sector is not comprehensive.

The main reason for this is the nature of tourism as a fragmented, broadly-based sector of the economy which is characterized by categories of employment which are problematic in terms of measurement. These measurement issues stem from the nature of tourism employment as being:

— Seasonal;
— Part-time;
— Casual;
— Self-employed;
— Family workers; and
— Part of the 'informal economy'.

In addition there are six characteristics of tourism employment that need to be taken into account:

— *Tourism employment is broadly based:* There is a danger in assuming that the above typical characteristics of direct tourism employment also apply to indirect and induced tourism employment which has been generated by tourism expenditure. Thus it would not be expected that the characteristics of employment in say, wholesalers, is the same as that in the accommodation sector.
— *Tourism employment is characterized by the self employed*: Employment in tourism reflects the domination of small and medium-sized enterprises (SMEs) in many industries serving tourism directly. Whilst there has been a growth in the concentration of the sector, the self-employed still represent a relatively high proportion of total employment. This is particularly the case for retail distribution, accommodation and catering.
— *Employment of women is important*: This is not only due to more women seeking to enter the labour force, but also because the nature of tourism employment is suitable in all categories – even in the transport branches an increasing number of women are employed.

— *Part-time employment is a feature of tourism*: This is due to the nature of the service delivery in **the sector and** makes the sector particularly attractive to women. In addition, part-time employment allows enterprises in tourism to adjust their staffing to the peaks and troughs in demand.

— *Seasonal employment is a feature of tourism*: This is due to the nature of demand for tourism that is seasonal in both the climatic, but also the institutional sense. As with part-time employment, seasonal employment allows enterprises in tourism to adjust their staffing to the peaks and troughs in demand and provides employment for those who are not available year round.

— *The spatial distribution of tourism generates jobs in widely dispersed areas*: Such areas may find other sources of employment difficult to source. This feature of tourism does mean that tourism employment is more significant and meaningful at a local or regional level.

In view of these problematic categories, statistical data on employment in tourism is not as comprehensive as in other economic sectors. In addition, as noted above, tourism is not a discrete activity which can be defined in terms of goods or services produced; rather tourists use a wide range of goods and services and are therefore customers served by a wide variety of people working in different businesses and services.

In order to determine the establishments and enterprises supplying goods and services to visitors, it is necessary to develop supply-side definitions of tourism. The leading supply-side definitions have been developed by the World Tourism Organization (WTO), WTTC and the Canadian government. The importance of supply-side definitions is clear. Tourism lacks credibility in government circles not only because the sector is ambiguously defined, but also because the data used to estimate the size of the sector are suspect.

There is an growing literature on this issue. Smith provides a clear account of the issues and approaches. He states that the real problem is that tourism has not traditionally been identified in national income and product accounts. This is because industries are traditionally defined on the product side. This is difficult to do for tourism given the varied products and industries involved - hence the creation of satellite accounts that try to bring together these tourism-related industries.

The most obvious approach to supply-side definitions is to allocate tourism consumption to categories in the Standard Industrial Classification (SIC). However, the treatment of tourism in the classification is problematic as the codes used to label enterprises only allow the classification of an enterprise into one category. The decision of which category to use is based on the primary source of income of the business.

Problems also occur when an enterprise conducts a significant volume of tourism-related business but earns most of its revenues from other sources. The ISIC is a generic SIC developed by the United Nations to provide a model for national SICs and to encourage consistency for international comparisons. It is based on the 'enterprise', the smallest legal entity that encloses and controls all functions associated with its business.

The enterprise is the owner of one or more commodity-producing units. It may involve multiple locations and/or multiple products. The fundamental characteristic of the enterprise is unity of ownership. The need to develop a supply-side definition of tourism led the WTO to begin a tourism-based modification of the ISIC in 1990. This modification has been named the Standard International Classification of Tourism Activities (SICTA).

The SICTA is essentially a subset of the ISIC consisting of those groups, divisions and classes that draw a substantial portion of their revenue from visitors. The aims of the SICTA are:

— To guide the development of the reporting of tourism in national accounts;

— To provide greater compatibility for national and international tourism statistics;

— To provide statistical linkages between the supply and demand side of tourism; and

— To permit clearer assessment of balance of payments conditions and the contribution of tourism.

The SICTA combines the supply-side and demand-side of tourism. The basic structure of the SICTA is drawn from a supply-side concept: establishments. However, these establishments are selected on the basis of a demand-side concept: the nature of their customers bringing together the demand and supply side. Data reported for each establishment should, ideally, be dis-aggregated to permit estimation of the contributions from visitors and non-visitors.

At a minimum, the SICTA can conceptually indicate whether any individual entry in the hierarchy (at each level) draws its revenue partially or primarily from visitors. The SICTA consists of four levels:

— The main division,

— The group,

— The main class, and

— The sub-class.

In addition, WTO proposes that where appropriate, suppliers should be distinguished by establishments in specific geographically or economically segmented areas (such as payments only in hard currencies) providing visitors with the goods and services they request and which cater almost exclusively to visitors, to be called Tourism Determined Establishments. The system also notes whether each category draws most of its revenues from tourism or only partially from visitors. The name of each category is also identified. The SICTA was adopted by the UN Statistical Commission in 1993 as a provisional classification.

From the supply-side point of view, the WTO proposes to distinguish the suppliers of services for which:

— their consumption by visitors represents a significant share of the total tourism consumption of all visitors:
— their consumption by visitors represents a significant share of the total domestic supply of this service, i.e. were it not for tourism, the level of the output of the associated activity would be seriously affected.

Statistics of employment, distinguishing paid employment, salaries and wages and other labour characteristics and conditions are already collected and analyzed by many countries for Tourism Characteristic Establishments, especially hotels, restaurants and travel agencies. The supply-side approach, together with capacity and utilization of accommodation allows the collection of employment data from standard sources.

A high proportion of the demand for these establishments may be Internal Tourism (inbound and domestic) and travel agents etc. also supply services to outbound residents, but some of the demand is local and in the usual environment of the residents of the country. There is still much work to be done to calculate Tourism Satellite Accounts (TSAs) for the principal countries, so the demand-side approach, while very important, does not yet provide data which can be agreed on.

For ILO, the supply-side approach with detailed statistics for the appropriate industries seems most appropriate, co-operating with the international agencies in developing these, TSAs and agreed demand-side data. There are still considerable problems in operationalising the above definitions and producing estimates of tourism employment – partly because comparisons are not between like and like.

The SICTA classification is primarily concerned with direct visitor spending and does not factor-in employment generated by indirect or induced spending. Estimates by WTTC include both direct and indirect spend. This has led to the Canadian employment estimates by the WTTC being challenged as being three times too large, whilst their estimates of employment growth in the US tourism sector have been criticized as underestimating the need. In addition, there is a controversy over the inclusion and evaluation of a range of categories. For example:

— use of consumer durables, e.g. vehicles also used for non-tourism travel; or

— year-round second homes.

Such decisions will affect the estimate of the total tourism expenditures, added value and estimates of employment for tourism. Estimates of tourism employment are particularly difficult because:

— most jobs which serve visitors also serve other markets;

— whilst a high proportion of tourist jobs are supported by visitor expenditure, some jobs are also supported by expenditure by governments;

— tourism jobs are created to serve visitors directly, but also tourism generates and sustains jobs in a range of supply industries; and

— jobs in tourism are not homogeneous – they can be seasonal, full-time, or part-time.

The use of broad-based economic data to estimate and infer information about the tourism labour market. This may be done by the conversion of tourism spending into the number of full-time equivalent (FTEs) jobs generated by that spending. This involves the estimation of tourism employment multipliers. It can also be achieved by attributing proportions of total employment in different industries to tourism. This method typically produces higher estimates of tourism employment than the multiplier approach.

A bottom-up micro approach which takes the sector itself as the starting point in terms of data collection through surveys and censuses. These data may then be aggregated and extrapolated to provide national estimates of the tourism labour force and its characteristics. This second approach only provides estimates of direct employment.

Computation of employee/sales ratios at the micro-level. Such ratio-based estimates assume the stability of the ratios. These are computed by the US Bureau of Labour Statistics. These ratios tend to be rather more stable for individual enterprises than for aggregations at the industry level. A proxy estimate is sometimes made based purely on the employment in hotel and catering. This is not satisfactory as it clearly omits the other tourism-related tourism sectors and will also include non-tourism-related employment.

However, this approach has been used in the past by both the European Commission and the OECD. These issues are highlighted when comparisons are made between different estimates. The only industry with world-wide employment, supply and demand data is the hotel industry, for which WTO with the International Hotel and Restaurant Association (IHRA) reported 11.3 million jobs.

Housekeeping Management

Recognising that the housekeeping department consists of only one person (the executive housekeeper), You readily see that planning, organising, and staffing functions are of first importance, and the efficient use of time is paramount. Not only is the planning of people functions important, but the design of systems, the establishment of procedures, the determination of supply and equipment needs, and reporting and coordinating relationships must be considered.

The executive housekeeper's experience usually begins by having the person to whom he or she will report (resident manager) introduce him or her to other on-board members of the hotel staff. These people are usually located in temporary hotel quarters such as a nearby office building. It is at this time that the executive housekeeper will most likely be given the tentative chart of hotel organisation, showing the positions of principal assistants to department heads.

Pay special attention to the positions of chief engineer and personnel director, which appear to be above the department heads and below the other members of the executive committee. The incumbents of these two positions are actually department heads, but by virtue of the fact that their staff functions cross all departments to which they will provide a staff service, they are (ex officio) members of the executive committee.

They are in fact middle managers with department head status. The executive housekeeper is on equal rank with the front office manager, with both reporting to the resident manager. The executive housekeeper will have an assistant, tentatively titled housekeeping manager. In addition, operation of the property's laundry will be placed under the direction of the executive housekeeper, requiring another junior manager, laundry manager, to report to the executive housekeeper.

Considering that we have a new property under construction that has not yet begun hotel operations, it is important to note the probable advance time when different members of the hotel organisation may have reported. The director of sales and marketing is usually the first major manager on the site, being there since ground breaking because advanced group room sales were begun at that time. The next major manager on site would probably be the chief engineer. This manager reports about the time the new building's foundation is completed and the first electrical and plumbing development has started.

The chief engineer must monitor the birth of the mechanical systems, since this person will be expected to know these systems with great thoroughness. Sometimes the chief engineer will work as an assistant to the construction manager until construction is near completion. The third manager to report will probably be the general manager, followed by the resident manager and director of food and beverage, and the balance of the department heads. The significance of knowing who reports when becomes evident when we realise that the executive housekeeper must learn in 6 weeks what several others have been exposed to for a far greater time.

For example, the executive housekeeper has to learn about available supply, storage, and security spaces before distribution of these spaces is undertaken to make sure that the housekeeping department is not slighted in the assignment of such space. Reporting relationships also are significant. Coordination between housekeeping and front office personnel requires the respect and understanding of each of the department managers for the others' responsibilities. The executive housekeeper will have many occasions to relate to other members of the total hotel organisation.

It is therefore important to know and become known to each of these managers, and a respect and understanding needs to be developed for each of them and their functions. Others should in turn develop an understanding and respect for the functions of the housekeeping department and its significance in the total operation. Becoming acquainted with the new surroundings includes obtaining a set of working architectural drawings of the rooms portion of the hotel.

Such drawings will allow the executive housekeeper to study the physical layout of the facility and will provide the basis for determining the scope of involvement and delineation of responsibilities of the various managers' areas. Once the executive housekeeper has an understanding of who is who in the organisation; has a knowledge of how long each person has been on site, how knowledgeable certain managers are, and how helpful they can be; has met all the members of the management team thus far assembled; and has a copy of the working architect's drawings of the rooms department and related areas, he or she is ready to be shown the temporary working area in which departmental planning may begin.

Given the various activities that make up the functions of planning, organising, and staffing, there will be a mixture of activities that take place at the same time. Whereas there is an obvious need to determine what is to be done and how to go about doing it, there is an equal and urgent need to, define the need for, establish the requisite qualifications of, and recruit the housekeeper's two principal assistants as soon as possible—the housekeeping manager and the laundry manager. Until these two managers are present, the entire planning, organising, and staffing function rests on the shoulders of the executive housekeeper.

Thus we see the immediate need to specify the qualifications of these two managers to the personnel director in order that advertisements may be placed and recruitment begun. Recruitment is an immediate concern and will remain a part of the daily concern of the executive housekeeper until these people are hired, usually within 10 days to 2 weeks. The work that must actually be accomplished for the entire property needs to be recognised and identified as soon as possible.

The executive housekeeper should make regular daily tours of the property under construction and, as soon as possible, draw up what is known as the Division of Work Document. This document is a recognition of what will be required in cleaning the property; all departments must become aware of this.

The executive housekeeper should present the division of work document to the executive committee for review, listing the areas by name, noting anything unusual about expected cleaning requirements, and offering a recommendation as to who should be responsible for cleaning and maintaining each area. Whereas most executive housekeepers are involved only in the guestroom portion of the hotel and related public areas, it is not unusual to be assigned the responsibility for nightly cleaning of kitchens, afterevent ballroom cleaning, swimming pool maintenance, and similar tasks.

Many times trade-offs are reasonable, such as the food and beverage department maintaining the employees' cafeteria at no cost to other departments and the housekeeping departments maintaining all public restrooms regardless of where they are. However, if the housekeeping department is expected to clean an area foreign to the rooms department, such as kitchens, banquet space, restaurants, or cocktail lounges, then budgetary compensation and personnel must be provided to the housekeeping department and charged to the department receiving the service.

It is always proper that costs be levied against the revenue generated in each of the various departments. It might seem most efficient to place all cleaning responsibilities under one manager for control, but employees are inclined to be more careful and make less mess if they are required to clean up after themselves. Thus departments charged with cleaning their own facilities create their own cost category for cleaning expense, which is to be charged against revenue generated rather than to another department.

Once the division of work document has been submitted to the executive committee for review and the executive housekeeper has made recommendations to the resident manager (member of the executive committee), the Area Responsibility Plan can be drawn up by the executive committee. This plan is an assignment of responsibility of the various areas mentioned in the division of work document and shows various cleaning area boundaries on a copy of a floor plan blueprint.

Such boundary lines are important to ensure that no space is left unassigned and that no overlaps in cleaning responsibilities occur. The area responsibility plan is usually the result of the advance thinking and planning by an experienced executive housekeeper who makes regular tours of the property. The plan should be forthcoming from the executive committee within the first week of the housekeeper's tenure. The next task of the executive housekeeper is to develop the housekeeping department organisation.

However, assistant managers are clearly in place, and the task of organising the laundry will be delegated to the laundry manager as soon as he or she is selected. The first-line hourly supervisory structure provides for evening operations (3:30 P.M. to midnight), linen room operations (communication central), public area and utility personnel supervision, and supervision of recreation areas (two swimming pools, whirlpool, game room, sauna, and associated public restrooms). The actual size of the largest part of the organisation (that which is associated with pure guestroom cleaning and servicing) is accommodated by applying a technique known as zero-base budgeting.

Zero-base budgeting refers to worker use that takes into account actual occupancy on a specific day or for a specified period of time. Worker staffing and eventual scheduling are limited on a daily basis to the service of that specified occupancy and no more. The next major planning step that the executive housekeeper must undertake is the development of the House Breakout Plan. In order to ensure maximum familiarity with the facility, it is highly recommended that the executive housekeeper personally develop this pictorial representation of every guest-room as it is located within the hotel.

This is done by making a line drawing of the guestroom portion of the hotel, showing the relative positions of guestrooms, corridors, service areas, and other areas significant to guestroom cleaning. As the house breakout plan is being created, certain criteria must be established: specifically, the workload of room attendants. The U.S. national average for rooms cleaned per day by one person ranges from 14 to 416 rooms, but the actual number may range from 13 rooms per day (8-hour shift) to a high of 20 rooms per day, depending upon the type and nature of hotel activity.

In resort hotels with many metal surfaces to polish, mirrors to clean, and multiple occupancy guests who sleep in late, the workload of a room attendant may be only 13 rooms per day. In transient operations of standard size rooms, where room occupancy consists primarily of business people who arise and vacate early each day, room attendants can clean as many as 20 rooms per day-and clean them well if properly equipped and trained for efficient operation.

In our model hotel, experience dictates that approximately 18 rooms per day would not be unreasonable, taking into account special areas of the hotel in which cleaning loads might be dropped to 17 rooms per day. Based upon the workload criteria, the house breakout plan can now show the facility divided Lip into room sections. A room section is a group of 13 to 20 guest rooms, reasonably contiguous to each other, that may normally be cleaned and serviced by one person in one 8-hour shift.

The room section will normally be assigned a number and for purposes of illustration will be cleaned by a person called a guestroom attendant (GRA). In order for the room sections to be grouped into logical units for supervisory and control needs, house divisions will be used. A house division is a group of four to six room sections with associated and/or specified corridors, elevators, stairwells, service areas, and storage areas. It may be assigned a colour or letter designation and placed under the charge of a supervisor.

For demonstration purposes with our model hotel, house divisions will be colour coded and placed under a supervisor known as a senior GRA or supervisor. The house breakout plan may now be completed by considering the size of sections, assembly of house divisions, location of contiguous rooms, position of elevators, and transportation from room to room. The house breakout plan developed by no means the only way the model hotel can be broken into logical work units. It does, however, reflect an efficient method of division of the workload. This particular technique also lends itself to a form of work scheduling.

Most hotel housekeeping departments will hire and individually schedule section housekeepers on an as-needed basis depending on occupancy. Whereas union operations may require the guarantee of a 40-hour workweek for regular employees, most union houses have few such regular employees. Union operations have considerably more people, referred to as steady extras, who can be called upon on an as-needed basis.

Nonunion operations seldom guarantee a 40-hour workweek but will staff in such a way (based on expected occupancy) so as to provide between 35 and 40 hours of work each week for their regular employees. Recognising that labour costs within a housekeeping department are the highest recurring costs in a rooms department budget, it is highly inefficient to guarantee a set number of regular employees 40 hours when occupancy is low. For this reason a practical number of employees will be hired based on expected occupancy for a given period of time.

Rather than scheduling housekeepers on an individual basis, housekeeping teams may be formed. A housekeeping team consists of one supervisor (senior GRA) who is in charge and one section GRA for each section within a division. Since a house division includes the cleaning and care of corridors, stairwells, elevators, and designated service areas as well as associated guestrooms, the additional position of section housekeeping aide is required on a team. This position may be filled by any person capable of performing the work set forth in the job description.

The assignment of regular teams to house divisions for staffing purposes satisfies the need for division cover age, but it becomes obvious that the hotel operating on a seven-days-per-week basis will require additional personnel to work when regular teams have days off. To accommodate days off, swing teams may be formed. Consider the requirement that no employee may work more than a 40-hour week without the provision of overtime.

It becomes prudent to assume that a 40-hour week consisting of five regular 8-hour days will be the standard and that the sixth and seventh day of work in a house division must be accomplished by using additional employees. The housekeeping department in the model situation will also operate a laundry. The laundry has about the same staffing requirements and will face the same situation of a seven-day operation, with employees requiring two days off each week.

Along with the development of the Table of Personnel Requirements, a set of Job Descriptions arid/or Position Descriptions must also be developed. This is done by developing a sequence of individual tasks for operations that may be grouped arid then assigned to a single person. The grouping of such tasks is the creation of the position and job description.

If one is to take full advantage of the motivators of achievement-growth, responsibility, and recognition-one must examine every job very closely in order to see to it that the factors that make up the job itself will form the "satisfiers". All too often, jobs are designed around people of special ability. This is not necessarily unprofessional, provided there is no possibility of losing the person for whom the job was designed. In most situations, however, this is not possible. When a person of special quality leaves or is transferred, we hope to fill the position with someone of equal capability. If no one can be found with the same abilities, the job must be redefined.

This is often time consuming and may cause some reorganising. It is a much wiser course of action to first specify the tasks that must be accomplished and then to group these tasks into logical units that have the lowest per unit cost. When there is a choice about which tasks should be combined into a single job, the criterion of *lowest per unit cost is* applied. Since cost is to be minimised, it is logical to design tasks and combine them in such a fashion that the lowest level of skill is required. For example, we would not want to combine the task performed by a guestroom attendant with those of a supervisor, because different skill levels are required.

Similarly, the tasks involved in the job of a guestroom attendant should not be combined with those involved in the job of a lobby housekeeper. The rationale is that it would not be cost effective to have people cleaning rooms one minute and fulfilling other maintenance tasks in the lobby the next.

Position Descriptions are sometimes written for managers, or for those who have management prerogatives. Such people hire, fire, set wages, and make policy. The Position Description type of document sets forth the basic function of the manger and defines the scope of the manager's responsibilities and authority. Specific responsibilities that have been created for the manager and the relationships to responsibility they have with other members of the organisation are listed.

There is usually a statement, referred to as work emphasis, about how a manager should allot his or her time and efforts. The basic function listed in each position description is a simple statement of overall responsibility. The scope helps the manager define the limits of managerial authority. What usually follows the scope is a group of specific responsibilities. Note that the terms "coordinate," "administer control," and "be responsible for" are used frequently.

They imply that the specific tasks have been delegated to someone who is working for the manager. The *standard form* first of the position descriptions for the department managers, then of the job descriptions for the working line personnel of the housekeeping department. These will differ when compared with those for the environmental services department. The environmental service department has similar requirements for job descriptions.

The same form for the job description (JD) is used whether for manager or for worker. The documents remain an essential ingredient for all departments within the hospital and all departments will use the same format. The JD provides a synopsis of the requirements for each job classification. It is used by the personnel department when they recruit to fill an open position, as reference for a current employee, and as a resource in conducting performance evaluations. The structure and number of job descriptions depend on the individual facility.

The human resources department often has a preferred format for job assignments; the number needed will depend on the size and structure of the department. Those presented herein are working job descriptions for an environmental services department in a medium-to-large facility. Departments that are structured differently may require more, fewer, or have differing types of job descriptions. The uniqueness within each facility must be taken into consideration when developing the job description.

Worker scheduling would be greatly simplified if such were the case. Everyone would have weekends and holidays off, and when doors of the department were closed, workers and managers alike could relax knowing that nothing was happening at the office. In hotels, hospitals, restaurants, and other seven-day operations, however, worker scheduling is a major task that must be performed with absolute regularity.

Not only must the manager and supervisor devote time and forethought to the task of scheduling, but they must also take into account the needs of people whom they schedule. For example, some workers may not be able to work on Tuesdays and others want weekends off; family demands and illness must also be recognised and accommodated.

Add to these concerns the problem of fluctuating occupancy, which has the greatest effect on housekeeper scheduling, and the manager has a full-time task that may not allow time for other less repetitive but more creative tasks. The manager who schedules a group of individual workers on a weekly basis and who must adjust schedules on a daily basis may well earn the label "tied down."

In order to improve this routine of scheduling and in so doing greatly reduce the time that management has to spend performing these tasks, you should try the team system of organisation and scheduling. A principal advantage to the manager is in being able to schedule a group of people as though it were one entity. It is true that not every person in the department can be handled in such a manner, but the majority of employees in a housekeeping department can be grouped for scheduling purposes.

Another advantage of the team system of organisation is the fact that cooperation and workers' morale will be higher as part of a small unit than as one in a large group of people. A worker who is a member of a seven-person team is much more likely to relate to team performance to which he or she can see a personal contribution than to a large organisation in which he or she is but one of many. The system of team scheduling and staffing also embraces the idea that the team will work together and will regularly be off together.

Having assigned teams to work in specific areas of the hotel, the teams become responsible for the entire cleaning function in their areas. The team-which has a supervisor in charge, several guest room attendants (GRAs) who clean guest rooms, and a section housekeeping aide who assists and also cleans other areas of the division such as corridors, stairwells, and elevators—becomes totally responsible for the entire division of the hotel.

Cleaning performance within the division becomes a primary responsibility of the entire team under the supervisor, and performance is measured on a team basis rather than an individual basis. If the premise that each individual worker wants to be a part of a worthwhile operation is true, team spirit will cause the entire group to excel. There will always be a few above-average GRAs who excel in rooms cleaning and take personal pride in their individual work; however, in the eyes of the guest, the reputation of the best housekeeper will never be better than the reputation of the poorest GRAs in the entire group.

GRAs, once they understand that their individual reputation is judged by performance of the poorest in the team, will become more willing to help the poorer performers to improve. It should not be surprising, therefore, to find many small disciplinary problems such as absenteeism and tardiness resolved at the team level because to be absent or late could have a negative effect on the team's reputation. Even though the entire department is one team and teamwork must be fostered at every turn, promoting teamwork within each individual team requires special effort.

Swing (or relief) teams, although not assigned to a regular division of the hotel, are as accountable as regular teams for performance and for condition of jointly used equipment on the days they are scheduled to work in a given division. This helps resolve problems that come up. For example, GRAs on occasion complain about the condition of "their" section after returning from scheduled days off, or about the condition of "their" maids' cart, vacuum cleaner, or other equipment.

Such complaints are often resolved when the regular GRA knows exactly who will be cleaning in the section when the regular team is off. Problems are much easier to, talk out when the same workers face each other and are held accountable for the condition of jointly used equipment. There are two major tasks that must be accomplished in order for the following complete scheduling system to work. One is the task of constructing a system for standing rotational scheduling. (The word "standing" is used to denote a continuous system, and the word "rotational" to denote the cyclical nature of the system that provides for two regular days off for people each week and for staff to cover a full seven-day workweek at 100 percent occupancy.)

The other task is that of providing tight scheduling, which is a modification of the rotational system to account for reduced occupancy. This will be accomplished by assigning extra days off when occupancy is low. The tight schedule is actually a daily modification of the standing rotational schedule based on occupancy. In new operations, these two systems are designed before opening and are then easily implemented on a given start date.

In ongoing operations, these systems may be used, but they require a thorough briefing of staff and an understanding by employees before they are implemented. Usually several weeks must pass after training employees on the scheduling system in order that the one-time shock of shifting from one system to another can be accommodated. Once the system is designed and employees are properly prepared, the standing rotational system is implemented on a given start date, which usually falls on the first day of the property workweek.

The hotel workweek has been established as beginning on Saturdays and ending on Fridays. Workers may work no more than five days in any workweek without drawing overtime pay. Days off will be consecutive unless the employee can be shown an advantage for having split days off. A condition of employment will be that all team employees must be willing to work their share of weekends.

Whereas the standing rotational schedule is a *permanent* system that, once established and initiated, continues to cycle on its own, the tight scheduling system is an *operational* system. It provides simple day-by-day modifications of the standing rotational schedule that are needed because of fluctuations in occupancy.

The tight schedule pertains only to team scheduling; it has no effect on the individual positions scheduled, since all positions other than teams are considered fixed and are not affected by occupancy. Recall that the task of specific designation as to who works within each team has been delegated to each team supervisor. Although this delegation is job enriching to each supervisor, control must be maintained to ensure equitable and fair rotation of the assignment of extra days off for team members.

Executives for Housekeeping

The overall goal of management in a profit-making operation is to increase the owner's equity by maximising profits. So, in turn, one of the major concerns of the executive housekeeper should be to maximise the productivity and efficiency of housekeeping employees. Theoretical production and efficiency methods in the workplace were first explored at the turn of the century by Frederick W. Taylor, whose classical scientific management concepts, although developed under industrial conditions, can still be applied today in the lodging industry.

Taylor analysed jobs systematically to determine the amount of work that each employee could produce. He did so by measuring the performance of workers in a given period of time. This allowed management to set standards of production and require employees to reach the preestablished levels of performance in a certain number of hours. If the productivity levels were above the standard, management could choose to pay bonuses to workers as an incentive to maintain productivity quotas.

If the productivity levels were below the standard, production methods had to be improved. This approach is still followed in well-managed housekeeping operations. For instance, the executive housekeeper can analyse the time required to efficiently clean one of the property's guestrooms and use that time as the department's standard for that task.

When productivity and quality exceed the standards, special recognition or extra compensation could be given for maintaining the productivity quotas. If performance falls below preestablished levels, the section housekeepers would need to be retrained or the method used to clean guestrooms re-evaluated. Frederick Taylor's classical scientific management approach dealt with techniques to increase productivity in the workplace.

At the time, workers had little reason to improve their productivity; on the contrary, they viewed the introduction of new machines and equipment to improve efficiency as a direct threat.

Toward the end of the 1920s, a new management approach developed as a result of experiments conducted in the workplace by Elton Mayo. The study concluded that factors other than the physical aspect of a job can have an effect on productivity, namely, the workers' social interactions and personal relationships. Mayo's study demonstrated that in order to increase productivity in the workplace, human relations factors must be considered.

That is, an organisation consists first and foremost of the people working in it and management must be greatly concerned with the social and psychological aspects of the relationship between the company and its employees. As a result, the human relations management approach was developed. This approach can be easily understood and applied from a housekeeping management perspective.

For instance, if the department manager does not consider the social needs of the workers a priority, workers in turn will not develop a sense of loyalty for their manager. If a houseperson who is scheduled to work the morning shift cannot find a baby-sitter for mornings, management should do everything possible to schedule this worker in the evening. If this were done, the employee would feel gratitude and therefore be more willing to return the favour by improving productivity. In other words, productivity can be greatly improved if management takes care of its workers.

The human relations theory allowed for an understanding of the dynamics of human behaviour which led to the premise that management must be aware that workers, besides being units of production, are social entities in their own right. Management, which until then perceived employees as mechanistic elements in the productive system, was now viewing workers as human components in the organisation's social system.

Although it is true that executive housekeepers must develop a keen sense for production in the workplace (after all, the main reason for lodging companies to stay in business is to generate a profit), they must also see housekeeping employees as individuals. Yet, without adequate productivity in the workplace, profits will be diminished, forcing management to pay insufficient wages and to provide inferior benefits. Then, adding concern for people to the management equation is imperative.

However, the real skill lies in finding a proper balance; for example, an executive housekeeper determined to please workers at any cost may not be totally successful, for employees easily sense when a manager is a "softy," not tough enough to have the work done fairly but efficiently. Another function of management is to see to it that all parts of a working unit are integrated as a whole.

Henri Fayol, of France, theorised that certain management principles can be applied to any type of business as well as to the various levels within the business. These principles apply, therefore, to the lodging industry in general and to the housekeeping department in particular. Fayol's book, Administration Industrielle et Generale, originally published in 1916, was not adopted in the United States until three decades later.

Fayol proposed that a manager must practice the following functions of management:

— Planning

— Organising

— Directing

— Coordinating

— Controlling

— Planning

One of the main functions the manager of the housekeeping department must perform is deciding what tasks are essential at any given time to keep the department running at peak efficiency. As the occupancy of the property varies from month to month, and even from day to day, forecasting labour and supplies needs must be done in advance to minimise costs.

The definition of planning is simple: deciding where one should go and how to get there. Planning, however, is not always easy for it requires the predetermination of strategies and policies necessary to fulfil company goals. When forecasting employees, for instance, the executive housekeeper must skilfully plan the scheduling of employees according to the property's up-coming occupancy.

If the hotel is full, all employees are needed, but only part of the staff is required when the occupancy is low. Regarding material, lack of planning might result in purchasing excessive amounts of guest supplies, for example, which means tying up cash that might be needed to pay salaries or to purchase new bed linens.

On the other hand, underestimating future occupancy may result in under-stocking supplies and running out of them when they would be most needed. Creativity is an important element of the planning function; it requires the ability of a manager to develop and implement different, more efficient solutions to operational problems.

A creative executive housekeeper is flexible in judging employee initiatives, encouraging workers to develop new ways to improve the efficiency of the department.A highly structured, bureaucratic housekeeping department might be efficient in production but would stifle or limit innovation. Creativity in planning should allow for diversity of ideas without attempting to rigidly structure the behaviour of employees.

Planning involves the achievement of short- and long-range objectives. A short-range objective might be to bring down the labour cost by one percentage point next month. A long-range objective might be to increase the productivity of section housekeepers by 5 per cent over last year's results by the end of the current fiscal year. The organisation of housekeeping is necessary in order to establish a pattern of relationships with other operational units and among the different components of the department itself.

The organisation of housekeeping includes the determination of tasks, skills, and personnel necessary to achieve the objectives of the department. It is the responsibility of the executive housekeeper to structure the department so that all work can be finished efficiently and on time. The first necessary step when structuring the housekeeping department is to determine the pattern of authority by drawing an organisational chart.

This follows the principle of unity of command proposed by Fayol which states that workers should be given orders only by their own supervisor. To this effect, the span of control must be clearly defined; this relates to the number of subordinates that a supervisor can oversee effectively. In the housekeeping department, when employees are well trained and dependable, the span of control can be quite broad.

In the case of new or untrained employees, the span of control should be narrow, usually four or five workers. Defining relationships within the department is also important because a strong cooperation must exist among its different units. For instance, a sufficient amount of clean linen must be made available to section housekeepers during the morning shift to set up guestrooms as quickly as possible.

However, if the soiled linen is not brought to the laundry room to be washed, dried, and ironed early in the day, the clean linen will not be ready on time. Another organisational task is that of creating descriptions of the jobs to be done (list of tasks) and the qualifications of workers who are to perform the jobs.

Matching the right person for each job that must be accomplished is a priority in the organisation of the housekeeping department. For instance, section housekeepers in lodging properties must clean between 12 and 20 rooms on average in one 8-hour shift. The importance of selecting people who are physically able to perform this strenuous job is obvious. The managerial function *directing* involves achieving the goals of the department by explaining to employees what needs to be accomplished, then facilitating their efforts to do the job.

Crucial to directing effectively is the ability of the manager to train, motivate, supervise, and discipline employees. Competent executive housekeepers will be able to reach higher levels of productivity from the housekeeping work force than managers who are not adequately trained to direct people. Without proper direction, employees tend to duplicate efforts, focus on the wrong priorities, and relate efforts to the wrong purpose.

An example of improper direction may be allowing section housekeepers to clean every guestroom (checkout and stay-over rooms alike) early in the morning when there are incoming guests waiting in the lobby to be checked in. Another example of poor management would be to play favourites with employees, which would lead to discontent among them.

As a manager, an efficient executive housekeeper should emphasise both the economic-technical system and the human aspects of administration. If we compared the housekeeping department to an orchestra, *coordinating* would be the act of bringing all the instruments together to produce a fine piece of music, that is, matching the individual work of the staff to the common goals of the operation.

Feedback is an essential component in the control process. In housekeeping departments feedback should be sought from guests, employees and other departments of the lodging operation. The need for executive housekeepers to control the activities of their department represents an important management function. Without controls there is no way of evaluating the degree in which the objectives set during the planning function are met. In other words, the actual results need to be compared to desired or anticipated goals and standard of performance. Labour cost percentages are typical standards of control; if the labour cost was set in the budget at 18 per cent of revenue and the actual labour cost is running at 22 per cent, the result are over budget and some corrective measures must be taken.

The position of executive housekeeper in the organisational structure of lodging operations is that of department head or member of the middle management team. In small properties, executive housekeepers report directly to the general manager of the establishment, while in large properties they report to the rooms division director.

Today's successful executive housekeeper requires skills beyond those of a person who is just in charge of keeping the place clean. Executive housekeepers cannot concentrate their managerial ability on technical skills alone-material, budgets, equipment. They also must concern themselves with people and with the conceptualisation of notions about the resolution of management-related issues. Executive housekeepers must have a thorough knowledge of how the job is done and how the equipment works, and also be able to exercise leadership and influence people to have the work done while being sensitive to the employees' needs. At the same time, they must be able to analyse situations, implement change, and effect innovative ideas in the workplace. A *supervisor* is anyone whose responsibility is to supervise; therefore every manager is a supervisor.

The definition of supervision is quite similar to that of management in that it is concerned with directing, facilitating, and monitoring the work of others in order to have the job done. The executive housekeeper's field of supervision encompasses three major components: the company's assets, the employees, and the guests.

Poor supervision of employees may lead to preparing guestrooms inefficiently, which in turn may create customer disloyalty and an eventual loss of profits. Executive housekeepers can effect supervision tightly or loosely. Supervision can be exacted by following prescribed rules and regulations or by allowing teamwork and decision making by line employees.

In the latter case, workers are expected to exercise initiative and self -coordination. Whether to use one style or the other should depend on the composition of the work force. When there is a substantial turnover of employees and their working skills are weak, supervision should be tighter than when the work force is well trained and reliable. Providing *leadership* is one aspect of management.

Leadership can be defined as the ability to lead people to willingly perform in ways to achieve the organisation's goals." One commonly encountered problem in the lodging industry is that of indifferent employees. Some of the reasons for this are the inadequate wages, poor benefits, part-time positions, and insufficient training so common to the industry.

In spite of these obstacles, it is the task of hospitality managers to create an appropriate environment in which employees willingly display a positive attitude toward guests and fellow workers. This can be achieved through proper leadership. There are three leadership styles generally used by leaders in human situations.

In the authoritarian style, the manager who dictates the tasks to be performed and the ways to accomplish them assumes the determination of policies; input from subordinates is not sought. The democratic style of management takes place when all policies are reached after group discussion and decision, encouraged and facilitated by the manager.

In the laissez-faire style subordinates have complete freedom for group or individual decisions where the manager does not take part in matters related to work. An executive housekeeper exerting the same leadership style in all circumstances will most likely fail to achieve optimum results in the workplace. As different problems require different solutions, a flexible approach should be used when leading people.

For instance, if a houseperson refuses to perform a task necessary for the normal operation of the department, the manager should compel the worker to do the job. On the other hand, if the same houseperson is performing the job satisfactorily, the manager should allow the worker to do the job without interfering. Several studies conducted to identify leadership traits have yielded a series of attributes inherent to their personalities.

Successful business managers generally are well educated, self-assured, decisive, risk-takers, power- seekers, problem-solvers, and good in their relationships with people. Besides these attributes, executive house-keepers should be good motivators, good communicators, good delegators, and good administrators of their invested power/authority. Employee *motivation* may be the greatest challenge that executive housekeepers can face.

Managers should not always try to motivate workers directly; instead they should create the right environment for employees to motivate themselves. The first step is to establish a climate of mutual trust and respect, meaning that employees should never be looked down upon from a position of superiority. Instead, managers should be characterised as fair, caring, and approachable individuals.

Good leaders must be capable of understanding people well and be sensitive to their individual needs and differences. Motivation is internal, complex, and individually patterned; what motivates one person might displease someone else, and vice versa. Before attempting to motivate workers, the executive housekeeper must provide for the satisfaction of their basic needs, which according to Abraham Maslow, theorist of the humanistic movement, maybe physiological, security-driven, social, self-esteem and achievement- driven.

It would be difficult to motivate someone feeling physiologically uncomfortable, for instance, a laundry worker labouring in a room without ventilation at 110-degree temperature. An employee working part-time without assurance of a guaranteed number of working hours per week might also be hard to motivate.

The same is true for workers who are shunned by fellow employees because of their ethnic background, employees who feel unappreciated, and those who feel they are not challenged to their true potential. It is therefore the duty of the executive housekeeper as a leader to facilitate the fulfilment of the individual needs of employees prior to attempting to motivate them. An effective, universal way of motivating people is providing them with equitable, if not generous, compensation.

It is axiomatic to assume that employees are motivated to work because of a need for money to live. However, greater financial incentives may not necessarily be the only motivators in all cases. For instance, a worker with job security and sufficient compensation may need additional challenges to get motivated in the workplace.

Frederick Herzberg worked on identifying the factors that motivate people. He proposed that employees may be motivated through job enrichment, that is, making the work meaningful. Herzberg found that factors people reported as providing job satisfaction include responsibility, achievement, personal growth, advancement, and recognition.

From this theory it follows that executive housekeepers should provide workers with jobs that embody responsibility, interest, opportunity, and challenge. The fundamental function of *communication* is to link people together in organisations in order to achieve a common purpose. The activity of a group would be impossible without good communication because without it coordination could not be effected. One of the attributes executive housekeepers must have is the ability to determine when and what to communicate to whom, as well as to know the available means for information transfer, including the use of both formal and informal avenues.

Communication depends on the way different people perceive messages, and even ideas. Workers of diverse geographical or ethnic backgrounds might interpret differently concepts such as "clean on time," or "efficient." Executive housekeepers must have the ability to convey messages to all employees so that they are unequivocally understood. Housekeeping managers spend most of their working time talking and listening to others; in some cases communicating represents about 80 percent of the work day. There are four types of verbal communication: speaking, listening, writing, and reading. Speaking and Writing are used to send messages, while listening and reading are used to receive them.

Of all these, face-to-face communication is the most effective. In order to avoid one-way communication, managers should strive to convey their message in such a way that employees feel free to express their feelings as well. There is a difference between getting someone to agree with the message sent and showing a willingness to accept possible disagreement. In the first case we are trying to communicate one way; in the second, we are being open to receive the employee's feedback in return.

Another condition for two-way communication is the ability to understand what someone is trying to say from that person's point of view. In other words, being able to empathise during a conversation is the key element for two people to understand each other. There can be several roadblocks to effective communication.

The status barrier can undermine willingness to listen patiently to workers who are perceived as having low social status, as, for example, the communication process that may take place between a section housekeeper and an engineer who might consider the former unworthy to listen to. In this case, it is better to use an impersonal mechanism like a work order to avoid any friction between departments.

The psychological barrier can cause communication distortion when one of the communicators has a preconceived, negative perception of the other person. If front office personnel perceive housekeeping room attendants as members of the cleaning brigade, they will always find reasons not to listen attentively to them.

Bibliography

Baum, T., Amoah, V. and Spivack, S., "Policy dimensions of human resource management in the tourism and hospitality industries", *International Journal of Contemporary Hospitality Management*, 1997.

Bramwell, B., "Sustainable Tourism Management Education in Europe", *Tourism Management*, 1996.

Bramwell, B., Goytia, A., and Henry, I., "Developing sustainable tourism management education", in G. Richards (ed.) *Tourism in Central and Eastern Europe: Educating for quality*, Tilberg, Tilberg University Press, 1996.

Brown, F., "Training and the EC (conference report)", *Tourism Management*, 1991.

Dahl, J. O., *Advertising and promotion for hotels and restaurants; a reference book for hotel and* restaurant executives, sales managers, advertising and publicity directors, advertising agencies, *publishers and students*, Stamford Conn: The Dahls, 1939.

Dahl, J. O., *Restaurant profits and management methods*, Stamford, Conn.: The Dahls, 1942.

Fellows, Charles, *Fellows' menu maker; suggestions for selecting and arranging menus for hotels and* restaurants, with object of changing from day to day to give continuous variety of foods in season, Chicago: The Hotel monthly, 1910.

Gray, Madeline and Vass De Lo Padua, *How to be a success in the restaurant business*. New York: Greenberg, 1946.

Hoke, Ann, *Restaurant menu planning*, New York, London: Harper & brothers, 1940.

Janet McKenize Hill, *The Up-to-Date Waitress*, Boton: Little, Brown, and Co, 1906

John Love, *McDonald's behind the Arches*, Toronto: Bantam Books, 1986

Leon Gottlieb, *The Best of Gottlieb's Bottom Line*, New York: Lebhar Friedman, 1980.

Newson, Carey, "Tourism without traffic: a good practice guide", Transport 2000, London. Oversize G155, 2001.

Pendleton, Tom, "Young People and Bicycle Touring", Velo City '01 Conference, Edinburgh, Glasgow, September 2001.

Prideaux, B., "The role of the transport system in destination development", (Elsevier) *Journal of Tourism Management* 21 (1), December, 1999.

Taylor, Gordon D, "Tourism and Sustainability - Impossible Dream or essential objective?", *Travel and Tourism Research Assocation*, Canada, 1991.

Index